RSAC

JAN 2002

ALSO BY SARA STEIN

My Weeds: A Gardener's Botany

The Body Book

The Evolution Book

The Science Book

Noah's Garden: Restoring the Ecology of Our Own Backyards

Planting Noah's Garden: Further Adventures in Backyard Ecology

NOAH'S CHILDREN

NOAH'S CHILDREN

Restoring the Ecology of Childhood

Sara Stein

North Point Press
A division of Farrar, Straus and Giroux
New York

North Point Press
A division of Farrar, Straus and Giroux
19 Union Square West, New York 10003

Text and drawings copyright © 2001 by Sara Stein
All rights reserved
Distributed in Canada by Douglas & McIntyre Ltd.
Printed in the United States of America
First edition, 2001

Library of Congress Cataloging-in-Publication Data
Stein, Sara Bonnett.
    Noah's children : restoring the ecology of childhood / Sara Stein.—
1st ed.
        p.   cm.
    Includes index.
    ISBN 0-86547-584-9 (hc. : alk. paper)
    1. Environment and children.   2. Child development.   3. Outdoor
education.   4. Outdoor recreation for children.   5. Human ecology.
I. Title.

HQ781 .S753 2001
649'.5—dc21

                                                        00-066832

Designed by Thomas Frank

For our children,

their children,

and those who used to be

(especially A. H. T.)

Contents

Noah's Children

Introduction

I wanted a Noah's Ark. I always had. One doesn't grow out of the story, or out of the tie between humans and animals that the story expresses, or out of the toy that invites children into a world where all animals are kin. Few children are given such a toy, but any child, if she knew that such a thing existed, would covet it, and sixty years is long enough to wait.

I could have bought one. A woodcraft company offered a Noah's Ark in its catalog. It must have sold well, because when the next catalog appeared, it offered as well a Noah's Ark lamp, Noah's Ark bookends, and a Noah's Ark shelf with glued-on animals to hang above a doorway. I laughed; then I felt a little sick. I'm too old for inauthentic.

So I determined that I would make an ark myself and whittle the animals.

The material is clear pine board, three-quarters of an inch thick for animals from elephant to fox size, a half-inch thick for smaller ones. The closeness of the grain is critical. You want the heartwood where the layers of the tree's growth are tightly compressed; the sapwood in the outer portion of the trunk is too soft and weak. The wood-carving knives and gouges are made in Japan, where steel for cutting blades is the best there is.

You have to hone your blades frequently to whittle well. You have to orient the shapes in such a way that narrow portions—tails and legs and pointy ears—go with the grain of the wood; otherwise, they break. Even with good wood and keen blades, you have to forgo details like cloven hoofs and flowing manes because they are too hard to carve—or too hard for amateurs like me. You can't keep the figures to scale: if you did, either the fox would be too small for your fingers to manage or the elephant too big to fit aboard the ark. The fattest any animal can be is the thickness of the board, so elephants and rhinos are narrower than they ought to be. The reality of the material constrains your designs, forces their stylized expression. You are making animals in abstract.

I whittle in the evenings, completing perhaps a pair of sheep or a single crocodile in a night. The busyness of the hands sets the mind free to ruminate. That happens with other forms of handwork too—sewing, drawing, shelling peas. Thoughts flow, images form, and every so often the mind awakens to notice what is going on within it. While whittling the second of the pair of sheep, hands concentrated on curving the flank and rounding the muzzle, my mind noted that my mind had created a flock of sheep, and then awakened fully to the fact that sheep are comfortable only in their flock. Now I have finished seven sheep, with the ram to lead them. One of the sheep is black.

There is no ram to lead one's flock of thoughts while in this peculiar state of mind. Each thought, indeed several simultaneously, stray as they will, nibbling at facts and memories, forming images, sounding phrases, occasionally straying into one another with a startled thump. Why is the black sheep the odd sheep, the bad one? Why is odd opposed to even, as dark to light and left to right? There are seven sheep and many more assumptions that, as I crook stray thoughts in my attention, tell me something of mental behaviors that may be as inherent to my species as the urge to follow the leader is to a flock of sheep.

For instance, I notice—and consistently in designing any animal—that I draw the head too large. I have in front of me my sketched design and *Walker's Mammals of the World* open to a clear photograph of an elephant, which is not a hard animal to draw. When I look at my drawing, it conveys true "elephantness." Any child would know immediately what animal it is. Yet the photograph shows the actual elephant's head to be a good third smaller. This happened with the great cats too, and with the hooved ungulates; even the sheep whose skulls are too woolly to discern have snouts too large for them. In the course of abstraction, I have unwittingly and unwillingly introduced a big-headed bias.

When I start to whittle the design in wood, I become aware of another difficulty. In spite of lack of detail and overly straight legs, the profile of the animal is convincing; the front view, though, fails to identify the species. It seems I know animals sideways, not face-to-face. I had just completed an embroidered quilt featuring my dog Girl in various attitudes and had sketched her many times in designing the squares. How many thousands of times I've looked straight into Girl's face! Yet I can't picture it to draw it.

And yet again, I can't draw owls in profile. Or monkey faces either. It is their eyes that prevent me. Some rule must say, If the eyes are set forward like our own, know the creature face-to-face.

Achieving a proper facial expression has proven to be exceptionally difficult even in profile. Because the figures are small and my hands too thick with the knife, usually I must paint the eyes and mouth. There wouldn't seem to be much of a trick to that: the eye is just a dot, the mouth a line. Yet if the dot is the slightest bit misplaced—a tad high or low, a millimeter fore or aft of where it ought to be—the animal is made ludicrous, not itself at all. I myself must look ridiculous as I try to paint a mouth. As I limn the ram's short-mouthed, sheepishly bland expression, I draw in my own lips for my hand's information. I stretch my lips wide and curl the corners slightly in mimic of the lion, and bare my teeth for the crooked grin of the crocodile. The result may still be glaringly wrong: the ram's too-long mouth makes him look overly intelligent and slightly mean; the croc grins broadly instead of menacingly. I cannot make a nasty polar bear. That species wears in real life, as in my wooden translation, a smile so foolishly innocent and friendly that my mind's eye won't let me depict it as the dangerous beast I know the polar bear to be. My reference is more deeply rooted in identification than in all that I have learned.

I won't keep my Noah's Ark when it is finished. I will have satisfied my craving in the course of its completion. Then I intend to give it to my newest grandchild, Ezra, knowing to a certainty that he will wonder at the story of the Deluge, that he will assume his kinship with other animals, that the eye dots and mouth lines I have given to their faces will convey to him the same expressions that they convey to me. He won't mind that from the front the wolf and fox are indistinguishable except by the color of their paint: like me and everyone, he will know them from the side. No one will have to explain to him the discomfort of the black sheep among its cream white flock. All of this is certain because Ezra was born human, and these biased perceptions and leaps to significance are written in his brain as the grain of the wood is engraved in the tree.

The boy will not understand, though, why his grandma paired the domestic pig with the wild boar and the present elephant with the extinct mammoth; or why I chose to whittle Noah and his family as australopithecines. The whittling has been simultaneous with the writing of this book, and my hands express my thinking as much as do my words. I've indulged in mismatched pairs as a reminder that relatedness extends vertically into the past, as well as horizontally across species. The wild forest boar of Europe was transformed into the barnyard pig nine thousand years ago by Stone Age farmers who earlier had domesticated cereal grasses. The mammoth elephant was the principal game of hunters who roamed cold grasslands ten thousand years before that, at the tail of the Ice Age. And long, long before that—some four million years ago—the first hominids, the australopithecines, ventured on a course that eventually enabled their descendants to hunt and farm.

In this deeper sense, every species is married to those that came before it, and I believe that history—that natural history—reveals why Ezra will so certainly love his ark.

The idea to write about the natural history of childhood arose from a conversation with a friend. I'd been reading a book called *Good Natured* and was immersed in the meaning of its subtitle, *The Origins of Right and Wrong in Humans and Other Animals.* I explained to her the evolutionist point of view that biology must be understood as a species' response to the challenges of its environment and that animal behavior, even the advanced and complex behavior we call morality, is rooted in biology.

She was frankly shocked. Morality, my friend insisted, is an outcome of human culture, and culture has arisen not in the natural world but in the artificial constructs of society and civilization.

But what could "artificial" mean? How might one obtain from even the whole universe something not within it, something outside the natural world? She was positing the dichotomy—spiritual or artificial as opposed to bodily or natural—that has prevented us from looking ourselves square in the face as a primate whose most extraordinary achievements are nourished by a genetic endowment that barely differs from that of chimpanzees.

I understood my friend's discomfort. People resist a biological view of human nature because it smacks of determinism: we fear that reducing humans to a mere physical apparatus would mean giving up our most precious hope, that unlike other animals, we are free to choose what kind of animal we are.

But there is a crucial misunderstanding here: the determinisms we are born with or that emerge in the course of our development merely direct our attention to and favor certain responses toward the social and physical features of the environment. They are biases: alertness to the color red, attentiveness to animals, comfort in snug places. But they are meaningless until culture supplies significance. All children are biologically cued to pay attention to animals; our culture's Noah story gives meaning to that cue; I, as an individual, choose to carve the ark.

Freedom of choice requires that we recognize the internal cues by which biology readies us to respond to the environment, and so realize the optimally responsive environment that allows the full expression of our human nature. What biology has to say about our relationship to the land we inhabit, to the plants that grow there and to the animals that share it, depends on what in the environment elicits the emotional arousal and creative impulse that is all biology can supply. We have been granted, through our intelligence, unusual freedom of choice, and this is a central issue in our ecology because, although we may be born to love our land as well as use it, nothing in the text forbids the abstraction of that love to scenes on calendars or denies the exploitation of resources until there are none left.

So much was clear to me from the outset. Yet all through the writing of the first draft of this book, I felt the tug of something wrong with it. Some days, my head was populated with children, particularly with those many who so soon lose the engrossment of their early meetings with the world and become incurious, detached, increasingly uncomfortable, and often, by adolescence, simmering with discontent. Other days, the images were overwhelmingly environmental—the sterility of suburbs especially and all the variety of life that can be described only in the past tense when speaking of that landscape. The lines of thought were parallel—both child and yard seemed to me dispirited, their spontaneity and liveliness unnaturally flattened—but parallel lines don't meet. Was the point where they could be brought together the angle of how to raise future conservationists? But how mean and arrogant even to consider raising children to that or any specific purpose!

I had been a writer for nearly thirty years. While our boys were young, I wrote for children and about them. It was only as they grew up that I turned my attention to ecology. This seemed a big change to me, this leap from children to nature, from raising humans to restoring land. And it was a leap: a leap over the gap that I now was finding so difficult to bridge. So I wrote and whittled, wrote and whittled, hoping that somehow in the hard thought that the one requires and the easy musings that the other allows, the whole would come together like strayed sheep that find their flock. Finally, with some two hundred pages typed and about that many animals carved as well, the lines came together, looped and caught each other, tied the knot.

Land is nourished or not by humans; humans are nourished or not by land. Place and occupant only seem separable because we have created such a distance between liveli*ness* and liveli*hood*. In creating that distance, we have unwittingly detached the nature of childhood from the sense it ought to make. Childish curiosity is to make connections, to realize the larger picture, to become able in the physical environment our lives depend on. We've removed the red from the fruit, the fruit from the tree, the tree from the wood, the wood from all the things a child might make of it, and so left fragments much harder to connect than laces on a shoe.

Just as I was intellectually grasping the wholeness of my subject, the emotional reality came home to me—literally arrived at my home: a band of wholesome children.

A Mr. Gwynn-Robson, from Guelph, in Ontario, Canada, had called and asked could he, on a certain date when he would be in my area, tour my gardens, and could he bring his wife and children, and could he bring also his wife's friend, and her husband, and their children?

"Sure," I said.

And sure enough they all arrived on the appointed day, in two cars, the parents with five children and an unexpected grandmother as well.

The youngest, Max, just two, was a sturdy boy incongruously mopped with flaxen curls far more unruly than his careful personality. The oldest, Anne, wore boots and overalls; she was twelve, dark haired, deep voiced, and forthright. In between were another boy and two girls, and the whole troupe of them were so cheerfully comfortable with each other and with the adults that I couldn't discern friends from siblings, or who belonged to which family.

A few of the carved animals lay strewn on a large, round coffee table, which the children immediately encircled like puppies around the chow pan. I said, if they wanted, they could go upstairs to get more animals (and the boats that I haven't told you about yet), so they hauled everything to the table and began to play: all five, all ages, both sexes. One or another—I don't know who did what—put each of the five great cats in a separate stall with its matching kitten; confined the crocodiles below deck in a covered hatch; lay the youngest Noah children to bed in a loft; filled a skiff with fish; hid the tiny rodents on a nest shelf planned for eggs; turned a sheepfold into a kennel.

These children didn't whine or bicker. I could hear them from my station in the kitchen, where I was chatting with their elders over coffee. I heard laughter and a bubbling of ideas. I glanced at them from time to time. They were a kaleidoscope of shifting symmetry, popping up here or there around the table without breaking the pattern of their play.

They were having such a good time that when we grown-ups began to move outdoors, I suggested they could stay in if they wanted, so long as one of the older children took responsibility for Max, who was too young to safely maneuver the spiral stairs. But one by one, they drifted out, too drawn by the next adventure to stay behind (Grandma took charge of her darling Max). They wanted to see the real animals, explore the actual ark: this was, after all, Noah's Garden; they were, after all, Noah's Children.

"Where do the snakes live?"

"Can we see raccoons?"

"Let's climb the rocks!"

"This swing is awesome!" (Our youngest son had made the swing and hung it from a shagbark hickory limb for his girlfriend when they were both sixteen.)

I hadn't seen the families' distribution between the two cars when they arrived. When they left, the two sets of parents climbed into one car, and Grandma with all the children piled into the other. The children did not want to be separated from one another, nor did Grandma wish to be separated from the young.

The following day, a neighboring family visited with their two children, six and eight, self-conscious boy and quiet older sister (dressed for soccer). There were still boats and animals on the coffee table. They looked at them, from a distance, without a twitch of eager hands. They went outdoors with us. They never left their parents' side. No rocks. No swing. No questions either. And no speaking with their eyes and smiles. Nor did their parents—the purpose of whose visit was to discuss the landscaping of a telephone installation adjacent to both our properties—wonder about much beyond whether they would be able to deliver their soccer daughter on time to Saturday practice. It was May. Rivulets of marsh marigolds flowed gold through the wetland. Frogs splashed. Bluebirds flew.

I can't say to a certainty whether the two from across the road were less content than the five from far away, but I can tell you for sure that the five made me happy and the two left me disheartened. I also can't say that there is a sure road to childhood content, knowing as we all do the losses, abuses, deprivations, injustices, and vicissitudes of temperament that make humans unhappy. Still, we have some generally understood sense that a raccoon pacing its cage at the nature center is less happy than a raccoon raiding our garbage, and that toddlers are more delighted (and delightful) than they will be a decade hence.

What struck me most about the Guelph children and their friends was their comfort—their open faces, their relaxed gestures, their unguarded ease among themselves and with us. And, indoors, their competence—politely asking for a drink but then fetching, pouring, carrying, and serving the soda pop themselves. And, outdoors, their freedom—to go their own way without us, fearless of snakes and bugs, eager for rocks and streams. Leaving aside for now the source of that comfort, it embraced all the generations present, from infant to elder (and me, a stranger, too), and hugged domestic ritual as easily as the whole outdoors. There was the same seamlessness in their moving from imaginitive play to physical exuberance as there was in their subtle slide from addressing peers to conversing with adults. Intonation varied, voices dropped or rose, but they seemed at all times to assume communication, as though listening and being listened to, understanding and being understood, were as much their natural medium as the air they breathed.

I appreciatively noted to the parents that their children seemed *normal*. They attributed their offspring's curiosity and content to homeschooling. I thought, Yes, but underlying that latest trend in education, mightn't there be a recognition on the parents' part of children's need to learn from the inside out, within their local environment and among those closest to them? Home is children's first school, parents are their first teachers, and the stuff and things by which the family leads its daily life are their first educational materials. It's not that homeschooling per se is superior to other forms of child rearing—the academic results are, in fact, equivalent, and the effort expended more than I, for one, would want to commit— but that education flows without a break from Max's curly toddlerhood to Anne's seriously idealistic puberty, enfolded in family intimacy and involved with their surroundings and growing in depth and scope with the child's mounting engagement. School is not the issue. The issue is how we can nourish that competent and comfortable engagement with the social and natural environment that is the biological significance of childhood itself. (But how words distort! I am frustrated that at this point I have to use two words, social *and* natural, because it will take me chapters and chapters to convey that our relationship with nature is social and that to be social is our nature.)

This book roughly follows a developmental order but in a somewhat disorderly way. Although it is possible to track, for example, language skills or social behavior in the "typical" child from birth to adolescence, it is hardly revelatory to do so. I'm after revelation. The reasonable transitions that "development" implies are far less interesting than apparently unreasonable bumps, quirks, and oddities of childhood that startle by both their ubiquity and their peculiarity. Why should a noisy toddler, only a few years later, assiduously practice sneaking without a sound? Nothing in the earlier stomping predicts the later hush. Childhood is emergent: this or that behavior pops out, unprecedented and yet complete, like whispering secrets or aiming pee. These oddities are the subject of my chapter-by-chapter exploration, and the material necessarily bounces more than flows because so does childhood. Steadily through the book, though, runs the quest to discover what childish urges and actions may reveal about young humans' expectations of their environment.

I start the story with Ezra when he was newborn, when he expected little more from his environment than what it readily supplied—the holding, feeding, crooning, gazing, and smiling that we humans, as biologically wired for such responses as he was to elicit them, could hardly have withheld. As the story progresses, though, children's expectations become more complicated and our responses to their elicitations less automatic—in fact, far from certain and even thwarting of goals that they, in their childish behavior, seem bound to pursue. I have tried to act as child translator, often by reference to our species' evolution and prehistory, and so through children's younger (and yet much older) eyes give you a fresh view of kitchen and climbing tree, suppertime, storybooks, salamanders—even staring contests and pierced noses—that accords with their primitive vision.

It is true that I would like this generation to steward the land—who would not? My reason, however, is not that I am a tree hugger or can claim to care very deeply about the desert pupfish. I'm concerned for our human habitat, which by its derangement isolates and estranges us like pacing animals caged from the heights and hollows that our nature urges us to seek. I worry about habitat as I worry about habitation and inhabitants: where we live and how we live is tied to what we are, and the more we realize how the loops entwine, the closer we can draw the strings and the more lovely the knot will be.

Perhaps it will seem myopic to focus on the near at hand while the Amazon jungle burns, but we can recite the tenets of Conservation, espouse its ideals, contribute through sorting trash and writing checks to the Sierra Club, yet still raise children who think that apples come from shelves and still not see that it is up to us to plant the apple tree.

"Us" is not just you, the parents to whom this book is most directly addressed, but for the larger cast of characters that people a child's world: aunts and uncles, teachers, coaches, guides; and neighbors who might let children trespass through their yard; and anyone at all who can see the fun of standing on one's head.

I write also, and certainly, for us elders, to whom little in this book will be revelatory except the validation of our memories' value.

Stewardship follows from a conviction of wholeness with the environment, and a child's environment is not off somewhere in the wilderness. It's home and yard and you. Neither are children figments of abstraction, as my wooden animals are, crammed as I have not yet described into boats and boxes totally unsuited to real living creatures. And yet children's shaping is similarly constrained by the nature of the material, and their strength is bolstered by working with the grain, and their authentic becoming the animals they are depends on our honest perception of them.

I load the ark not only with graven images, but with meaning: with knowledge of human nature, with appreciation of natural history, with acknowledgment of the connectedness of all forms of life.

And, as is natural to my kind, with moral significance.

Born Human

Ezra was born old. It was astonishing. Everyone noticed it.

He looked nothing like his youthful parents—Joshua the curly haired, whose smooth and smiley face still prevented him from buying beer without proof of age, or Laura, his mother, who sometimes was mistaken for Joshua's kid sister.

Ezra clearly was going on eighty. Sad and knowing worry lines furrowed his brow row after row to where the hairline receded beyond his high-domed forehead. His eyebrows arched sardonically, and when he lifted one in seeming skepticism, the lines lifted with it in a unison of doubt. His ears were generous; his nose prominent too. His lower lip protruded slightly as if in puzzlement.

He had skipped a generation: line for line and feature for feature, in every expression that fleetingly crossed his world-weary face, Ezra was the seeming clone of his grandfather Henry, who was approaching eighty. The old man cradled his newborn image and with a smile, introduced the baby to his ancient species.

Ezra was born human. It was worthy of note, but no one remarked on it.

Unlike the intense scrutiny with which we seek in every newborn evidence of descent from close kin, we overlook entirely the much more dramatic evidence of a baby's descent from a primate species that first appeared in the fossil record two hundred thousand years ago. Babies much more resemble one another in that ancient genetic endowment than they resemble anyone in their families. No one remarked on Ezra's ability to cry, nor did anyone pause in wonder that the crying was so powerful as to compel two grandmothers, two grandfathers, and two parents to fairly leap to his attendance.

The adults, in fact, didn't notice the odd ways they themselves were behaving—bobbing their heads at Ezra, arching their eyebrows, lifting their voices to a singsong croon, grinning eight inches from his face. The behavior would be absurd in any other context: imagine greeting a friend that way. We reserve this greeting for babies, although it may be elicited by puppies too.

Ezra was captivated. He spent long moments gazing at each face so vividly presented to him, and as he held the image with his eyes, his body relaxed and occasionally a smile trembled at the corners of his mouth. He seemed to appreciate his audience's approaches, as though he had come prepared to greet his fellow humans. Yet he wouldn't have been able to do so without their unconscious but considerable help.

Newborn babies—Ezra was one week old at this first meeting with his grandparents—can't focus on an object that is much closer or much farther than eight inches from their face. Peripheral vision is still undeveloped: they see what is straight in front of them, unaware of anything that lies to either side. They follow a very simple set of rules for visual exploration: provided the light is not too bright, they open their eyes, keep them open, look for the light, and locate an edge. They are then constrained in their infant curiosity to stick with that discovery, examining just the near vicinity of the edge without exploring the remainder of the shape. This primitive set of rules might fix Ezra's gaze on Laura's hairline or on Grandfather Henry's chin. One wouldn't think that line of attention was much of a greeting.

But as though to put our every feature on display, we slowly weave and bob our face within the baby's narrow field of view, and from this animated sight also come sounds that happen to be pitched within the baby's preferred range of hearing. Although he can hear low rumblings and dull thumps, again a perceptual rule forces his attention to the lifted tones and singsong tunes that biology prescribes to adults greeting babies. The face has depth and contour, color too, bright flashing eyes and teeth, and—at eight inches—breathes a human scent. The adult so ludicrously bobbing for the baby makes his face into a super-object that certainly riveted Ezra's attention more than any other attraction his doting family could devise.

Ezra's inborn package of preparations to meet his species was not limited to near-face encounters: he accommodated our cradling arms, slumping into them even in the midst of a stiffening cry. Here again, we "knew" how best to mesh with him. When we picked him up, we automatically crooked him in the left arm to hold him against the heart without having to be told that the thump of his life before birth would soothe the baby. It was natural too, when he was distressed, to walk or rock him in imitation of his swaying prenatal environment. More tellingly, it was also natural to hold this potentially bipedal animal upright in our arms, with his head supported on a shoulder. This posture, while calming, prolonged his periods of alertness as though the upright vantage point provided him with a more coherent and engaging point of view than he could achieve helplessly floundering on his back or belly.

I couldn't tell whether Ezra knew his mother in any special way: he was an easy baby for anyone to care for at that age. But breast-fed babies recognize their mother's milk by smell from less than two weeks old—and would rather hers than any other's. And certainly nursing provides more time to get acquainted than other activities do: Laura nursed him whenever he wished, often every two hours, sometimes more frequently. At intervals as he suckled, she jiggled him. Had she been asked why, she would have said that the jiggling was to wake the baby up, get him going again when he paused during the meal. All mothers say that. But slowed-down videotapes of nursing babies say differently: the jiggle precedes the pause; the baby looses his grip on cue. During the interruption, the mother leans her face toward his, captures his gaze, and chats with him. From the very beginning, mealtimes are social times; they nourish bonds as well as bellies.

One other phenomenon is worthy of note: there are babies who are pretty at birth; frankly, newborn old-man Ezra was not among them. "Comical" was the best compliment I could honestly offer. His other grandparents could do no better. Joshua and Laura, though, seemed to have developed a sudden immunity to aesthetic judgment, a sort of baby blindness: their infant was perfectly beautiful to them.

We don't know what ancient ape we are descended from. We are certain that our closest living relatives are chimpanzees, for they differ from us genetically by barely more than 1 percent. Descending vertically down four million years through the branches to the trunk of our own family tree, we are fairly sure we have identified our likely hominid progenitor, a humanlike species called *Australopithecus afarensis*. Presumably this species differed even less from the apes of that time than we differ from chimpanzees today, and yet *A. afarensis* was already a stunningly different animal. It walked on two feet: the family Hominidae is defined by gait, not brains.

A. afarensis is best known as "Lucy" for the nickname given to the first specimen of her kind to be unearthed, in 1974. Since then, many others of her species have been found. They are just fossils, of course—mineralized teeth, skulls, hips, limbs—mere anatomy. Yet their bones have yielded intriguing clues to their way of life and suggest that Ezra's social readiness in part dates from that time.

Lucy stood between three and four feet tall and weighed about fifty pounds. Males, though, were a good deal larger. That contrast in body size usually indicates that males compete for females, as do chimpanzees. These males, though, lacked fangs. Maybe this was just a physical adaptation to tougher foods than most apes eat: fangs get in the way of grinding molars. A more intriguing explanation for loss of weaponry is that cooperation had become more pronounced than competition. Chimpanzee males cooperate in pig and monkey hunting and in raiding others' territory and defending their own. When it comes to sex, though, they turn fiercely against each other. *A. afarensis*'s smallish canines hint that males of the species may have come to some agreement about apportioning females. Their larger body size would remain useful in gang assaults on predators, such as the leopards that prowled their savanna habitat.

Chimpanzees have been seen ganging up on a leopard to scare it off with sticks. *National Geographic* ran footage of chimps attacking a stuffed leopard. It was pretty funny: there they were, the bunch of them, jumping up and down, hollering and throwing sticks. There was plenty of racket, but the sticks mostly missed. Chimp thumbs are too short and at the wrong angle to firmly grasp a club; they tend to toss ineffectually underhanded.

Here Lucy's group differed radically. Their arms, in keeping with their arboreal-ape past, were still long in proportion to the rest of the body, and the finger bones were curved for easy hanging from a branch. It's thought that *A. afarensis* was still at home in trees, could climb and swing from branch to branch with confidence, and perhaps ascended to safety for the night. But the thumb was longer and had rotated to a position that allowed a grip on sticks and stones powerful enough to hold the missile through windup and release. Dental weight has been added to this skeletal suggestion: carbon-isotope analysis of *A. afarensis* teeth shows that the species must have eaten either dryland grasses or grazing prey. Since electron microscopy shows further that their teeth lack the type of wear associated with abrasive foods, it seems likely that these early hominids included meat as well as vegetables in their diet. That doesn't prove they hunted: scavenging carcasses was pos-

sible if other wild and hungry animals could be beaten from the
meal.

About a year after Lucy was discovered by paleoanthropologist
Donald Johanson, his expedition came upon a group of *A. afarensis*
apparently drowned and buried in a sudden flood. There were
thirteen individuals—nine grownups, four children, and one
baby—presumably related and traveling as a band. The site of their
burial is now a dried-up riverbed in searing wasteland, but in their
day the habitat was grassy savanna similar to game parks like the
Serengeti and thronged with ancestors of the elephants, giraffes, zebras, pigs, and lions that I'm whittling for the ark. All of these were
originally forest dwellers and so was whatever ape it was that
spawned the hominids.

It is commonly said that hominids "moved" from forest to savanna as climate dried and trees had trouble growing. That can't be
so. Nothing—not a pig or a grass or a Lucy—could have made the
transition from woodland to grassland without serendipitous preparation for it. Rather, those species that could persist in spite of what
was happening to their habitat stayed on. Those that couldn't died
out. Chimps remain only in habitat that is still as it had been. For
hominids to have persisted where forest thinned to woods and then
to grassland, they must already have taken up a way of life that
worked as well for them in the forest as it would on the open plain.
Australopithecines must have descended from the arboreal highways
of their origin before the canopy vanished. But what is the use of
walking in the woods?

When biologists note a behavior that is shared by two related
species that in other respects have diverged from one another, they
conclude that both species inherited the conserved behavior from a
common ancestor. Thus, if flocks of sheep and goats are made up
of related females following one male leader, and if in both species
the male leads his flock along a route of greening grass within a circumscribed home range, biologists assume that the common ovine
ancestor was similarly sheepish. For all the stunning difference be-

tween hominids and apes, the genetic overlap is so nearly complete that we ought not be surprised that we show behavioral traits in common.

One of these is food sharing. Chimpanzees are not notably generous, but cooperating males do sometimes parcel meat out among the hunters according to their rank, and a courting male may offer a morsel to his love. His love is likely to copulate promiscuously if he's not around to interfere, but sometimes short-term faithfulness is assured by whisking the female away on "honeymoon" while she is in estrus.

If only that chimp—that chump—could be sure he was responsible for her pregnancy, it would be in his interest to continue to provision his mate and the offspring she produced. His provisioning of both—especially with high-protein meat—would favor the survival of his genes in the next generation and the descent of his good nature through succeeding ones. This is all that animal evolution is: some structural or behavioral individuality is transmitted to descendants who are thereby more likely to survive and reproduce. Nothing is foreordained; nothing is either on purpose or to a purpose. And yet the accident of a little extra generosity might bias the future of the race.

Look at us now! Note our courtings with candy, our marriage feasts, our festivals of food and family reunion! We are breadwinners, providers; we bring home the bacon.

And recall now the suckling infant reminded with a jiggle to stop and socialize: food sharing and social eating are so deeply ingrained in our species that it is inconceivable in any culture to invite a guest without offering food or to turn our backs to one another during a meal or to nurse a baby without pausing for a chat.

And now consider Lucy: hips and legs and feet had been reshaped for walking but so had her hands been reformed for grasping. Imagine that her ape progenitors were a species of more than usual generosity yet no more able to walk and haul than an ordinary ape—which is to say, a few yards with a light load. Given the behavior of food sharing, any slight anatomical change that made it easier for an ape to carry food would favor his descendants. The behavior, though invisible in fossils, drives the reshaping of the bones until by small increments over a million years or more a straight-legged, strong-handed Lucy walks into the fossil record.

It's a good story anyhow; no better one has been suggested. And it makes the point that we don't have to look for physical pressures like climate change or scarce resources to drive evolution: an animal by its culture can create the pressures that drive its own selection. If that were not so, we would be at a loss to explain how an Ezra ever arose from a Lucy, for his skull is nearly the size and shape of a bowling ball and her brain was no bigger than an ape's.

I next saw Ezra when he was three months old. It was June by then and, in his North Carolina habitat, already sweltering. I'd been summoned to baby-sit, and I sat most of the week indoors breathing at the air conditioner. There wasn't much to look at except Ezra.

He was quite changed. The worry lines were smoothed by baby fat, and new creases had appeared around his plump wrists and thighs. I won't say he had become handsome: he resembled Maurice Sendak's rendition of himself as an infant, a definitely round-headed Eastern European look. Adorable, though, especially when he smiled.

This he did at every opportunity. He smiled at my face; he smiled at his toys; he smiled at lamps and kitchen pots and window blinds. He fairly chortled to have his diapers changed. If you want to see how hopeless it is to deny biology, try keeping a straight face to a smiling baby.

Ezra had few motor skills. He could grasp an object but couldn't reliably hold on to it or bring it to his mouth, and his interest was only briefly sustained by any of his toys. His legs were strong and he delighted in digging them into my lap to stand while

I supported him, but he couldn't turn over, creep, or sit. His vocalizations had become charming: I would reproduce them for you here if I could spell those deliciously wet and gurgly, airy or chirruping sounds with which, though lacking a shared lexicon, we nevertheless communicated very well. He slept much less than half the day. The rest of the time was devoted to socializing with smiles.

Yet smiling is not entirely written on the infant brain. The motor pattern is built-in, as are patterns for those pouts and puzzlements that so amused us as they flickered across Ezra's newborn face. Blind infants, however, don't smile either easily or well. By Ezra's age of three months, some—not all—smile to their mother's or father's voice. The smile remains muted, not infectiously radiant as Ezra's smiles were, and appears reliably only in response to tickling, jouncing, nuzzling, and similarly hilarious baby games that threw Ezra into chortles on the changing table. Some blind babies don't smile at all. None smile to strangers, and none initiate smiled greetings with even those they know the best. The pattern for smiling may be inborn, but we are born also with the biological expectation that someone will smile back. Failing to receive that visual reply, this and other communicative facial expressions fail the child born blind.

I mentioned how hard it is to present a straight face to a smiling baby. Hard but not impossible. In an experiment that was tried (and quickly abandoned), researchers asked mothers to approach their infant and, instead of joining him in mutual greeting, keep a blank face. The experiment was almost immediately terminated because it so upset the babies (and their mothers too). Absence of expression is unnerving to so communicative a species even when, as infants, we haven't yet learned in much detail what is being communicated.

I recall an episode with Ezra sometime later that was as hilarious to us as belly nuzzling was to him. He was in his father's arms. I handed him a wooden toy. Somehow he lost it on the way to his mouth, and startled as it loudly hit the floor. We laughed. He laughed with us. Then a look of utter bewilderment crossed his face: What was the joke? This made us laugh all the more, but he did not join in. Not all laughter is socially inclusive, as not all smiles are friendly.

The root meaning of a smile is suggested by chimpanzees, who grin to disarm aggression. Theirs is a one-way grin, from inferior to superior in deference to his status, as though the smiler were claiming the innocence of a baby too helpless to be harmed. Our two-way smile signals that both parties have friendly intentions and so serves as a mutual invitation to approach each other safely. The hundred muscles of the human face eventually learn to modify that meaning: we disarm in the sense of embarrassing or frightening the other person, as when we curl the lips to deride or threaten, and we invite in the sexual sense of leering. These complex expressions were not among those that Ezra could produce in infancy; they remained to be learned in the complicated context of his culture. Biology is parsimonious. Given the fact that a human infant is inevitably born into a human culture, nature has only to provide the rudiments of what that culture can be expected to provide. Its rules say to reach and grasp; we say which objects to place into the baby's ready hands.

Yet we are compelled to place *something* in his hands. In time, biology will urge Ezra also to aim and throw. The fact that accurate throwing is no longer critical to our way of life won't stop him; the fact that his parents don't throw things won't dampen his pleasure in the practice. And we, helpless to deny human nature regardless of the culture we occupy, will express through ball games the rewarding skills that once might have served us in the hunt.

The nature/nurture controversy still lives, but its death is overdue. Culture *is* our nature. We come biologically prepared to express and elaborate our human nature through our culture, and all cultures are rooted in the kind of animal we are. How deeply rooted, and in how nourishing a soil, is another matter. In an old-fashioned village, Ezra's innate assumption that everyone he meets is to be greeted might remain true. I've been told by a native of the island where we summer that it can take an hour to pick up groceries because of the social exchanges everyone expects. In a modern urban culture, Ezra's enthusiasm to greet would be altered, and the assumption in general abandoned.

At three months, this baby's every inborn expectation was being met. He was born to be social and was born into a sociable family. He was rocked, stroked, talked to, and played with in just the ways that came most naturally to them—and that they could hardly help and that he could not help enjoying. But there will emerge as Ezra grows through childhood very many other inborn rules, biases, urges, and behaviors that will mesh less easily with adult responses and that may be ill expressed or poorly supported by the surrounding culture. What are we to make of a child's urge to climb trees?

In the two million years since australopithecines became extinct, various hominid descendants have walked the earth. All but one are fossilized in oblivion, dead ends without descendants. A single branch of the hominid tree continued its evolution to what we think of as the flower of creation, *Homo sapiens sapiens*: modern humankind, ancient Ezra. Environment—climate, diet, disease—has impressed on us those minor alterations we call race, but in intelligence and aptitude for the human way of life, there has been in the intervening two hundred thousand years no further evolution of our species.

Ezra's brain is the same size and structure as that of early man; so are the childhood behaviors his brain prescribes. Yet those inborn preparations to join his species' culture must now serve his participation in a culture very different from the foraging way of life that was ours for nine-tenths of human history, and very different too from the farming way of life that we followed for nearly all the remaining ten thousand years and that is still followed by the majority of our species. The rapidity of cultural change during the previous century has been breathtaking enough. Now, to be born into the twenty-first century presents a challenge to human nature that children have never before been asked to meet.

Or, more accurately, Ezra's birth poses a challenge to us to meet his expectations in circumstances that biology has no reason to expect.

Ezra came to visit for Thanksgiving. He was by then nine months old and crawling. His exhilaration was evident and exhausting, for his territory had expanded from lap size to house size. The landscape he had visually inspected was now his to physically explore, and the objects he could investigate were whatever he could reach.

Within the four-day weekend, Ezra scraped a cheek against the fireplace logs, blackened an eye on a wooden chest, pinched a finger in a drawer, and bumped his head quite a few times under the coffee table. He cried and kept on going: wool rug to wood floor, flat surface to ascending stairs, one room after another through a terrain of chair legs and lamp wires where everything was novel.

Ezra's other grandparents arrived for the holiday with gifts for him: a truck and a "talking" toy.

The truck made Ezra mad because, although he grasped that it should roll, it rolled only when it was upright, and it kept falling over. The talking box was a hit: when he pushed one of the raised figures on the panel, it lit up and spoke. "Night night," said the moon when Ezra pushed it. "Baby," said the baby when he pounded it. This lit-up noisy toy interested Ezra for quite a while—meaning, at that age, a good five minutes. But what did it convey?

"Dog," said the dog in the box, and the real dog, Girl, replied by growling, hackles raised, at the strangeness of the noisy box. Ezra pushed the button again, and it said "dog" again. But when he reached for the real dog, Girl wagged her tail and licked his ear. She wandered off and he crawled after her, squealing with excitement. After many tries, he caught Girl's thumping tail and tried to use it to pull himself up to stand. Girl did not say "wruf, wruf" as the dog button does on another version of the talking box. When she did bark, her sharp yip startled Ezra and make him blink, and the bark had meaning: Girl was demanding to go out.

Whenever Ezra caught sight of Girl, he broke into grins and gurgles, and one or another of us said, "Dog!" That weekend, Ezra learned his first word: *duh*. The word came from us, not from the box. It signified dog, not button.

He found Girl's ball to play with. Whereas the truck rolled only when it was upright and being pushed, the ball rolled in any position and continued to roll when Ezra let go of it. It was a solid rubber ball, and it smelled of vanilla. Ezra mouthed and licked it nice and slimy. He dropped it from his high chair, laughing at its loud and lively bounce. Down on the floor, he rolled and chased the ball. A great joke to Ezra was that Girl, too, played ball.

The kitchen revealed to Ezra's exploration the most amazing things. Drawers to push and pull, open and shut. Inside the drawers, clanking pot lids, nesting cups, a whisk. The whisk made different noises depending on what it was banged against: tile floor, metal stove, wooden drawer. The rolling pin rolled but differently from ball or truck. It took some muscle to pick up.

One morning, Laura called a friend from the kitchen wall phone. She was holding Ezra in her lap. He was, of course, enchanted with the coiled wire. To relieve her of his grappling entanglement, I handed her the portable telephone while Joshua took the child, still grasping the wire. Laura continued her conversation in the next room. Joshua let Ezra listen in. His face turned wondering, eyes wide, jaw dropped: his mother's voice! She hung up and reappeared at the kitchen door. He chortled at the rejoining of her voice and person.

I find it striking that the least educative of these events was Ezra's brief engagement with the talking box which, according to the brochure that accompanied it, was "Designed to Develop Minds." The mind the manufacturer intended to develop was set on a goal to which "Little Smart First Words Plus" was irrelevant.

Ezra was bent on getting acquainted with his habitat. His approach, as well as his parents' cultural mediation, was similar to the early adventurings of young chimpanzees.

In a television program that followed the one on leopard-attacking chimps, the camera recorded a youngster holding a stout piece of branch by both ends, as one would hold a rolling pin, and bashing it against a nut to try to crack it open. The branch, though, was slightly curved, and the concave portion didn't make sufficient contact with the shell to break it. The youngster's mother watched his efforts for a while, then came over, took the implement, and turned it around so that the convex edge faced downward. She then handed it back, and the chimp, using the demonstrated grip, cracked the nut.

Chimpanzees use a variety of tools: stripped stalks of grass for "fishing" termites from their holes, chewed wads of leaves for sponging up water, sticks and stones for frightening off their enemies. The use of tools is culturally transmitted. Implement and technique may differ from one tribe to another and must be taught to each new generation. The young chimp's mother was purposefully introducing him to a material aspect of her culture.

A second scene showed another youngster repeatedly climbing a springy sapling to make it bend and bounce him. He was not shown how to do it; the adults were taking their afternoon rest while he explored through his own play a property of wood that might serve him in the future.

These two scenes summarize a good portion of what is going on as a baby becomes able to move about and handle objects. A human mother might reorient a spoon her baby is holding so that the bowl, not the handle, is aimed toward his mouth. Or she might just keep an eye on him while he discovers on his own the properties of metal, wood, and rubber. Ezra's habitat didn't yet extend much farther than our habitation, and it seems right to me that his natural and cultural education should have begun there. That he was drawn so particularly to the kitchen seems reasonable too: it's where food is stored, prepared, and eaten; where everyday implements are kept and used; where there is fire as well as water; and where, in chatty cooperation as we work, we reveal an ancestral way of life.

Yet in a perversity of our culture, the kitchen is hardly the favored arena for infant education. We go to great effort to create a playroom or a nursery—a world apart decorated in baby colors, filled with baby toys, and tinkling with a musical mobile that tires our adult ears. In spite of evident protest, we confine babies to playpens and infant seats as often and for as long as they will stand for it. "Is it true," a Japanese mother is said to have asked an American visitor, "that in your country you put your babies to sleep in cages?"

There is more to this isolation than the attempt to physically separate the infant's sphere of activity from our own. We also create a cultural divide. We give babies food that we don't eat, unspillable cups that we don't drink from, and implements that we have mastered in forms that require no mastery. Pablum is not a new invention; cups and spoons sized for baby hands have been around for ages. But "junior" foods intrude upon the time that infants used to share, in mashed or minced form, the food on our own plates. With the advent of infant ergonomics, babies are no longer required to learn the wrist-turning tricks of spooning food into the mouth or tipping cups correctly. Ezra, at three months, already was learning to hold his bottle, but by Thanksgiving he had been supplied with bottles that yielded juice no matter what the grip or angle.

These seem small things, and I don't suppose a baby's humanity is warped by drinking from a sippy cup. But Ezra, by nine months, had quite a mind of his own, and there were areas of disagreement.

He didn't want to sleep in a crib. It happens that I don't have one. He slept here on a futon on the bedroom floor, and he slept well, nestled like a puppy in the spot he had chosen among the quilts and pillows. He didn't cry when he woke up as he did at home caged in a crib. Why should he, when he could call and crawl to us so freely?

At home, Ezra fought being strapped into his high chair. Our
high chair is the old-fashioned kind, with a tray that lets down over
the baby's head. No straps, no adjustments. Not safe, either, not a
place you'd leave a baby while you answered the telephone. But
Ezra was fed there without a fight, since there was no restraint to
fight against. Usually we were eating too, or food was on the table.
He wanted what we ate, even though the unfamiliar textures of
cheesecake, oatmeal, cranberry jelly, and mashed potatoes resulted
in some of the funniest wry-mouthed expressions of distaste I've
ever seen on any infant's face. It was as though he *would* like our
food, was determined to eat what we ate regardless of how hard to
mouth or strange in flavor it was compared to the baby foods he
was used to. He dove headlong toward our drinks, and we were
constantly grabbing glasses from his clutch.

Through all of these endeavors, from tonguing for beer to
climbing stairs to groping through pocketbooks, it was adamantly
clear that Ezra intended to join us in whatever capacity he could,
and he resented distractions from that goal. Toys are distractions.
They are among the ways we try to keep babies safe from, but
therefore also ignorant of, the actual world that we and they inhabit.

A story Laura told me sticks in my mind for its near uncanni-
ness. A friend of hers, noting how delighted his infant daughter
was with his key chain, had an identical set made for her. The same
chain exactly, with every key on it. She refused it. She wanted *his*
keys, the original and authentic.

Babies are born human. They are driven by their nature to join
the culture of their birth, to eat its food, listen to its music, handle
its implements, explore its materials, and navigate its habitations.
But while we can't avoid sociably introducing ourselves to babies
through smiling and many more intricately patterned and unconscious responses, our built-in program for introducing the material
culture seems less delineated. We have choices, and I think the
choice to insulate babies from our habitat is a wrong one. I wonder
whether the creation of a separate babyworld is the first step toward

what we have come to call alienation. I strongly suspect that the nursery is an intellectually inferior milieu for an infant's rapidly developing brain.

Newborn babies have at birth the full human complement of brain cells—neurons—that will constitute intelligence, but they are not intelligent. Most of the neurons are sparsely branched, not elaborately connected with one other or not connected at all. It is the connections that make intelligence, and babies must construct these through their own experience. I mean "construct" quite literally. The growth of intelligence is physical, structural: real.

It is also accurate to say that the brain is an intrinsically curious organ, for from the very beginning and throughout life, neurons actively seek contact with one another. They grow and branch toward one another, almost but not quite touching across the gaps called synapses. When two neurons' approach is rewarded by a chemical signal across the gap between them, that contact is strengthened: a connection has been learned. The learning arouses more curiosity, more reaching out between sender and receiver until, as with friends who have come to know each other very well, they meet in embrace. So neurons registering the feel of a ball simultaneously with other neurons registering the sight of a ball literally connect touch with vision. That's a terribly simplistic description, though.

As Ezra played with the ball, signals were arriving to his brain from his eyes, ears, nose, mouth, and fingers: the ball's look, sound, smell, taste, feel, and motion. The sensations did not arrive whole, as the mind experiences them, but in scores of fragmented data from specialized sensory neurons that fire to particular wavelengths of light, frequencies of sound, molecules of scent, and aspects of touch. These raw data were arriving by separate, incoming pathways into processing centers in Ezra's brain where, for example, signals arriving from three kinds of cones in his eyes were being constructed into his experience of red by contacts among receiving neurons.

Such basic learning is itself a feat, yet these early connections are merely a fraction of the entire collaboration among neurons that one is dimly aware of when thinking *ball*: all the kinds of ball, all their sizes, materials, colors, and actions; and thoughts of the games they involve; and comparisons among other ball-like objects; and the abstractions by which such comparisons can be made. And yet even this exercise in conscious thought can't convey the number of contacts necessary to experience *ball* as a baby is only beginning to do. Each neuron in the brain—there are one hundred *billion* brain cells altogether—may eventually receive signals from a hundred thousand other neurons. Each of those receivers may contact a hundred thousand others, and any of these may also reach for one another and disperse signals on and on through networks of communication too intricate to imagine.

A baby's brain grows to nearly three times its birth weight in the first year. By the age of two, what had begun as a mere tracery of neurons will have become more thicketed and more broadly communicating than it ever will be again. The vaunted "creativity" of toddler play is exactly the astounding multiplicity of connections they grow during these first years among the neurons in their brain. Everything seems possible to toddlers: every substance edible, every object animate, every use potential, every similarity compelling.

But though the brain at birth is structured to seek such connections, and the baby's active explorations make them happen, it is we who provide the arena for their happening. Chimpanzees are naturally surrounded by the substances, materials, and objects that they must learn about to grow up chimpanzee. We now live removed from the basics of our own way of life, but babies aren't warned that they were born in the computer age, when barks and meows come from boxes more often than from animals. All babies are ancient. Toys won't deter them from reaching for our tools. Playpens won't extinguish their urge to explore our habitat. But to whatever extent we do succeed in keeping them in babyland, to that same degree, we lessen the significance of what they learn and detach the learning from its cultural context.

One example: among infants' built-in equipment is a preference for the color red. Among languages that have only one color word—all have words for black (dark) and white (light)—the word inevitably means "red." So the significance of the color red must run deep into our evolutionary past, and the best guess as to why is that it signifies ripe fruit. I notice this when scanning the near landscape: anything red leaps to my attention. I run my eyes over the talking-toy brochure that came with Ezra's noisy box, and sure enough the overwhelming color is red. The manufacturer knows what appeals to the infant—to the human—eye. The red portions of the toys, though, have no particular significance. On one, a steering wheel is red; on another, the frame around the display screen; on a third, wheels and a handle; or on others, the base, buttons, speaker, or the whole body of the toy.

A friend has twin daughters who, at the time of the following event, were about a year old. To keep them occupied before they went to day care in the mornings, she sat them on the kitchen counter where they helped themselves to fruit and breakfast cereal while she finished cleaning up. The fruit bowl was kept on the kitchen counter too, but on this particular morning, it held cherry tomatoes and hot cherry peppers that she'd bought the day before. Of course, one of the girls helped herself to what she thought was a tomato and bit into a cherry pepper instead. It was unfortunate; she cried. But not only did that daughter learn to discriminate between the same-sized, same-colored fruits, so did her observing twin. Red signifies "ripe," but it does not always signify "safe." Our culture, in fact, uses our special alertness to the color red to warn of danger, and red is metaphorically anger's color too. The "hot" experience of red pepper, even the observation of someone else's experience of it, spliced into a cultural intelligence more neatly than the experience of a red plastic toy can possibly do.

Helping a friend with minor repairs one day, I was stymied by some loose screws holding the hinges of a wooden cabinet door. I tightened them with a screwdriver, but they wouldn't hold. They'd been

tightened too many times; the holes were stripped. I hied to the
hardware store for plastic plugs. You hammer these into the holes,
then rescrew the screw. Of course, the plug has to fit the hole, and
these didn't.

Along came a handyman who had more experience of wood,
holes, and screws. He said to dip the end of a wooden matchstick
in glue, pound it into the hole, break it off at the surface, then rescrew. Wooden matches aren't round; they're square. But wood is
compressible. These kitchen matches were longer than a screw
hole, but wood is breakable. Even pounded in, there might have
been gaps between the round hole and the square peg, but the glue
filled in and bonded wood to wood. The screws held fast.

I would like Ezra to learn, as his brain develops, the complexi-
ties of approximation, the many and often overlapping qualities of
materials, the creativity of their multiple and possible connections.
Some connections will prove false. The young chimp bouncing on
a springy sapling may assume that all slender trees support him, until the day one cracks and dumps him to the ground. So Ezra may
suppose vanilla-scented balls taste like vanilla-flavored cheesecake or
that round red apples bounce like round red balls, but reality won't
confirm such over-eager connections. Lack of confirmation—lack
of any experience of bouncy apples and delicious balls—will be reflected in fewer firings of those connections, of a weakening of signals or their inhibition, and finally the baby's brain will prune away
the possibility that apples are elastic and balls are food. Children
don't thereby become sober realists. Rather, the traces of what
might be so but really isn't remain in playful hovering, in the as-if
imagination that allows a child to jokingly offer Grandma a rubber
ball to eat.

I'm on the Grandma list now of mail-order toy catalogs that
heavily tout the capacity of toys to teach facts and foster creativity.
I threw one away this morning after I'd gotten to the "Best for
Baby" page that depicted an "activity center." It appeared to be a
cross between a high chair and a car. That is, it was shaped like a car

(red) with a tray (yellow). To the car was attached a crank (green) and to the tray a telephone receiver (blue). Baby is strapped into the seat for his/her "activity."

All the toys on the page were in the four primary colors, and all were made of plastic. Plastic, because it's plastic, can be molded into objects that, were they real, would be as fundamentally different from each other as a ball is from a bat. The brochure that came with the talking box described the whole line of talking toys. In Ezra's age category, beginning at six months, these included a talking "Book," "Telephone," "Toy Shop," "Farm," "Home," "Bug," and "Ball," as well as Ezra's new "Little Smart First Words Plus" that says "night night" when you push the moon. The display for the next age category, beginning at nine months, opened with a "Laptop" that says numbers, shapes, and colors, makes animal noises, and plays five built-in melodies selected by five keys (all yellow) to "encourage musical discovery."

I was appalled.

I so enjoy being appalled that I look at every catalog that comes before I trash it. Through endless repetition, I have learned that it is terribly, terribly important that babies learn the names of primary colors and geometric shapes regardless of what vehicle is used to teach them. Yes, vehicle: one is a shape-sorting truck that, when the correct block is inserted through the correct window, says the name of the shape. "Triangle," it teaches. I look in vain for any equilateral triangles lying around the house—or for any truck with triangular windows.

Abstractions are constructs of the brain. That is, they are recognitions of underlying qualities that are derived from many experiences of imperfect objects that approximately share the quality. The intellectual feat is not in learning *round* from a disk that fits a hole—common pigeons can do that—but in deriving *round* from objects as dissimilar as coins, wheels, pancakes, buttons, and their spherical equivalents, snowballs, oranges, and Christmas ornaments. Plastic perfection limits the concept.

Ezra anyway had no concept of *truck*. He had no way of con-
necting a wheeled vehicle with how he had gotten from North
Carolina to New York for the Thanksgiving holiday. What intrigued my grandson at nine months would equally have engaged
an ape, for the young human has as yet no imagination, and the ape
at any age will have less imagination than a child of three. I've said
I have no doubt that Ezra will love his ark of animals, but it wasn't
in his mind yet to love them any more than, a month later at his
first Christmas, he loved the stacks of blocks his parents gave him—
the blocks that were, as Laura remarked, no more to him than a
trove of wooden teething toys.

There remained the problem of Christmas.

Having spent the week after Ezra's Thanksgiving visit writing
this diatribe against plastic, this disquisition on the limitations of
toys for infant adventurers, I couldn't very well buy a jack-in-the-
box. But gee, it was cute!

I found in one catalog the most darling sit-on train: hard wood,
shiny paint, big wheels. It looked like a baby locomotive, its features exaggerated and plump. And oh! The stuffed animals! Laura
and Joshua had taken Ezra to FAO Schwarz, where they were
crushed in a stampede caused by a woman stumbling on the escala-
tor, but they emerged at last with a stuffed woolly mammoth.

Adorable!

Ezra sucked the tusks.

The trouble with toys is that they are so age appropriate for
grownups. One has to force oneself not to get silly over barnyard
sets or at least not to indulge oneself in one now, when the recipi-
ent doesn't yet know a *duh* from a donkey.

I steeled myself. I ordered a steel wagon from a serious catalog
of professional tools. It was designed for nurseries—not the kiddy
kind, the bush and tree kind. Very heavy-duty. So heavy that, when
it arrived in two boxes, I couldn't carry the bigger one. That box
held the wagon body and the wheels. The second box held all the
other parts.

I'll spare you the assembly details, except to remark that the instructions were written in a semblance of English translated in Taiwan. But I got it together at last, all sixty-three pounds of it, and gave it to Ezra, and noticed that he didn't notice it. What is a wagon to an infant?

A wagon, Ezra, is to go outside.

Outside! Outside!

Ian at two: big for his age, with feet still bigger, plump faced, eyes set wide apart, hair straight and of a forgettable color. Yet who could forget a boy so vigorous, so delighted with purple asters, hunting for honeybees!

Ian arrived one Sunday evening with his little dog, Gunter, his mother, and his father, who is a plantsman and photographer. The family was harried and exhausted: their car had been stolen in Boston, along with cameras, stroller, car seat, dog crate, and the seeds that, collected at the Arnold Aboretum, had been half the purpose of their travel. The other half was to photograph my garden for a magazine, but the light was going by the time they got here in a rented car, so I offered dinner and asked them to stay the night.

Before we could so much as settle the parents with a glass of wine, Ian began: "Outside! Outside!" Outside were flowers. "Smell good!" Ian said, pushing his flat nose deep into sprays of asters. He stroked sweet everlasting, pulled me by one finger from flower to bush to grass, touching, sniffing, picking red apples from the Sargent's crab. He heard a noise. I told him, "Cricket." We looked for it but couldn't find it. Ian hit the lawn and said, "Run!" so we ran through the grass to the pond, where we sat on a rock at the shore. I was barefoot and splashed my feet in the water. I took off Ian's shoes, and he splashed too. Gunter joined us, carrying a rawhide dog chew. He dropped it in the water. I reached for an oar in the rowboat moored at the rock and retrieved the rawhide for him. This delighted Ian, this simple feat.

On the way back through the terrace garden, I caught a toad and carried it in for him to examine in the lamplight. "Frog," he said, and I said, "Toad." I expected the frightened toad to pee in my hand—and thought that would delight Ian too—but instead the toad cried: short yelps of distress, sounds I'd never heard coming from a toad. Ian touched it gingerly, saw the toad blink, and touched again to make it blink again. We released it among the flowers outside the living-room door.

Now it was dark, and Ian's parents told him to stay inside. He was past the kitchen cupboard stage; he already knew his whisks and rolling pins. My husband, Marty, took him upstairs to the attic where we keep the boys' old toys. After several trips, Ian had accumulated a fire truck, a pull-toy alligator, and an antique steam-run tractor. He liked each for about a minute but then again, "Outside! Outside!" We opened the terrace doors as we often do on warm evenings and turned on the outside light. There was no contest between toys on a rug and toads in the jungle. We could not keep Ian in.

And the next morning, hardly awake, with soaked diapers under his pajamas, Ian's first words were again, "Outside! Outside!" He heard a noise and correctly pronounced "cricket" even though we never had located the chirper. For the next three hours while his father photographed, Ian tirelessly explored the paths, the pond, and the terrace garden where, although he was big for his age, he easily became lost among the towering flowers.

As the sun warmed the terrace, bees began to arrive at the goldenrods and asters. Soon there were hundreds of them, honeybees and bumblebees and varieties of wasp swarming the flowers, their buzz swelling with the heat. I saw that Ian was trying to catch a honeybee, and warned his mother, but she merely remarked that if he got stung, he would learn that bees are not good things to try to catch. We stood and watched him, his cupped hands snatching at the loud flowers, happily repeating with every try, "I missed!"

I have never since my own childhood so sharply felt the contrast between inside and outside. After the family left, I looked at the fire truck on the living-room floor, at the wooden high chair pulled up to the kitchen table. The light was outside. The breeze was outside. The noise, the only noise—the chorus of cicadas, katydids, and crickets—was outside. Smells were outside; motion was outside; life was outside. Inside is shelter from all these things, roof against the rain, walls against the night, a bed against the hardness of the ground. But to Ian, inside was not where he lived.

Outside: how it has shrunk! New houses seem to have gobbled the land to fatten themselves. They have grown enormous. A house twice the size of ours where we raised four children is now considered modest. Some of the houses in the new developments here are more than three times bigger. They display themselves to one another over bare lawn. Their size and ostentation say something sad to me: indoors has grown more important than outdoors used to be.

The original farmhouse still stands on one of these developments. It is tiny! Yet farm families were large: six children, ten. How did they fit? The five children in my father's farming family could have told you: they packed in for meals and overnight; otherwise they were outdoors. Smaller still than farmhouses and going back much farther are the oval adobe huts the Maya still inhabit, as well as felt-covered yurts, snow-block igloos, deer-hide tepees, and the steppe homes built of mammoth bones and tusks during the Ice Age. For most of human history, people have spent the majority of their time outside.

So you'd expect that we are born to love the great outdoors— and Ian supports that view—but the disturbing absence of children playing on what land is left in the new developments contradicts

the expectation. Or maybe children's expectation of the great outdoors has been contradicted. I think of Grandfather Henry:

Henry is not an outdoor man. He exercises for his health but
sticks to the pavement. He doesn't do yard work or even sit outside.
He doesn't feed the birds. He doesn't like to touch the soil. He
startles when Girl approaches him and will only with urging pat
her head. Actually, Henry is scared of dogs, even small friendly
ones.

There is every reason for Henry to suffer a general discomfort
with the natural world. His only intimate experience of the countryside was two years spent hiding in a dugout beneath a Polish
farmer's barn to escape the Holocaust. All the rest of his immediate
family perished. So he wants to be indoors, safe, and I don't blame
him.

I don't blame any of the many people who live with such discomfort in the suburbs—pruning wild shrubs to ornamental buns,
demanding leash laws, zapping insects in the night. It is not their
fault that they were given so little experience of nature that they
distrust the outdoors, or at least whatever lies beyond the patio.

That's not to say their distrust is natural. Even at nine months—
even at three months—one could always soothe Ezra when he became fretful by taking him outdoors. Was it the breeze on his
cheek, the sunlight? Perhaps the motion of leaves, the liveliness: he
loved to look at foliage and flowers. And why not, since he is the
child of a grassland species? And why shouldn't he come to feel
easy with animals too and understand as Noah did that all of us are
on the ark together? But then, why shouldn't every child smile like
the very sunshine?

For the same reason that lights do not turn on unless the switch
is flicked.

I do not think that lawns can flick that switch. And if children
are to make contact when they seem, like Ian, so ready in their
fearless sensuality, then I think the switch must be within their own
reach, not someplace they must be taken to.

I have watched another boy, Sam, grow from babyhood to three years old. Sam, too, likes to be outside. There are woods and meadows where he lives, a marsh, a stream, and ponds. I've seen the sky there filled with dragonflies. Since Sam was a baby, his mother has walked with him daily on paths through these wilder places, first on her back, then in a stroller, now hand in hand. These are walks, though; Sam plays in his yard.

The yard is a lawn. There are two trees, a tire for him to swing on, and toys. The toys come in and out, from rug to lawn—trucks and other vehicles, the same kinds of toys that attracted Ian. I haven't watched Sam play indoors, but a truck on a rug isn't much different from a truck on a lawn. Sam can't get lost among flowers in his yard, can't smell or stroke anything but mowed grass. Of all the bees that might visit there—giant shiny carpenter bees, furry bumblers, emerald metallics—only the ill-tempered yellow jacket might come to bite his sandwich, and it would surely sting the hand that tried to catch it.

Already Sam is learning that the real "outside" is where you go, not where you live. It isn't that the distance is far: the meadow, with its butterfly weed and butterflies, is right across the road. But Sam's immediate world, the one he can touch and smell and venture on his own, lacks the "outsideness" that so excited Ian.

Ian had impatiently downed some juice and suffered his diapers to be changed before his mother let him out through the kitchen door into the morning. The door opens on an herb garden. There were a huge rosemary bush that miraculously had survived two northern winters; savory, lavender, and thyme in bloom, all attended by pollinators; sour sorrel, fragrant basil, and anise leaves to taste. That late summer morning, a trumpet vine was still hung with a few flowers visited by hummingbirds and many green pods the size of small bananas. Even standing on the seating wall that surrounds the herb garden, Ian's head was barely level with the New England asters just beyond, and the flame honeysuckle vine came above his knees. Behind him as he looked over the stone terrace was a row of sunflowers; goldfinches had been coming daily for the seeds. Below him was a hole in the ground where a chipmunk stored acorns and hickory nuts in caverns so commodious that the Franklin tree in that corner was dying from the desiccating air around its roots.

He clambered off the wall into vegetation waist high to us but over Ian's head. There was fruit to be found: cranberries, bearberries, wintergreen, and bright crabapples that he tried to feed the dog. Earlier, there would have been blueberries, huckleberries, Juneberries, and strawberries as well—all of them delicious and safe for toddlers to eat. The garden is paved in stone, and the paths are narrow. He brushed against the bayberry and caught the fragrance of the leaves. There is an aster, called silky aster, whose leaves are as soft as mole fur, and another, stiff aster, whose leaves are resinous and sharp. Both pearly everlasting and sweet everlasting were in bloom. Their texture is tissue papery. Ian loved best the feel of milkweed silk and how, loosed from his fingers, the seeds rode the air.

One morning was not enough for Ian to explore this yard. He did not, for instance, climb the boulders or discover the birdbath, the mosses, the cranberries, or the ants that were guarding the trumpet-vine pods. How much longer would be needed to explore this yard-size garden not only as it was on that September morning, but how it changes through the seasons of the year, how the nodding onions slowly lift their blooming heads, how the winter wren runs across the paths like a hurried mouse, how the bluebirds introduce their babies to the bath, how the squirrels plant nuts among the herbs, how the monarch caterpillars chew the milkweed leaves, how the cedar waxwings in November devour the crabapples' red fruit in an orgy that continues for a week!

We didn't plan the garden with children in mind: we planned it for wildlife. But I saw that day with Ian that the needs of toads, chipmunks, ants, and wrens coincide with the delights of wild toddlers. For instance, splashing in the birdbath, which is set low in a

rock outcropping. Scrambling up the rock as chipmunks do to hide
under the branches of the weeping hemlock. Digging in the sand
between the stones like toads do to make their burrows. Crawling
through the grasses to find sweet fruits or the elusive cricket. And
sipping nectar. Nibbling leaves. Collecting acorns. Catching bugs.
Hunting. Gathering. Bathing. Hiding. Hoarding. Exploring.

Ian was rather like a puppy just venturing from the den, discovering what there is to eat and where water is and how to get from
one place to another. Shortly, most mammals put what they have
learned to use in the serious practicalities of survival. Humans remain playful and make more of their explorations than is strictly
necessary for survival. Ian fingered milkweed silk, then let the fluff
float on the breeze. Some weeks later, our granddaughter Phoebe
used the silk to line a "bird bed" in a bower she had contrived.
Some hundreds of years ago, settlers cultivated the novel plant in
hope that it would become a commercial crop for stuffing mat-
tresses. There's a developmental direction here from the sensual
through the symbolic to the practical. Whereas Ian explored what
the stuff is like, Phoebe played with what its softness implied about
its use, and the settlers experimented with how the material could
be exploited.

I don't mean to suggest that toddlers should be given experience of milkweed silk so that they will eventually make money in
the mattress business. I do suggest that toddlers build from their
sensual experience of the natural world ultimate connections with
it. Asters, as it happens, do not smell good. Sniffing flowers,
though, was the essence of Ian's relationship with them, reflecting
both his understanding of flower*ness* and his experience of himself
as flower sniffer. Perhaps in another year, he will differentiate between the aster, which smells, and the lavender, which smells *good*,
and later still will make the connection that the "smell good" of
lavender flowers is the good smell of lavender soap. The point is
not the intellectual achievement, but that the child, by his own
sniffing through the garden, can make such connections himself.

They are his, part of him, the flower hound who sniffed along a trail to its conclusion.

Think of the difference if, on the family's drive home, they had stopped to visit the herb garden at the Cloisters in New York, and the parents were to have told the boy, "This is lavender; it smells like Mommy's soap." That is an experience but one far removed from that of plunging mind naked and open nosed into the jungle of one's garden home. Our propensity as adults is to educate, as when I could not help but articulate a difference between *frog* and *toad*. But at every stage, children's intimacy with their own surroundings precedes the ability to grasp how that knowledge is formalized in our culture.

Ian was on the verge of connection. He came upon the crabapples in idle exploration and liked their color and that they could be plucked. His mind leaped: they were food, perhaps to feed the dog. The day that Phoebe made her bower, she went straight for the red fruit to decorate a cake. I use the apples to make jelly. The juice that Ian drank that morning was apple cider.

When hunting, as when gathering, Ian was after something bigger than a bee. Like younger Ezra, the whisk-wielding noisemaker, or older Phoebe, the floss-gathering bed maker, he was formulating some sense of himself regarding bees. Their and his quest was less to discover what the object is than what can be made of it: a noise, a bed, a captive. Children milk the environment to build themselves from the outside in, filling themselves with their own sensations of the world and the sense of their actions on it. This brave taking—I would almost call it a greed for wholeness—isn't something we can do for them. Toddlers are adamantly self-propelled; so, intrinsically at any age, is growth itself. What we can do is create an environment that is inherently functional. Outdoors, in our own yard, that means an ecosystem that is at least as useful, engaging, significant, and social a place as the kitchen is indoors.

What if all the yard had been a lawn? Lawn said, "Run!" to Ian; it had nothing else to say. Its very blankness makes a point: indoors

is by comparison the more interesting place. Of course, the household habitat is engaging only incidentally. We grown-ups employ a
variety of substances and implements but not because we intend to
give children joy in smearing ointment and unrolling toilet paper.
Some tribal societies consider that all household possessions belong
to the children, since it is they who must come to use them. I can
imagine Ezra or Ian finding that a natural point of view, but ours is
not that sort of culture.

Our culture makes the point that much of what most interests
children is not obtainable *by* them. It's our cotton balls and cinna-
mon sticks, not their free-for-the-gathering furry mullein leaves or
minty wintergreen. What rolls or smears or makes a noise when it
is squeezed is a truck we've bought, a set of finger paints, a stuffed
animal—not the log or mud or toad that children might obtain for
themselves. They can't even get some berries for their breakfast unless we buy the fruit.

We're well aware that children of Sam's or Ian's age want to
splash, dig, swing, climb. So we make the yard a playground: provide a sandbox, a wading pool, a junior gym. We toddlerize it and,
as with playroom and nursery, thereby draw a boundary between
our and our children's world. Parents, when planning their yard, are
careful to site the children's play area within supervisory view from
the house (often ironically from the kitchen and adjoining patio).
The intervening space is where nothing grows and no one lives,
where children have no reason to play nor adults to linger. We say,
by this distancing, Go *away* and play; we grown-ups don't swing;
you kids don't barbeque.

Where is the common ground? Where is the place that they and
we can come together within our shared environment? Where, in
fact, is the environment?

The rocks that Ian might have climbed that morning are home
to a large but harmless blacksnake; the sand he might have dug is
punctuated with ant hills; the water he might have splashed in
quenches chipmunks' thirst. The connection Ian was beginning to

make between what grows on trees and what comes in jars is empowering and joyful—not to mention potentially practical. And what a shock of recognition the boy must have experienced when the toad blinked, when it cried! Yet even so, in this natural play yard simultaneously occupied by so many forms of life with so much to reveal, the fact is that the biggest, most dramatic, engaging, and interesting creatures in the garden that morning were us: we who plant and care for it, pick flowers and take pictures of them, grow plums and cook them into jam, watch over a toddler as he pitches into this sensual and self-formulating feast. A garden is in no way a wilderness: no matter how natural it may be and how well it functions ecologically, it can't be divorced from the humans who made it and maintain it. We are essential to the ecosystem, a large presence among the many others that children encounter as they gulp for wholeness with their environment. We all had business to be there. So, therefore, had the garden business to be there, since it served us all, ants to Ian, and we had made that be so. The terrace is a working garden: it works; we work. We can also work to take functionality from the environment, and that is what we mostly turn our labor and our money toward when we force it into lawn. But when we excise the usefulness of our environment, we also excise children's potential usefulness within it. We disable both.

According to our own metaphor, humans were created in the Garden where surely there were fruiting trees, frightened toads, and buzzing bees. If I read Scripture right, the onus of our expulsion was responsibility for ourselves in those gardens where, forever after, we would have to work to grow. It seems to me an obligation, literally and figuratively, to plant in ground and child seeds to grow them back together.

"Outside! Outside!" said Ian of the greater complexity and liveliness that awaited his exploration there, but to Sam, as to other youngsters in the suburbs, beyond the door is a small and empty world, and it is not Outside.

A Chosen Land

Joshua wanted to see where I had lived as a child. Summered, to be exact, but summers were my life then.

I knew the way there as intimately as can be known to someone who has walked and biked the roads a hundred times or more. I knew the way by slope, the uphill pump and downhill coast; by bend and bump and shoulders of skiddy sand. I could re-create in my mind every feature along the route: the crumbling limestone bank where mullein thrived, the dirt shortcut best avoided in deerfly season; the tussock marsh, its basking turtles, its redolence of mud. I could still feel—pumping hard now, getting up momentum in the dip where horsetails grew—the muscle it took to get up that last hard hill past the rock outpost that had attracted my father to this piece of land even before electricity had found it.

So it was with confidence that I turned the car onto Limestone Road.

Immediately, I was lost. The limestone wasn't there. Had it been buried under this other road that had usurped the way? I backed around and tried again and, back on track, came to the marsh—or to where its ghost shape was outlined by a ring of houses. The dirt shortcut a mile farther on was paved, and this formerly nameless track had been named Limestone, while what had been Limestone, continuing around the bend toward the old schoolhouse, was named something else, and the schoolhouse was gone. The hard hill was still there, and the rocks. My parents' driveway had become a road.

Pentimento.

As I drove up the road that had been driveway, through the development that had been farm, I experienced a *pentimento* of the mind. I saw the houses, the plantings, and the lawns, the new picture that had been painted over the land, but beneath those crude strokes there reappeared to me the earlier and more intricate design.

A fine old apple tree shaded the corner of a new home, and there were the whole arc of apples my father had planted. Where was I? I was driving through his vegetable garden, crossing rows of cabbages and kohlrabi. Behind the next house, to the rear of a great lawn, was a small pile of stones. How well I knew those stones! The potting shed in front of them, the barn, the rock-lined pit where we burned the household trash. The stones were those a farmer once had piled from his fields, and below them the land cut abruptly downward to a low meadow. I couldn't tell whether the stone steps my father had laid to ease the descent were still there. Certainly there was no trace of the peach orchard the steps had led to, and of course, nothing left of the little horse he had made for me out of an oddly angled cherry trunk or of the privy he had built or the elderberry bushes where, sitting on the warm splintery privy hole, I used to watch the blacksnake sunning in the morning.

The road ended in a cul-de-sac near the boundary of what had been the twenty-acre farm. I turned around and drove back through once-were woods, past the disappeared, the reappeared, the detail of what was no longer there.

We continued on to visit my parents' graves at the cemetery down the road a piece. But which road? There were new ones everywhere, and I was disoriented, lost on the green-smeared, house-spattered canvas, able to find my way only tentatively, as a girl on a bike peddling this curve, that dip, over the bridge that spanned the brook where watercress once grew—and didn't any longer, for brook and bridge too were gone.

Only the cemetery hadn't changed. The low wall, the broad steps, the iron gate, the cheerful horse chestnuts, and the gloomy spruces: they were as solid as they'd ever been, unmoved. I knew exactly where to find my parents' burial place and walked directly there, spotting my sister's grave right away.

But you see, my sister isn't dead.

I can't explain my sister Susie; she's a little loony sometimes. I suppose she must not want to leave the design and placement of her tombstone up to surviving kin. The stone had apparently been there for some years; it was aged already with moss and lichen, though the stone was yet undated. Its solidity struck me: the future carved crazily in granite.

I figure Susie was about five and I three years old when our father fell in love with the rocky farm and bought it from Tony, the Sicilian who continued to live there and work the land until he died. I have in my mind an even earlier sketch of the land as it was then, when Tony farmed it and before my father began his own repainting. I noted on my drive by the property a Bartlett pear my father had planted on what is still front lawn, and I supposed that beneath the lawn is the septic system that served the first toilets the land had known. I imagined through the turf and tiles the seep of water that once emerged through rushes and was the frog pond.

The house had changed considerably, but I could restore in my mind the previous layers: under the newly grandiose living room, my parents' flagstone terrace, and scraping away that image, Tony's rhubarb and onion patch that the terrace had covered over. Chickens, the kind now stylishly called "free-range," pecked among the tomato vines located approximately under an enormous extension built against a background of walls that step up the high outcrop. This structure was once my father's flower garden; it is now the site of a swimming pool and children's play yard. Beneath those overlaid images, I could only barely recapture the stonework as it had been when I first saw it: the foundation of a three-tiered barn where lived cows, barn cats, and Roosevelt the horse.

I don't think it is just my imagination that is richer than the present reality of this new development. The land really was richer than it is now. For one thing, it smelled: manure, onions, chickens, privies, smoke, hay. The ground was bumpy, rutted, obstacled with barways, woodpiles, barbed wire, arbors, ditches, walls. And it was littered, too, in the choicest places for a child's rummaging, with rusted buckets, horseshoes, and broken implements. The land was in motion, happening: water rose from the ground through a spring, fell from the sky into a barrel. Heat was from fire, fire from wood, wood from trees that were felled, sawed, split, chopped. Eggs came from—guess what!—the rear ends of hens.

Tony had no life "style," as we call our ways of life these days; he merely lived. After he died, somewhere in his eighties and to- ward the end of World War II, my parents overpainted the land considerably, though not to the extent that it is encrusted now. At least carrots were still roots that we pulled from the soil, scallions in June were onions by October, and if my parents' weekend and va- cation inhabiting of what became their country retreat precluded the keeping of a cow, so did the lack of a rail line or highway to New York in that rural area preclude the rapid development of sub- urbs that was consuming farmland closer to the city. Throughout my childhood summers, milk still came from mooing cows that manured the nearby fields.

With us that day on the drive and in the graveyard was Ezra, a babe-in-arms innocent of the ghosts of past and future that I could see so clearly. I wish I had more to give him than a granny's recol- lections. I want him to have what has been most important in my own life: my treasures of frog pond and dusty chickens, my savor of wild grapes. I want him to have experience as prickly as burrs, as juicy as peaches ripe in the sun, as real as the rear end of a hen.

Writing now, months since that revisitation, two images linger most poignantly: the small pile of stones and my sister's grave. I've been haunted by a sense that they have something in common, deaths past and still to come that pair unmarked cairn with incised tombstone. The conviction of connection and the elusiveness of its identity have been troubling me for days. This morning, bittersweet arose through the murk.

Ezra, I want to give you bittersweet, the American kind, Celastrus scandens, *that used to sprawl over the stone pile and that we used to clip for Thanksgiving decoration in autumn when the orange husks opened over the vermilion fruit. I'm sorry to have to tell you that the vine has moved from rubble heap to endangered species list and sorry to inform you that as your great-aunt Susie fulfills the prediction on her tombstone, so will the general death of our granny generation kill even remembrance of the vine.*

As antidote to this nostalgic, sentimental, subjective, romantic, and verging on maudlin exercise of mind, I booted the computer, clicked to the Web, typed in a URL, arrived virtually at Amazon.com, and electronically ordered *Crabgrass Frontier* by Kenneth T. Jackson. The book materialized in forty-eight hours, delivered by UPS.

The volume, published in 1985 and therefore somewhat outdated, remains nevertheless the authoritative history of its subtitle, *The Suburbanization of the United States.* The story was more thought-provoking than I had imagined: it was not merely the redressing of the land but a mask pulled over the human face as well.

Jackson begins his account with a description of the pre-nineteenth-century "walking city," one in which home, office, workshop, store, and public building were mixed together and crowded into an area that could be crossed by foot in a few hours at most. As Jackson remarks, a dot on the map was then an apt symbol for a city: one stepped off the dot into a cow field.

My city was the dot called New York. According to Jackson's history, the dot had smeared over the surrounding countryside by the time of my childhood several decades into the twentieth century, but that was not my experience of it. My workplace—my school—was half a mile uptown. The amusements of movie houses, museums, and Central Park were closer still. Most of the stores and services we used were within a one-block walk: grocery, fishmonger, bakery, pharmacy, newsstand, florist, bookshop, tailor, and shoemaker. I hung out at the shoemaker's often, taken with the scent of leather and the cobbler's skill.

Two blocks away were Rohr's Coffee Roasting Establishment, Paprikas Weiss spice store, and the German butcher where I was sent for pork sausages and calf liverwurst made on the premises. Proprietors of these shops lived above their workplace or in the immediate neighborhood. Social distinctions may have been clear to the adults, but they were not to me whose life was peopled with soda jerks and janitors more intimately than with guests who came to dinner parties after I was put to bed.

Come summer, we went to the "country," clear off the city dot. From just north of the George Washington Bridge, the trip was green, grassy, and undeveloped all along the Sawmill River to where the parkway terminated at the village of Chappaqua. Then the road narrowed, and shortly—stopping first at the icehouse to specify the size of chunk we needed, watching the iceman chop the block, wipe the sawdust from it, and carry it with tongs to the car—we turned onto a one-lane dirt road, where we were likely to get stuck behind a herd of cows ambling toward their barn at milking time.

Both these worlds were transparent: a child could see how things are done. City streets were as open to my exploration of the community economy as country lanes were open to my investigation of rural ecology. In one milieu, I saw how shoes are made, and in the other, I came to know the animal that shoes are made of. I didn't think of shoes as cowhide, nor did I think of cows as leather. I doubt that I ever, as a child, explicitly realized that human livelihood depends on other lives, but the connection was implicit in the to-and-fro between the city and the country even if I was only aware of flowers in fields and florists, milk in udders and bottles.

This pursuit of connectedness is what Ezra had begun as he explored the utensils and materials of domestic life and that Ian, too, was after as he ventured outdoors into the natural world. The pursuit ought not to end; it is the very purpose of childhood. But it does come to an end in suburbs because the connections are not there, and children growing up in these unlively places lose that sense of purpose.

Chappaqua, just halfway between New York and the farm, was one of the early "railroad suburbs." I had a friend who lived in Chappaqua—skinny, freckled, red-haired Kay—and Kay and I had fun there. It was a prewar, precar suburb. Its steep streets ran downslope to the shops and station, and just beyond the crest of the hill lay open countryside. The suburban ideal could perhaps be perceived in the neatness of the yards and the freshly painted faces of the homes, but suburbs as we know them now grew up with the automobile—or, I should say, grew *out*, for the ideal was exactly to distance the family from the workaday bustle that connects people with their environment.

Americans chose to live in separate, spaced-out houses rather than clustered villages; they wished to be removed from stores and workplaces rather than reside among them. Jackson's chapter exploring this choice is called "Home, Sweet Home: The House and the Yard." In it he describes a phenomenon that was, if not peculiarly American, most intensely so: the paired idealizing of domestic life and nature.

Before people could get around by other than hoof or foot, any concept of the nuclear family as the fundamental social unit was pretty much swamped by economic reality. Households were the source of their occupants' livelihood, whether the work conducted there supported a farm, a store, an inn, a trade, or a manufacturing business. Occupants included extended family as well as unrelated employees, apprentices, servants, and their spouses and children. Privacy was not easy to come by nor was it much valued when the welfare of the individual was so visibly dependent on the welfare of the entire production unit. No matter whether society entertained the notion that parents and children are the central family unit, the reality was that hardly any home housed just Mom and Dad with kids.

I'm reminded of a scene I witnessed in a nursery school. Two girls were playing house when an uninvited and unwelcome boy asked to join them. "Okay," one of the girls responded, "here's your briefcase, now go to work." Jackson approaches his subject from many angles and over many pages, but I think this scrap of social savvy expresses in a nutshell how it became possible to actually live the dream of private family life. During the nineteenth century, as trains and, later, streetcars made possible the separation of home from workplace—and it was the men who went to work—women were left with a domain that was far less constrained by demands of productivity and that might be developed along other lines. There was born what writers of the time enthusiastically and unembarrassedly called "the cult of womanhood."

Catharine Beecher, in her popular *Treatise on Domestic Economy, For the Use of Young Ladies at Home and at School*, advised on every detail of home management in the belief, fervently shared by her readers, that a well-kept home is the wellspring of family bliss and personal morality. Hardly hidden in her and others' prose was the conviction that women were more pure than men, more capable not only of leading a virtuous life, but of creating the orderly surround that would mold the moral character of husband and children. With co-author and younger sister Harriet Beecher Stowe, Catharine further added in *The American Woman's Home, or Principles of Domestic Science* that her advice was most applicable to "those living either in the country or in suburban vicinities as give space or ground for healthful outdoor occupation in the family service."

Among those healthful occupations was mowing the grass. An example of how utilitarian sheep pasture became idealized as lawn is this passage, quoted by Jackson from an 1860s text extolling the lawnmower:

Whoever spends the early hours of one summer day, while
the dew spangles in the grass, in pushing these grass cutters
over a velvety lawn, breathing the fresh sweetness of the
morning air and the perfume of the new mown hay, will
never rest contented in the city.

It's hard to realize now just how deliberate and radical this social
experiment was. New housing types were introduced: the villa was
a landed rural home with the grounds immediately surrounding the
house dedicated to "recreation and enjoyment, rather than profit";
the bungalow, a smaller and more modest building, was a one-story
home set in a garden. There followed colonial, ranch, and cape
styles, but despite their rural references, none of the floor plans
originated in country living. The too-public front porch was removed; such conveniences as laundry, breakfast nook, nursery, and
patio were added. Frederick Law Olmsted, among the prominent
designers who defined for their generation both the nature of the
suburban ideal and the ideal of suburban nature, was particularly
adamant that the various functions of a household be segregated in
separate rooms. He was equally insistent that residential communities be segregated from commercial enterprises. Designers and de-
velopers in general rejected the urban grid. They placed residences
along winding ways that followed the natural contours of the land,
set them well back from the street, and wrapped them in lawn. The
effect was to give homes, even ones on smallish lots, a greater sense
of privacy within a rural setting. So was the bosom of the family
artfully covered in belief that, within its sanctuary, might more
freely beat the passion for purity—of air, morals, and bed linens—
to which suburbs still aspire.

Victorian sentiments about women seem quaint to us now,
when little girls playing house are so likely themselves to end up
with the briefcase they foisted on the boy, yet we do not question
other assumptions that support the suburban dream: a suburban
community is "safe," "clean," and "healthy"—the ideal place to

raise children. These children are innocent; they must not, for example, be subjected to gruesome fairy tales or fornicating dogs. They require prolonged protection from matches, knives, and electric sockets—and all through childhood from germs, bites, pesticides, and pedophiles. They grow in stages, at each of which they benefit from certain age-appropriate toys, games, and storybooks. These boys and girls have neatly divisible talents as well: eye-hand coordination, large-muscle control, attention span, and language, numerical, and social skills. Needless to say, they wish to be in the bosom of their family.

No one who has the slightest recollection of childhood will recognize in this description their own experience of being a child. It is far too static, passive, and clean. But then, so is the environment we have chosen to create. Suburbs are static by design. They are not supposed to change: the grass is not to bloom or go to seed; the shrubs are to keep their clipped shape year after year. Nothing in this landscape can get along without us; it is a passive thing, helpless to feed or water itself. Our job is to keep it safe and orderly: kill the bugs, rake the leaves, mulch the beds. We do not let our yard soil itself with work, like growing beans. This is the understanding of our neighbors as well: a suburb is intended to be an island free of commerce, cows, and people who hang their laundry out to dry.

An insidious environmental notion underlies these ideals of yard and child: it is that both nature and human nature are entirely shaped by our external influence; they cannot run themselves; they must be made to grow. Yet however we lay on the fertilizer, spray the herbicide, water, and mow according to prescribed regimes, clover still comes in: it is not in the nature of grassland to be lawn. So it is not in the nature of children to sit still and be civilized.

There is an environmental way to envision children, but it is subtly different from the view that they are what we put into them. Living things take from their environment what they need, and what they need is what their nature leads them to take. Grass takes all the nitrogen you can give it, but it only seems to need such care because it is not in its natural environment, where it would be free to take nitrogen from clover or from sheep manure in the pastures where lawn grass evolved. Children take all the toys you can give them, but they only seem to need such lavishing because they are not in their natural environment where they are free to take their pleasure from toads and splashing water or from the social engagements of the close and working communities where our human race evolved.

We were in a rain-forest village between a river and the sea. The villagers were mad for soccer: the center of the dirt-path town was the soccer field, where children played the game and so did their elders. They grew chickens and bananas and ate fish caught from the river. Pulled up to the shore were dugout canoes made by burning and scraping out logs of a particular tree, known for its resistance to decay. We were looking for a guide who could take us by dugout through the numerous channels that lace intricately from the river through the lush forest. We were directed along this path and that, past the post office that was the postmistress's home, where she sold stamps through her open window. The guide was the son of a famous one before him, who had shown biologists where the nearly vanished Atlantic green turtle still hangs by a thread to one ancient nesting site. For hours and hours, he paddled us through the riverine jungle of howler monkeys and trees hung with epiphytes. Ashore, on tracks barely visible to us, where villagers hunting and harvesting on days-long forays into the forest have been killed by jaguars at night, he showed us poisonous yellow frogs and named the strange flowers. We pulled back to shore at the end of the afternoon. I asked, When are children allowed to paddle on the river, to navigate alone its backwater wilderness?

At the age of seven, he said.

All peoples raise children through a series of formalities that acknowledge their growing competence and changing status in the society. A baby is a baby until she can leave our arms; a toddler is a toddler until he can leave our sight. Both are preschoolers until they leave on the bus. Six years old—seven in Tortuguero—is the age when we consider children to be emotionally and intellectually ready to take on a new level of independence and responsibility: climb into the dugout and come home with fish; climb aboard the school bus and come home with grades. You'll appreciate the difference.

My father gave me a wristwatch for my sixth birthday. That was an acknowledgment of my ability to tell the time and a conferring of responsibility to be on time. But more indelibly impressed in memory is the tantrum I had some weeks before, when my father told me he would not give me boxing gloves for my birthday because girls can't be boxers. I had expected to change into a boy when I turned six.

Children are not rational. They are internally driven, given to magic, as prone to grief and fury as to childish giggles, and daring, dirty, sexual, primitive by nature. When the nuclear family retired to its private home, these are the aspects of being human that were hidden behind the walls.

One image included by Jackson in *Crabgrass Frontier* is an 1855 Nathaniel Currier print titled *American Country Life* that shows father, mother, son, and daughter surveying their property. The little girl is picking wildflowers while her older brother whoops it up, waving his cap as he runs across the grass. Their home stands behind them on a hill, shaded by large trees. Below the house, cows graze while a group of workers fork hay into a wagon. According to Jackson, the print was "enormously popular." Though sentimental in the extreme, the depiction struck me as otherwise not unlike my family's cow-country home on the hill above the old farmhouse where Tony used to live.

I spent portions of the last year house hunting with a friend for her escape place in rural Vermont. At the top of her list of desirables was an antique farmhouse privately located well back from the road. There was a fruitless search! Antique farmers built their homes practically *on* the road. Front yards were nonexistent. Back yards were barnyards. My parents did not encourage me to enter Tony's home. It smelled: cats, wood smoke, root cellar, rotting wood, garlic, and Tony himself, who did not bathe all winter for fear of pneumonia. I simply could not understand my parents' reluctance to breathe deeply of this rich odor: that is how different children are from civilized adults.

After Tony died, my parents "renovated" his home, which originally had been built by bachelor brother veterans of the Civil War. I place "renovated" in quotation marks because they actually gutted and reconstructed the whole interior. There hadn't been any living room in that house. There was what I suppose today would be called a "great room," but honestly it was just a kitchen with a few chairs drawn around a wood-burning stove: the only place in the house warm enough to sit in the winter. In summer, the cool place to sit was the porch, ten feet from the road.

They named their transformation the Cottage and decorated it with hooked rugs, tavern chairs, a collection of chalkware cats on a hanging shelf in the living room, and a trestle table in the dining room, where arguments were held. Loud arguments, unheard by neighbors, with door slammings compromised by quaint Early American latches that didn't work too well. The summer I was thirteen, my father renamed the house Casa Morosa—house of gloom. There was nothing really so awful going on except that Susie and I were dating local brothers, going to square dances, necking in their car. That hadn't been in the rural picture, and our parents were unprepared.

I was unprepared for their reentry into my life.

Memories from before the age of six are necessarily fraught with parents—telling stories, wiping tears, tying shoes, and warning, chastising, insisting, tangling, because you need them to, into the intimate precincts of your life. But then you are six. You can tell the time, you can cross the street, you can ride a bike, and you go.

I had been free for years, secret and unsupervised, a wild child bashing bikes with boys in Central Park, catching frogs with Tony in the pond, digging maggots out of cowpats, chasing kids with poison ivy, eluding old Miss Todd who disliked children leaping from the hayloft in her barn. Miss Todd remains etched on her porch, watchful and scolding. Mr. Rothschild, proprietor of the neighborhood stationery store in the city, similarly guarded candy bars and comic books from our restless hands. Must children steal and trespass? I know none who haven't.

I know no children who, let free during those years from six to twelve, would honestly tell their parents all that they'd been up to when they were out of sight. A child-advocacy book published in 1957 is titled *"Where Did You Go?" "Out." "What Did You Do?" "Nothing."* The out and the nothing is what suburbs don't supply, since there is no out where children are unobserved and nothing they can do that is uncivilized.

But I did not live in the suburbs. Given the freedom to muck about in both urban and rural environments for all those years, I arrived at the age of thirteen supposing that I would be allowed to continue doing so, when WHAM!, the trap snapped shut on my freedom.

Adolescence is among the more difficult subjects of this book because it is experienced by American parents and children as a discontinuity: not merely a "stage," like the terrible twos, for which texts on child rearing prescribe various management techniques, but more like a disease that must be suffered. I suffered; my mother and father suffered too. Now, though, looking back, I can see why.

Whether children are let loose to grow their story in privacy from adults or have no choice but to develop their sense of self under observation and supervision, the story is biologically supposed to pause at the joining of the younger generation with the elders who have raised them and continue with the saga of their own reproduction. Had my parents ever gone to a square dance—and I cannot tell you how unimaginable that is—they would have seen a continuity of generations that has nearly been extinguished in our urban and suburban cultures. Everybody dressed for the dance in dirndl skirts and peasant blouses, checkered shirts and jeans. Everybody means every age: there were courting couples in their teens, young brothers and sisters allowed to stay up late on Saturday nights, and parents, and parents' parents, all linking elbows, letting go, weaving with and swinging through one another in the movements of the dance—and who knows who's kissing whom in the culminating figure called Birdie in the Cage.

I grew up at geographically opposite ends of the social experiment called suburbia—thirty miles south of Chappaqua, New York, and thirty miles north of it. My father was a Mormon farm boy from a hick town in Utah, my mother the product of the Brooklyn Jewish ghetto. The suburban culture, already at that time older than either of my parents, was unknown to them. Or so, from each of their perspectives, they would have claimed. But, in fact, they had discarded both plowing and pushcart ways of life and had chosen to live in the void between them that is suburbia now.

The farm was geographically rural but functionally suburban. Rail service, at first desultory, improved to the extent that my father commuted to the city by train in his latter years. He continued to raise vegetables, but we did not depend on the land's productivity for our nourishment. There were dances, parades, fireworks, civic ceremonies. My parents took on the zoning board; they wanted to abolish quarter-acre lots because they feared development like the summer colony a mile down the road.

This was where Mr. Hauser, a building superintendent by occupation, over his brief summer's respite built a plywood boat for himself and us children to fish for sunnies in the lake. This was where Bobby Bowen's mother and I gathered elderberries along the road to turn into wax-sealed jars of jam. And those were the years when, there and everywhere, creeping upon us were the separation by social class, the segregation by age, the closeting of adults' work, and the denial of our own productivity that have been the hallmarks of the suburban ideal.

I think of Uncle Paul. He was an upright, uptight, buttoned little man who lived in a darling cottage in Bronxville within walking distance of the station, a half-hour commute to his law firm in Manhattan. I remember Uncle Paul with bitterness for marrying my loose-limbed, seductively improper, flapper sort of aunt Aileen and thereby conferring on her and forcing her conformance to his Bronxville snottiness. I remember Uncle Paul with some amusement for the dwarf conifer collection he coddled in his "rural" back yard. But I remember Uncle Paul best, and most amusedly, dressed as an engineer in visored cap and blue-striped overalls with a red bandanna at his neck, running his model railroad.

The railroad, OO-gauge and skillfully constructed from kits, filled a whole room on a waist-high plywood base shaped to allow access deep into the miniature landscape, which also was handmade to scale and in detail worthy of an architect's model. There were hills and woods, bridges and tunnels, a railroad station (of course), and farms with barns and cattle, a tiny village, a steepled church:

Bronxville, circa 1890.

And now, 1998 in a Midwestern town I will call Lakeville: *

I arrived on a Thursday with a day to spare for sight-seeing before the Saturday symposium I'd been invited to address. My hostess delivered me to my lodgings as the cold March evening fell.

I wheeled my bag along the corridor beside an atrium greened with plastic philodendron, past rooms with blinds closed for privacy, to number 217. I slipped the card into the slot and opened the door on darkness. There was no window.

That weekend I inhabited an "as if" environment. There was no dawn or dusk, no weather: television was my "window" on the world. There were irksome inconveniences: an angular bathtub that didn't accommodate the human body, a straight "hook" on the door that couldn't hold a towel.

I emerged in the "morning"—so said the digital clock—for breakfast, retraced the corridor past two women taking their morning walk on treadmills, followed the "Boardwalk" along its

glassed-in view of the parking lot to what was advertised on the
room-service menu as the Continental Breakfast Room. Again, the
slot, the card, the windowless closet. Styrofoam cups and Coffee-
Mate. I was staying at the newest and the best hotel in this well-
known city suburb.

The very word "suburb," though, doesn't adequately describe
the form of landscape that surrounded the hotel. The original suburbs that so rapidly filled with urban escapees were like Chappaqua
and Bronxville used to be, enclaves within the rural countryside,
near a village and a railroad station whose window boxes spilled
with geraniums in summer. Here there was no break between the
city and its sprawl nor any indication of where one town ended and
another one began except the changing names on post offices and
firehouses. After we had been driving from the airport for close to
an hour, I asked my hostess when we would see any opening
among the commercial strips, the blocks of lots and houses. "You
won't find that here," she said. The nearest open land was forty
miles away.

Impressions piled up like ice against the shore of this lakeside
community: a child home from school roller-blading alone along
sidewalks that converged on the horizon; the feeder in a back yard
where all the birds were city sparrows; the repetition of clipped
shrubs; a threesome of canvasbacks bobbing against the steel side
of a newly built marina. The town—the whole surrounding net of
streets and malls—had once been a vast marsh. I was shown what
remained of the marsh during the Friday tour: ten acres scheduled
for development.

The Saturday audience was large and stood to clap when I had
finished. That doesn't happen often, not when the subject of a
speech is ecological restoration. An older man said I'd made him
cry. That doesn't happen often either.

I was uncomfortable. I'd been annoyed by the hotel, its eu-
phemisms and plastic, its hermetic atmosphere. I'd been sick to see
fake ducks on lawns where at this very time of year countless flocks

of waterfowl had once descended in migration. I'd been incensed as well to find that the famous "Great Meadow" at an estate I toured was nothing but a lawn. In short, I'd enjoyed two days of withering contempt for these people who had let their surroundings slip into virtual reality, and here they were, hanging on my words.

I realize why: this audience was the most engaged, most moved, most deeply comprehending of any I had ever spoken to precisely because their habitat was so disengaged, unmoving, incomprehensible. I'd had lunch with the mayor and other town officials that afternoon. Talk was about the spring flood that was expected soon, the chore of pumping basements, the cost of metered water that, by July, would have to be expended on irrigating lawns. Lakeville had originally been a cluster of summer bungalows where vacationers came to boat and fish and hunt the wild shore. There were still those who remembered the marsh before it was drained and channeled, when it neither dried nor flooded at any time of year.

Now residents were at a loss, felt dispossessed, missed the missing birds that only some of them had ever actually known. Their dispossession was real: it was not only forty miles to the nearest cow, but half a century since their grandparents might have milked one—and the residents certainly didn't have any notion of what the Midwestern sky looked like blackened by passenger pigeons or even what their city pigeons taste like as roast squab. Ironically, but truly, they hungered for a glimpse of wild fowl in a land of chicken nuggets.

The physical isolation of suburbs from the plant, animal, and manufacturing resources that actually support them and the length of time that has passed since those connections were common knowledge have begun to drain the sense from our lives. Is it butter or "butter"? Only the label can tell.

Times have always changed and people have often changed their habitat. In the past, culture has helped us bridge these gaps in time and space by relating what our elders did to what we teach our children, by tying what we do to why and where we do it. Despite the gulf of time that separated old Tony from the little girl I was and the span of road and difference in culture that separated the city from the farm, Tony made sense of things for me. One keeps chickens in the garden because they eat the insect pests. Here is how to kill a chicken, clean the innards, get the feathers off.

It was of no practical importance that I learn to chop and pluck. Those days were past for my city-bred generation. What is important is that I realize that the meat was once a bird. Trading money for food merely culminates a story that started as an egg.

Or is it an "egg"? When Joshua was a teenager, he took a summer job at Friendly's. His work was to prepare the restaurant's specialty salad of lettuce and tomato topped with slices of hard-boiled egg. He brought this wondrous egg home for me to see. It was shaped like a knockwurst and measured about a foot in length. An extruded, euphemistic "egg."

But what salad eater could tell?

Back home one early dawn, I drove through town while people were still sleeping. I passed raccoon-proof garbage pails placed the previous night along the curb for morning pickup, starlings rising from a street-tree roost, crows picking at the night's roadkill, an injured deer limping through the gate of someone's driveway. This is our habitat, and we no more ask why these animals thrive where suburbs spread than a child questions why light appears when he turns a switch. Human curiosity is such that we wonder only when what we are used to changes, and we did not grow up with purple martins in the yard and skies black with pigeons.

I was astonished to learn some years ago how passenger pigeons became extinct. I had thought—so we were taught—that they were all just shot: shot by the bucketful, shot by the barrelful, extinct by extermination. The reason is actually more subtle.

The shooting season for passenger pigeons was spring, when vast migrating flocks assembled at traditional staging grounds prior to pairing up for breeding. Thus assembled, they were easy to shoot in quantity, and their ranks thinned. What was not realized was that the pigeons' thick assembly was a necessary stimulus to breeding. Without that period of crowdedness, hormone levels did not rise high enough to permit their reproduction: passenger pigeons became extinct through disruption of their social lives.

We are accustomed to thinking of habitat as physical resources—food, water, and shelter available in quantity and quality according to the needs of each species. We understand easily that habitat destruction, as in the draining of the Lakeville marsh, makes land uninhabitable to many kinds of plants and animals that previously lived there and that when all such habitat is gone, so too vanish those inhabitants unable to live elsewhere.

Less evident are changes to the environment that alter behavior. Coyotes, who as far back as natural history knows have hunted surreptitiously alone or in pairs only, now boldly hunt in packs where, previously, predation by wolves prevented such gregarious and vulnerable behavior. Coyotes have penetrated eastern parts where they never lived in the days of wolves and have developed a taste for house cats in the suburbs. Deer, extinguished in southern New England and New York during most of my lifetime, have lost their fear of humans and have risen in modern suburbs to the highest population density ever recorded for the species. Purple martins, which originally nested in tree cavities, switched first to hollow gourds provided by Indians, then to birdhouses built by settlers. They no longer congregate in housing farther than fifty feet from human habitation or more than a mile from the communal box where they were hatched. With our failure to continue the martin-house tradition, the bird has become a rare to vanishing species in the suburbs where I live.

Purple martins were common at farmyards and village greens when I was growing up, so I notice now that they are missing. Children were common too: city children on the sidewalk playing hopscotch, jumping rope; country children in the village racing to the ice-cream shop; children going fishing and children going

walking and children going nowhere, doing nothing, sitting on the
stoop. So I noticed when, as Friday's raw March weather in Lakeville changed suddenly to a warm and sunny Saturday, the children
of the neighborhood did not come out to play.

Joshua and Laura moved to a Boston suburb when Ezra was five
months old. Their first experience there mimicked mine at the
Lakeville hotel. They were put up in a corporate apartment until
they could find a home of their own. They arrived to a cof-
feemaker set to make the morning brew; to beds made up with
fresh linens and towels stacked for use; to wrapped soap and dispos-
able shower caps. The lamp shades were brand new, still bound in
plastic wrap. They called me that evening to marvel at their sanitized and air-conditioned digs.

They called again the next morning: cockroaches had crawled
from the baseboards in the night.

At last, they found a home on a half-acre of outdoors. It is a dis-
reputable bit of land. The stone wall that bounds the yard along the
street is built without cement. It houses chipmunks, maybe snakes.
The lawn is dreadful, gone to moss in the sour and sandy soil, good
for nothing but replanting with ferns and sedges, coral bell and
columbine, mountain laurel, shadblow, blueberry, and hazelnut. A
brook—tiny, to be sure, and not strictly theirs—runs across a corner boundary of the lot through a small wetland where noisy frogs
disturb the night and children get their feet wet. The back yard is a
mess. A child might get scratched picking blackberries there. And
what with all the deadwood lying about in the far and woodsy portion, it might occur to Ezra (looking now into his future) to build
a lean-to, and what then? What if the children on the other side of
the brook, who have such excellent play equipment in their own
groomed yard, were then to wade through the skunk cabbage, hack
a path through the brambles, and join him in his hideout?

I started out with passion to preserve my childhood landscape
only to discover that the passion is to preserve childhood itself.

Girls and boys, come out to play! But they will not unless we summon them with the piper's tune of mud and rushes, not sprinklers mechanically circling an uninhabited lawn.

I want a word and cannot find it. What is the opposite of *to tame?*

If our children are to grow up at home in their environment, in appreciation that its sharing among other lives is essential to our own life and livelihood, and with the intelligence to wisely manage it, we must wild the land.

The Name of the Snake

I stayed up late one night whittling animals. By two o'clock, my hands had become too sore to continue, but my mind wouldn't stop. I leafed through *Mammals of the World*. There are two volumes, 1,300 pages, 1,000 genera, 4,000 species. Bats alone number 942 species, bettered only by rodents, which boast 1,687. And these are just the furry creatures, the order Mammalia, which are eclipsed in number by 20,000 species of fish, 6,000 species of reptiles, and 9,000 species of birds.

I began to jot down on the back of an envelope other animals I'd like to whittle. Emu and ostrich; penguins and the fabled but vanished dodo; tortoises and turtles; the egg-laying, ant-eating Australian echidna. A serpent! And gorillas (because they are easier to carve than other great apes) as well as a cute little armored armadillo. I added a triceratops, a dinosaur that so resembled a modern rhinoceros that the two would make a credible pair. Then I thought Ezra might like to reassort the animals for a barnyard and would therefore need chickens, ducks, and geese. I added a workhorse, a Percheron. Then he, still mateless, called for a wild horse of the Asian steppes, and horses led to cows and bison. I went to bed at three o'clock well aware of a throbbing arthritic thumb and the impossibility of representing for the ark even the major groups of good-sized animals, not to mention mollusks, crustaceans, arachnids, and a zillion insects.

Our own species, the only extant hominid, falls at the end of volume I, taxonomically lower in evolutionary order than even rats. Yet we the wise have by an extraordinary and largely invisible evolutionary course come to name all the others. Our minds work according to a sort of intelligence that no other animal has. We are the symbolic species; we mentally manipulate experience through language. We conjure rubber apples as easily as those two words are put together and so convey both what is and what is not to ourselves and one another. Or we actually make material what had been mental image, as I chip an extinct dinosaur from a piece of tree. Extinct dinosaurs exist only in the human mind.

Think of that.

"I saw it! I saw it! I saw it!" I cried when, as a little girl in overalls, I ran breathless to my father from a large slithery thing I'd uncovered beneath a stone in a damp corner of the garden. "It" was merely a spotted salamander, and my father knew its name.

Consider the emotion the salamander aroused and the odd words I chose to express it. I wasn't exactly afraid: awestruck better describes my sense of simultaneous shock and fascination. The seemingly inarticulate cry, "I saw *it*," accurately conveys the sense that *it* was something I expected to see, as though someone had often described to me a rainbow and I finally saw one. In this case, though, the sense of recognition and the awe the recognition inspired was rooted in biology. Humans are predisposed to respond dramatically to sinuous shapes.

I say dramatically rather than fearfully because our predisposition is less fear at first sight than it is a readiness to become frightened. The awe I felt was a phobia waiting to happen if the salamander had lunged at me, or my father had considered it dangerous, or teased me with it, or warned me to stay away from such disgusting things. He took my hand; we lifted the stone. The creature was not so large as it had seemed. *Spotted*, my father said—and sure enough it was spotted with yellow polka dots—and *salamander*:

a pretty name, that one, and I have been fond of salamanders ever since.

My dog Girl learned *rabbit* by a single remark the first time she roused one in the meadow. She got so excited at the thought of rabbits that we couldn't use the r-word in conversation, or even mention its homophone, *rabid*. Ian too, immediately at first exposure and without so much as a single repetition, learned *toad*. At first thought, it would seem that both child and dog had learned the name of the animal.

But their achievements are in no way alike, as I learned from *The Symbolic Species*, a difficult book by neuroscientist Terrence Deacon about the evolution of language. I had to read it several times, get through brain anatomy, neural processing, development of the neocortex, and apes, aphasias, icons, and indices, before I began to understand what a symbol is and why language is so different from other forms of animal communication. I had this difficulty in spite of having read about the subject ever since ethologist Konrad Lorenz wrote about signaling among jackdaws; and in spite of having dabbled in Noam Chomsky; and learned on the way curious things about Creole languages, American Sign Language, the "talking" parrot Alexander, vervet-monkey calls, the signage that apes have been taught to use, and the postural/gestural/vocal communications of baboons and wolves. I had always been interested in language. I had never understood what it is.

Girl once learned the name of the mouse. "Mouse," I would say, and she'd race to the cupboard where several times she had caught a mouse trapped in a mop pail. After a while, though, when no more mice appeared, she lost the word. *Mouse* indicated the creature only as long as the sound of the word and the presence of the animal were temporally connected. She runs to the door when I say "out" and comes to the kitchen when I say "biscuit." But if I begin to say "biscuit" when I'm ready for a walk and "out" when it's time for her snack, it will take her only a few days to switch her behavior. To a dog, words point to an object that is available or an event that is about to happen, and if the object isn't available or the event doesn't happen, the words become pointless and are erased from memory. The word by itself does not make sense to a dog; it responds to the sound only in the here-and-now context of what the sound indicates.

You need no external context to get the sense of *cricket* even if you haven't heard or seen one in a decade. In fact, you need never have seen one at all, as you have perhaps never seen a cricket-hunting wasp, or a flying flower, or a gigantic rabbit: symbols are internally related to one another in the mind, and their meaning is derived from those mental relationships, not from their relationships in the outside world.

That doesn't mean experience is unnecessary to learn language. The internal system of reference is built from the ground up, so to speak, from *cricket* pointing to cricket and *wasp* to wasp, to both words' relationship to *insects*, and *insects*' relationships to *flying, hunting, flower, rabbit, gigantic*. A dog can learn the word *bad* but can't combine that sound with another it has learned to mean, for instance, *bad biscuit*. It knows without understanding.

Some talented apes, with enormous patience and effort on the part of their teachers, have crossed what Deacon calls the "symbolic threshold." They can use hand signs or computer lexigrams to combine words in meaningful ways: "drink juice," "eat banana." Once they get the trick of language, they can make up phrases they have never heard and may spontaneously remark on the world around them, as when Koko the gorilla insults people who have annoyed her by calling them "dirty toilet." Yet transcripts of what passes for conversation between Koko and her teachers are at the level of "me Tarzan, you Jane." She may have language, but she can't use it with anything like the fluency and ease of an average two-year-old, and whereas a child's learning to speak seems natural and effortless, the process of teaching an ape is painfully arduous.

First, the ape student—most have been chimpanzees—has to

learn the signs that stand for things: for instance, lexigrams on a keyboard that indicate various foods, such as *banana, peanut, juice*, and simple action words like *eat* and *drink*. Each sign is taught separately, until the chimp, when offered a type of food, can reliably ask for it. Then it is given a full keyboard with all the lexigrams it has learned, and the chimp is free to combine them in any way. The result is a high percentage of absurd requests—"eat peanut juice"—and these impossible requests are not rewarded. Thousands of trials and errors later, the smart student finally gets it: banana and peanut are related to one another; they are solid foods; juices are liquid. You eat the one and drink the other: aha!

From then on the teacher can add symbols for any number of eats and drinks, and the ape no longer makes mistakes. New categories—tools, toys—can be added too. The chimpanzee's learning has suddenly become efficient because the words—the lexigrams—are no longer "point-to" objects on the keyboard that have to be learned painstakingly by rote, but have been mentally organized into a meaningful system from which they can be retrieved quickly, without trial and error, and into which new symbols and categories can easily be incorporated. But why was it so hard?

Although primates are among the most intelligent animals, their cortex, the outer "cap" of the brain that surrounds the inner portions—and especially the front part of the cortex that bulges human foreheads—is not nearly as well developed as it is in us. It's not that the cortex is the seat of intelligence: like other mental functions, including language, the processing of any sort of task is widely distributed in the brain, with different areas handling different aspects of the problem. Neurons in the cortex, however, branch through every level of the brain, contacting older and more primitive areas such as those that create emotion or control stereotyped movements. By selectively suppressing activity in deeper structures, the cortex allows the animal more flexible and purposeful control over its responses. The expansion of the cortex in primates was likely driven by the demands of an arboreal life. Stereotyped movements, like a horse's trot, would not swing an animal accurately through the trees. Horses merely yank and munch their food; primates must use their hands and mouths in any number of ways to pluck, peel, and otherwise process the foods they eat. Social demands must also have played a part: as we all know, some urges have to be suppressed in the interest of getting along.

A wonderful example of ape limitations in this respect is the chimpanzee who, coming upon a cache of bananas, wanted to keep it for himself. Usually, when a chimp finds a bonanza, it utters a loud food call that brings others to the feast. The call, stimulated by the quantity of food, is automatic. This chimp, knowing the call was coming, slammed his hands to his mouth trying to keep it back, but it burst out anyway. The difficulty for language-learning apes is similar: they want that food. To get it, they have to press the lexigram that indicates it. They're too intent on the external relationship between key and snack, too focused on rote learning, too gripped by the immediate result to sit back and think about what they're learning. They come to know the trees but must be forced to see the forest.

Picture the animal wracking its brain under the burden of memory that rote learning entails. It has to remember not only all the combinations that worked, but also all the combinations that didn't work. It has to review each association one by one and compare it to a memory of reward or nonreward. There are so many details to keep in mind! Finally, in the struggle to think about what it has learned, the ape stumbles on the pattern, and what a load is then off its mind! It no longer has to keep track of dozens of lexigram-food-yes-no associations but can retrieve what it wants from the symbolic system of solid/liquid that it has constructed.

Only once has an ape gotten the trick of symbolic representation without formal teaching. He was an infant pigmy chimpanzee—a bonobo—named Kanzi, and he was quite a pest. Researchers were trying to teach language to his foster mother, but during the lessons, Kanzi, scrambling up her back, climbing on her head, jumping on the keyboard, utterly distracted her. She never learned the task. But Kanzi did. Just by observing his mother's lessons, he picked up the trick as effortlessly as human children do.

Possibly bonobos are more intelligent than ordinary chimps, but Deacon thinks Kanzi's youth—he was the equivalent of a toddler—was also in his favor. Like a human toddler, he was restless, didn't pay attention to anything for very long, and hadn't yet a mind for details. You could say he wasn't very good at seeing the trees. For that very reason, Deacon suggests, the forest "popped out" of the background. It was simply easier for Kanzi's immature brain to recognize the overall regularities in the situation than to dwell on the details.

Of course, Deacon is going from this line of reasoning to an explanation of why young children learn language with such ease compared to older children and adults: they can't keep a lot of details in mind; they notice global qualities; they grasp the big picture. Children don't need explicit teaching to learn language nor is it necessary to posit any special "language organ" in the infant brain. They naturally stumble onto symbolic representation because rote learning is too hard.

This appears to be another of those things we "know" about young children. We don't expect them to learn a great many things by rote until first grade, when they are six. In the meantime, while they are picking up the trick of language, we help them along by speaking "Motherese." We use short sentences and repeat them often; we speak slowly and, by the exaggerated lift and fall of our voice, we emphasize the salient features in the string of sounds:

"Wanna go outside?"

There comes a time during a child's second year when suddenly her language-learning brain realizes that every object has a name. She points; you say.

I can't show anything to my dumb dog, Girl. She just doesn't get it. She can stiffen and point her body toward a rabbit noise or scent, and she recognizes that posture in other dogs as indicating prey, but the gesture is instinctive, automatic, stereotyped, and inflexibly aroused by rabbits. The index finger indicating an arbitrary object makes no sense at all to her: the gesture is uniquely human, as is the toddler's purpose in identifying what is pointed to without any other motivation but to learn its name.

Implicit in the pointed finger is sheer curiosity. We not only can make sense of things by relating them symbolically in our brains, we seek to accumulate many symbols for the reward of representing their relationships with one another. We want to understand the meanings of our world. Girl does not wish to know the meaning of a rabbit. She just wants to chase and catch it. The rabbit "smells good" in a sense quite different from Ian's remark about flowers. He, the sniffer and plucker, already had a relationship with flowers, yet the aster that he claimed "smells good" really doesn't nor did he try to pick or taste it. His interest was in fitting this particular object into the higher-order category of flowers.

Indoors during the pointing period, we are able to give two-year-olds the names of every sort of object: *spoon, fork, knife; television, radio, telephone, clock*; the names of every item of clothing and the titles of every storybook. And not only *book* but *newspaper, magazine, page, paper, pad, pen, ink*, and *crayon*. Three-year-olds may pick up twenty new words a day.

But what is *outside*? A bush or a tree, a squirrel and grass, birds, bugs. When people lived by foraging, children's elders could—in fact, had to—give them names for hundreds of plants and scores of animals. My father learned from his father, who hunted and fished as well as farmed, what grew and flew and swam and ran, and passed down their names to me. It's extraordinary today how few people know even common trees by name. Or rather, they may know the words *oak* and *apple*, and can relate those words to the higher-order categories of plant and tree, but without really having the sense of what the object is like. The word is there; the reality is missing.

This is a problem with symbolic representation: it is facile, often superficial, and can exist independently of correlation with the real world. An example was given to me by a naturalist friend who leads walks through the Wisconsin prairie:

One spring over the space of a week in apple-blossom time, he guided a total of two hundred schoolchildren and their score of teachers through a field where an old apple was in full performance. He described the tree as so weighted in bloom that it seemed the branches bent with the load, although it is the many years of heavy fruiting that bow old limbs nearly to the ground, giving the apple tree that classic form that is displayed in picture books and posters at elementary schools to depict the seasons. Who is not familiar with that illustrated tree, green leafed in the summer, red fruited in the fall, brown branched in the winter, pink budded and white blossomed in the spring? Here was the real thing, the very model, and sweetly fragrant too, humming with delighted bees and loosing petals like snowflakes on the breeze.

The naturalist coaxed the group around him and asked for hands: Who could say what tree this was? He repeated the question at every outing, addressed it to the teachers too, and in all that week, no hand was raised. Not one child or adult could identify an apple tree. They had the word, but they had missed the "point-to" experience that made sense of apples to Ian that morning in the garden.

Another problem with our word-bent minds is the tendency to see forests more easily than trees. Just the opposite of apes who get stuck in details, sometimes we have to be forced to notice them. Ruby fruit and emerald beetles may grab our attention, but someone literally has to point out to us the sycamore or sumac. *Then* we see it. This is an extraordinary result of naming: the name determines the perception of the object that is named. To those who can discriminate vegetation only in broad categories—tree, vine, underbrush—a roadside is no more than a green blur. Learn sumac and the scene sharpens. Learn two dozen roadside species and what had been carpeting resolves into tapestry. To name something is to know it, to make it leap to awareness.

Often, it is to see it at all.

I've always disliked "being educated." I find it an infliction to walk the woods and fields with a guide pointing and saying. I prefer to notice for myself and then to engage the attention of someone who can enlighten my curiosity. I think that's probably the way with most children.

My father did not set out to teach me the names of flowers; he set out to walk with me. That was before I was old enough to take off on my own—four or five. I collected flower names offhandedly from him, secondarily to sipping nectar from a honeysuckle or dabbing my fingers with the orange sap of bloodroot; or he might show me, opening the layers carefully, the heart within the heart of bleeding heart, and so I learned the name.

Ian in the garden may find lavender and honeybees, and almost anyone can drop those names into his collection. Soon, though, and with that close sightedness typical of the young, he will find beetles too, along with snails and salamanders that are all beneath most adults' notice and that few of us know anything about, neither what is the use of them or even what to call them. Then what are we to do?

My father, having led me through the flora, fell into step behind me as I explored Arthropoda.

He had the agricultural attitude that bugs are pests. He sprayed cabbage worms with the same fervor and revulsion that homeowners now spray ticks and with as little concern for the other species that necessarily die with them. He knew few insects and no spiders by name. My father was, moreover, a fastidious man who warred with houseflies and washed his hands after each encounter. Yet, when I pushed past him to where he really didn't want to go, he handed to me, like a relay runner, a net, cork mounting boards, mounting pins, an insect guide, and a prescription for chloroform. I became a bug collector.

I was by then years past the point-and-say time where we left Ian in the garden, but from my early learning of the flower language, I had inferred the underlying grammar of the living world. I knew not only that everything has a name, but also that it has a place, a habitat; that it has a way of life; that it has relationships with its own and other kinds: that it has meaning. In other words, I had at my disposal a symbolic system into which potentially I could fit any novel creature that I came upon. Or so I thought.

My father could name for me only big, dramatic insects like walkingstick and luna moth. There is just one bloodroot—*Sanguinarea canadensis*—but katydids, one of the names he knew, are only a fraction of the long-horned grasshopper family Tettigonidae, which is further divided into eight subfamilies. You'd have to be an entomologist to identify any but the commonest katydid to the genus level, much less to name its species.

At the height of my bug-collecting years, I hoped to become an entomologist, but a full collection of all the insects that have been cataloged in this country would come to nearly ninety thousand specimens, not counting mites, ticks, spiders, millipedes, centipedes, and numerous other arthropods that have more than six legs. Just the true "bugs," the order Hemiptera, in North America includes two suborders, forty families, and forty-five hundred species. My father knew the broad and common term "stink bug," but the chance that a particular species of this large family would actually be depicted in the guide was slim. To the best of my recollection, my specimen boards and boxes never amounted to more than sixty or seventy species (most of them unnamed) compared to the fourteen hundred insect species that Frank Lutz, a onetime curator of entomology at the American Museum of Natural History, identified in a suburban New Jersey yard that measured seventy-five by two hundred feet—a mere third of an acre.

So I gave it up. But the symbolic stickiness of things learned in childhood assured that my interest would not be extinguished by time and distance nor my respect for insects daunted by the few who eat my crops.

I look up names and I look up meanings. I looked up *respect*. The word is derived from the Latin for "to see" and contains the sense of seeing again or anew. The experience of naming can be like a double take: you see, you name, and see again with the sense of what you saw.

There was a wasp on a trumpet-vine pod one weekend last fall. She stayed most of the day, licking the sugary sap that the pod exudes. The wasp was very beautiful—metallic blue black, with transparent navy wings that flickered as she ate. Thinking her so singular that I might find her portrait in my insect guide, I thumbed through the many wasps. There she was: Steel-blue Cricket Hunter. Reseen, respected.

Her scientific name is *Chlorion aerarium*, which I must say is confusing: *chloro-* means greenish yellow, as in *chloro*phyll. The only chlorion in *Webster's Third* is a greenish yellow bird. The only wasp in my guide that shares the same genus name is *Chlorion cyaneum*, a.k.a. Purplish-blue Cricket Hunter. Was the namer blue-yellow color-blind? Or do other members of the genus come in leafy colors?

The wasp was licking the pod she stood on. I have watched ants do that many times and have read about the reason for it: the pod, by attracting predatory ants to its sweet exudate, gains their protection from herbivores like caterpillars that would chew its flesh. Unlike ants who eat such prey, this wasp does not eat meat. The adult subsists entirely on sweets. She hunts her prey to provision her larvae, and she certainly was not doing that here: crickets forage on the ground and eat garbage, more or less, not hard pods swaying ten feet up a vine.

The Steel-blue Cricket Hunter returned daily over the ensuing weeks. I took to watching her with binoculars. She would visit vari-

ous pods but spent most of her time on the one where I had first noticed her. Small red ants, and also large black ones, frequented the
pod. She appeared not to mind their presence. On occasion, though,
another wasp would alight, this one a yellow jacket of the genus
Vespula. The Cricket Hunter at first seemed to tolerate the yellow
jacket as she had the ants. Then one day the two wasps bumped into
one another coming around the pod, and the Cricket Hunter
snapped at the yellow jacket with her sharp black mandibles. She
snapped rapidly, twice, and the yellow jacket beat a fast retreat. The
Vespula was persistent, though, and returned as many times as she was
chased away, landing always on the opposite side of the pod where
she was able to get in some licks before she was discovered.

After some days of this snapping over sweets, I noticed a change
in the Cricket Hunter's behavior. She began to keep watch from
the stem of the pod where she could see in all directions. Now
when the yellow jacket landed, the Cricket Hunter attacked immediately regardless of their distance from each other. Ultimately, the
common wasp retreated for good; the hunter had won unchal-
lenged possession of her pod.

Only once while I was watching did the two actually tangle.
Mostly, the Cricket Hunter snapped in her enemy's face, just
threatening. Neither tried to use its stinger. I found this odd because yellow jackets are apt to sting viciously and repeatedly on
slight provocation, like finding my lip in their beer.

If and when the Steel-blue Cricket Hunter went hunting, I
didn't witness it, but the guide explained the procedure. The wasp
digs a burrow, "tossing out quantities of sand and pebbles," then
hunts for a grasshopper or cricket that she anesthetizes with her
sting. She drags the living body to her burrow and attaches an egg
to it. Each egg hatches into a larva that eats the meat, pupates over
the winter, and goes forth as an adult the following spring leaving
the empty cricket shell behind.

Here the information in the guide ended, but my curiosity did
not.

As a bug-enchanted child, I used to open mud daubers' nests that I found under windowsills and in the holes of hose bibs. Each cell of such a nest contains an egg and a meal of anesthetized spiders. Other wasps feed caterpillars to their larvae; some feed them cicadas. I thought of how kittens learn from their mother's provisioning what prey they are to seek. Might it be that the wasp's natal meal determines the kind of meat the female will later hunt to provision her family?

There is the question, too, of why yellow jackets are so aggressive. Whereas mud daubers and Cricket Hunters are solitary wasps that, having provisioned their larvae, leave them to fend for themselves, yellow jackets are social wasps who keep house among their daughters and feed their brood on picnic fare and masticated prey. I wonder if motherly protectiveness necessitates their sting?

I stumble occasionally across answers to such questions, but that's not the point. Connections can't be made, and questions arising from them can't be asked—nor can thoughtfulness itself arise—from seeing a whatever on a something-or-other for which one knows no names.

Identifying a plant, bird, or butterfly can be quite tedious for an adult. Field guides have what's called a key that you follow through a process of elimination to arrive at the correct species. The identification depends on the details: alternate or opposite leaves, four petals or multiples of three, leaf edges smooth or serrated. I walk with a group of women who love the process and appreciate the detail. Often, though, I point out to them a plant that I know by name, without knowing any of the details by which it could be keyed through the field guide. I just know it. Because my father taught me the plant when I was a child, I know it holistically as Ian knows "smell good" without having had to analyze the syntax of verb and adverb. Plants my father didn't teach me are less "inside" my mind, and often if I don't see a particular species from one year to the next, I forget its name. Things we learn as children get glued to the self. I don't just identify blood-root; I am in identification with it. My father, by offering me the name, gave me the soul.

Jean Piaget, in *The Construction of Reality in the Child*, says that children believe the name of an object is *in* it—*is* it—much as we feel that the name of a person is that person. He doesn't mention something else that I'm sure is so: that children expect adults to know the name. They expect our introduction.

When introducing your child to a friend, you wouldn't merely point at her and say, "That's Betsy." Introductions imply attitudes, the incorporation of the name into some category of emotion and system of behavior. Ian said *frog* and I told him *toad*; he touched the toad first gingerly, then more certainly to make it blink. Together, we set free the frightened animal in the garden. That was considerate behavior toward a toad.

We talk of "socializing" children, by which we mean not only distinguishing among people by name, age, sex, role, and personality, but also learning appropriate behavior toward others in a variety of circumstances. If we are to achieve a similar degree of civilized behavior toward other species, we will similarly have to socialize children in the natural world even if that entails, as in moving to a strange land, forcing ourselves to become acquainted with the inhabitants.

But thinking back on the spotted salamander episode now, in the context of years of urging people to naturalize their land, I see that it illustrates an essential obstacle to that quest. Natural habitat comes with natural inhabitants, and some of them are ones that humans naturally avoid.

The tendency to avoid sinuous creatures is not only powerful, but easily generalized. Thus, the city acquaintance who, upon exposure to suburban "wildlife," became hysterical about a caterpillar looping along the windowsill. A potent readiness to fear is also aroused by spiders, and this fear is easily generalized to any multi-legged crawler. My acquaintance found all things that coil or creep equally abhorrent and consequently groomed her yard to lifelessness.

She may have been an extreme case, but it's fair to say that many, if not most, inexperienced adults, when exposed to snaky, scurrying, or spidery creatures, are driven by the unmodulated primitivity of their prewired vigilance to the worst assumptions. This phobic response to "vermin" has contributed to a sterile landscape in which no child can have the experience of turning a stone to find the salamander that, if properly introduced, might convert innate awe to cultivated interest.

Spiders and serpents loom large in mythology and psychology because they loomed large in our evolutionary history. Although humans long ago passed the point where instinctive response strictly rules behavior, we have only very recently lost the continuity of naming that, in previous generations, tempered such inborn cautions with traditional information. Like the acquaintance who mistook a caterpillar for a snake, we have become at the mercy of primitive short circuits uninsulated by culturally transmitted knowledge. I can see that for those adults whose terror is insurmountable, the dilemma seems unresolvable: how can they introduce a child to a snake while running in the opposite direction?

But isn't this dilemma the same one my father faced? Children whose parents introduce them early to the ordinary and unmenacing life around them can seek their own snakes.

I received an article from my son Lincoln. Across the top, he had written, "Funny stories of suburbanite alienation. Thought you'd enjoy."

The article was about homeowners' run-ins with wildlife: the man who paid $350 to have a nesting raccoon removed from his basement window well; the woman who shelled out $1,000 to seal her chimney against a marauding squirrel; a couple who faced an estimated $3,000 to rid their attic of bats. I believe these figures; I know how much it cost me to install a deer fence. The total annual cost of wildlife-related damage in the United States, according to the article, is close to $3 billion (not including the cost of removing the heart-rotted trees and stone crannies that these animals might have preferred had they been available).

The expense of wildlife control isn't funny, but some of the victims' remarks were hilarious. Of the squirrel who dropped down the chimney, the homeowner said, "He smudged black soot all over my furniture and then hid in our fake ficus tree." This woman's four-year-old son, she recounted, sought safety from the squirrel on the kitchen counter, where he huddled "in fetal position." The couple with the bat problem engaged their grown son to rout the colony with ammonia. The wife claimed the fume-dazed bats "dive-bombed him like crazy." And—this regarding woodpeckers drumming on an enraged homeowner's shingle siding—"As much as we love the little bastards, they're killing us. It's us against them."

He had, in fact, pulled a shotgun on them.

Attempts to plant the seeds of biophilia in such alienated ground are likely to fail. It may be too late for even the four-year-old, so tightly curled that he'd be hard to straighten out. He's being raised with an attitude. "This whole nature thing," declared his mother, "is a pain in the neck."

One can't be sure from such remarks that the adult is against nature—as long as it isn't in her own back yard. The woman may well support saving owls and old-growth forest. She perhaps looks forward to the coming year, when her son will learn in kindergarten about bees and apple trees. She may support his education with books about animals and visits to a nature center. But she has already missed a period in her child's life when he was avid for sensual experience of the natural world and eager to name the creatures in it: to have the soul of the squirrel, to identify with it, to feel *its* fear. The squirrel still would have had to be removed from the house, but the experience would have deepened the boy's understanding in a way that phobias and fake ficus trees preclude.

Children's attitudes are influenced by parents, and I suppose had

Ian's mother hated honeybees, she might have screamed and rushed him back inside, compromising his pleasure in that dangerous garden. Yet it wasn't necessary, either, that she love bees; her neutrality was sufficient support for the boy's self-education. Provided, of course, that he had access to a classroom—and not the school sort and not a nature center, but some small wild place where he might on his own come upon, and touch, and pluck, and sniff, and come to recognize with intimacy and by name a common apple tree.

Compared to the hunger with which Girl gulped the word *rabbit*, her appetite for words like *sit* or *stay* is nil. She has learned other ingestible terms—*water, biscuit*—more easily than commands, yet only *mouse* and *rabbit* have elicited in her such immediate grasp and such excitement. Her behavior, when she's allowed to explore rodent and rabbit habitat, also differs from her behavior elsewhere. She races and leaps through woods, seldom pausing to investigate anything at all, but in a meadow, she will often walk slowly and deliberately, ears forward and nose down, every sense alert for signs of prey. And this dog, who will not venture from the sofa on a rainy day and who further insists on being covered with a blanket if the house is chilly, will wait for hours in any weather at a burrow entry for a vole to appear. Girl loves that habitat and the prey it harbors: she has her own aesthetic.

I don't think it's stretching the term "aesthetic" to apply it to even so lowly a creature as a spider or a fly. In late winter, skunk cabbages bloom in wetland woods, and in the same vicinity, the carrion flies that will pollinate them are emerging from their overwinter sleep. The flies' parents are long dead; there is no one to teach them what to eat and where to mate even if their fly brain had the capacity to learn. Yet they will be "attracted" by the meaty color of the skunk cabbage's hooded blooms, by their fetid smell, and by the heat the flowers emit to melt their way through frozen earth. These are hard-wired preferences. Whether they will guide a particular fly to a newly emerged skunk cabbage or to a newly dead corpse may be a matter of chance, but chances are that most flies will follow their aesthetic to a suitable food and mating site.

Animals are necessarily endowed with mental schema that guide them to optimal habitat. A cobweb spider may not be aware of joy in corners, but it is primed to notice a corner, motivated to approach it, and prepared to use it. Our aesthetic similarly guides us to our natural habitat, to landscapes that share features with the grasslands where humans originally evolved and in which most peoples over history earned their living.

Shown slides of various landscapes, people generally find most beautiful open, grassy land that is gently rolling, dotted with single trees and groves, and flowing with water. This is true whether they are urbanites or farmers, inhabit mountain or desert, belong to our culture or another, or have ever even seen in real life anything like oak parkland or African savanna. The response is physical: heart rate, blood pressure, and hormone levels are affected. Mental patients are calmer and surgical patients heal faster if their window overlooks open countryside; even framed landscapes affect recovery. The suburban scene seems to be related to such preferences: it is lawn grassland, specimen-tree savanna. We consider waterfront property the most valuable of all.

Girl would not be moved by a painting of the prairie any more than she would rise to the bait of Beatrix Potter's Peter Rabbit. Dogs haven't that capacity for visual abstraction. We do, and not only do we respond to representations that match our mental diagrams, we are far more talented at creating abstractions than at reproducing visual reality. Compared to actual savanna, the flattened surface, geometric shrubs, and isolated trees of our designed landscape are as conventional and simplified as a child's crayon drawing. As with the apple tree we've never eaten from, lack of actual experience of land where we both live and earn our living has left us with an impoverished abstraction.

Biology is odd in that it doesn't necessarily link inherent preferences to the purposes they might serve, or even determine that preferences march in lockstep with each other. Girl's relish in rodents was aroused independently of grassland habitat, and her interest in grassland habitat was evident long before her discovery of rabbits. Given a lively meadow, though, it was inevitable that tall grass and small mammals would coincide and that she would herself link habitat to prey. The sketches merely guide the dog to the experiences that will, when combined, help her to hunt.

We also are biologically primed to pay close attention to living things. Ezra nearly leaped out of arms to get to Girl; that first word *duh* remained his only word for the next three months. Ian immediately learned *cricket* and *toad*, even discriminating the latter name from the previously learned *frog*. There was a garden; there were creatures in it: Ian the infant hunter tried to catch the bees.

In the ordinary course of ancient events, people's attraction to open habitat along a waterway would have brought them to a wealth of living creatures, some to fear and some to eat but all requiring close attention to learn what each was like. But just because animal alertness and habitat preference happened to coincide in the hunting way of life does not mean that hunting is the only possible result. Biological guidance is independent of cultural interpretation: later in human history, linkage resulted in domestication of both the land and the food animals that lived there. Today it nourishes bird-watchers, naturalists, and the cultural move toward conservation. But without linkage of the landscape with the creatures that live there, children can grow up loving lawns as an ideal and owls in the abstract without even a dog's understanding of mice in the meadow, much less the necessity of rodents for the owls' survival.

Words without experience are insufficient. Nameless experience is insufficient too. Neither interest in animals nor delight in landscape stands alone in guiding us toward respect for the environment. They must meet in culture. The garden that attracted Ian, the place where scene and word and creature came together for him, is after all a landscape I planned and planted: it is a cultural creation. And if our ultimate relationship with other forms of life is molded by the cultural milieu in which we grow, I think even squirrel-fearing grown-ups might begin by cultivating their garden.

I heard the darnedest story from a woman in Ohio. There she was, sitting at the kitchen table having her morning coffee and admiring the garden she had planted in a bed below the window, when along came a yellow butterfly to sip from a purple coneflower. Leaning closer to the window, she saw a praying mantis lurking on the stem. In an instant, the mantis leaped upon the butterfly to eat it. She saw in that microcosmic event—saw and realized simultaneously—the nature of nature.

There is more to the story (there always is). First, the flowers: this woman had always lived in the city, hadn't so much as gone to summer camp or ever vacationed in the country, but when a new job took her to a Midwestern suburb, she planted this little garden bed for the simple reason that she had always liked flowers. Not so simple, though. I have known people who are phobic even toward birds and butterflies, who they fear might swoop at them. I have never known anyone to be afraid of flowers. Strange fruits, yes, and mushrooms, and generally unfamiliar vegetation, but not flowers. You never hear anyone say, "Ugh! I hate flowers!"

Quite the opposite, we make love with flowers—court with them, apologize with them, greet with them, celebrate with them. Since we only occasionally eat them (though most don't know it, cauliflower and broccoli are flowers), there has to be another reason that they mean so much to us. Possibly in our prelinguistic past, flowers indicated food to come, as apple blossoms indicate the future fruit, or possibly the attraction goes back further still, to ape days when flowers were commonly eaten. But never mind, there it is: we are flower people.

The more immediate question is why the microcosmic scene the woman witnessed was a revelation. Might there lurk in urban minds and even in adulthood some switch that electrified her realization of the natural world? I asked her to tell me more. She had learned somewhere along the way—in school, she supposed—about predator/prey relationships and also knew the praying mantis by look and name. What captured her comprehension, though, was the close-up drama: she was forced to switch her mind-set from sweet-sipping butterfly to meat-hungry mantis, recode from experience what she had previously known only in the abstract. She was compelled to *re*spect, to take another look.

And with what result? In this rare case, the adult was converted to the child's view as it is before the overlay of taught meanings obscures what is real about the world. She was back in the global mode, soaking up the grammar of the world without having tediously to memorize its vocabulary or analyze its rules. She "got it"—and by the way replanted her yard in ecological accord with the vision she had had.

I don't expect this result to happen often; the lesson is that there is an entry point for parents who do not now, and never will, love snakes and spiders. They have only to begin as the woman from Ohio did, with a bed of flowers.

Flowers don't lunge or bite or pee on you. They stay put; you may hunt for them but needn't chase them. The hunt is leisurely, a stroll through mail-order catalogs and nurseries that offer native plants. The pictures have identifying captions; the pots have labels. Many of the names are already familiar: aster, goldenrod, milkweed, sunflower, lily. Some come in many species: the milkweed whose seeds Ian lofted on the breeze was butterfly weed, a brilliant orange species that is one of five milkweeds he might have found here. You get to choose. You get to know the flowers—planting them, watching them grow, picking them, calling them by name. Your vision improves: the scale changes. Yellow dots in the center of the black-eyed Susan resolve to bunches of pollen grains ripening there. Movement resolves to a bumblebee gathering pollen for her brood. I hope your curiosity will be aroused. I hope it will lead you afield—field guide in hand—to learn more names, to see more closely, to sharpen your perception of that green blur outside.

Sharpened perception is irreversible and may lead to sudden comprehension, as when a child, having tediously memorized the alphabet and the sounds the letters stand for, suddenly extracts meaning from the written word. Landscape learned unit by unit as separate species similarly becomes legible, meaningful, and personal. I remember the thrill of sounding out words; I remember as well the thrill of deciphering where in the vast text of landscape to find the salamanders I had come to love.

Let me now tell my salamander story in different words:

I was shocked by what biology told me was a serpent. I ran to my father. I had expected the serpent; I also expected adult interpretation of it. My father's interpretation overrode the biological program, and set the course of my future learning. He was handing on to me the living world for my belonging.

The obligation to name is no doubt much older than the story of God's instruction to Adam in the Garden, and only recently have we failed to heed it. We neglect the obligation at our peril: those who don't know the names for the plants in the landscape don't see the landscape I see and carelessly cut it. Those who know no insects by their names crush them indiscriminately.

I've been reading up on insects ever since I last pinned a beetle to a board. Entomologists collecting in such places as the rain-forest canopy and old-forest soil now estimate that there are thirty million insect species, most of *them* unnamed. Whole ecosystems, including North American ones, would collapse without the seed-planting, soil-aerating, plant-protecting services of ants. No one has to tell me to hold the insecticide: I understand why not to spray my land. I learned it from flowers named for me by my dad. I learned it from bugs and beetles that he didn't much like himself. It was generous of him to let me. It was courageous.

It is this courage that I ask for.

Safely Gathered In

The list of animals grew. The more I finished, the more there were to add, for those left out would not be able to come aboard the ark. The urgency of the endeavor caught me by surprise. There had to be animals from every continent; I carved a group of penguins from Antarctica. There had to be reptiles and birds, not just mammals, and snakes and lizards as well as turtles, and then I also had to whittle frogs. I found myself grouping and regrouping the finished animals, uncertain whether the wolf belonged with his prey, the flock of sheep, or with his kin, the other canids; whether the horse belonged with farm animals or with the wild equines. It seemed unfair that there were baby polar bears but no baby panda and wrong that the group of small mammals lacked opossums. If someone idly fingering my work removed an animal from its place among the others, I had to put it back right away. They had to stay together, don't you see?

Samantha, our son Aram's child, was the first to play with the whittled animals. There was no ark yet; she didn't know the story of the Deluge anyway. To Samantha, the animals were the people in her life. They were her friends at day care lining up in pairs to go outdoors. One was the teacher who called each child by name to join the morning circle. Another was a child who strayed from line and

circle, and had to be found and brought back into the group. Most
often, though—indeed, dozens of times a day—Samantha chose
three figures to play Mommy, Daddy, Baby in a narrative that was a
ritual attempt to keep the three together during an angry and
frightening divorce.

The gist of the story was that no matter what—no matter fighting, no matter shouting, no matter being "bad"—a baby's mommy
and daddy are hers forever and will always take good care of her.
The game was intense, insistent, played out with any available characters: the whittled animals at my home, but elsewhere the stuffed
animals she carried with her and, on one memorable occasion,
without any props at all: "Let's play Mommy, Daddy, Baby God-
zilla," begged Samantha in the car en route to visit cousin Ezra. She
did not ask me to play the game with her; it was always her father,
Aram, who played both parents to her enactment of the baby. In
real life, Aram had moved out of the home. The play did not acknowledge that spatial separation.

We were sitting together on the couch at Joshua's house when
Samantha addressed to me directly a series of statements regarding
the permanence of kinship.

Her daddy is a grown-up, but I am still his mommy.

Yes.

And Grandpa is still his daddy.

Yes.

And we still take care of him.

Yes.

And even though he doesn't live with us, we are still his
mommy and daddy.

Yes.

Aram is *her* daddy, but he is still *our* child.

Yes, Samantha, wherever he goes and whatever he does, he is
and always will be our child.

In fact, Aram had brought Samantha east from California to
demonstrate his childhood. He read to her the storybooks that had

been read to him; he showed her his old stuffed animals and the cupboard in his bedroom where his teddy bear still lives. He told me that he wanted Samantha to know that her father came from somewhere that was hers too, a family home. But I think really it was Aram our child who needed to come home.

The first of our sons to marry stunned us by deciding that he and his woman would pronounce themselves man and wife. How could he have been so thickheaded?

Marriage is conferred on a couple by the community. Without that consent, they may mate, but they are not married. When a couple is married, they are assigned reproductive rights and economic obligations. Others' roles also change: parents become in-laws and ultimately grandparents; brothers and sisters become uncles and aunts; their children are cousins. In other cultures, many other categories of kin may also take on new roles. Agreements are reached among the families or between whole villages; goods are exchanged; alliances formalized. How elaborately the ritual is conducted and to what extent it dictates the future behavior of the participants vary greatly from one culture to another, but marriage is universally practiced in all societies and always with the intent that the community at large recognize the exclusive sexual relationship that the rite confers.

Sexual exclusivity addresses a problem that arises whenever the young of a species requires guarding or provisioning by both parents: the female can't afford to mate with a male who won't support her children, and the male can't afford to support her children unless he's sure they're his. Among the animals I've whittled, whistling swans and gray wolves are examples of species that form lifelong bonds. Swans jealously guard their mate from others' sexual advances and, to avoid continual harassment, they isolate themselves during the breeding season. Sexual jealousy and isolation are not options for wolves because they hunt cooperatively and provision the young communally. In wolf society, only the leading couple breed; sexuality and fertility are suppressed hormonally in subordinate members of the tribe. As the dominant couple ages, subordinates replace them, so there is a sort of reproductive taking turns that works because group size is small and leadership is brief.

Marriage is fundamentally unlike either of these strategies for assuring paternity. It places the responsibility for reproductive integrity not in the couple's bond to one another, or in their privacy, or in their ability to suppress cuckoldry, but in the whole and public community in which they live. Marriage doesn't assure monogamy; it does greatly increase the chance that infidelity will be discovered and the cheater publicly revealed.

Marriage is also unlike pair bonding in that it relies on promises: the vow "I do" is only one of many made explicitly or implicitly among many people regarding their individual and group behavior in the future. A sign like the sound, *rabbit*, that I voice to indicate to Girl that a rabbit is nearby—right here, right now—won't suffice: if the sign is "I do" and then I don't, the sound I made becomes pointless and forgettable. Only symbols have the indelible quality that remains even when what they originally referred to is far away and long ago. I am as married now as I was forty years ago no matter what events have intervened and regardless of the fact that the object of my vow is now overweight, balding, and approaching seventy. The community's continuing interest in marriage also dictates that Aram and his wife, though they may divorce, will not thereby be freed from obligations to each other and to their child.

I was puzzling my way through Terrence Deacon's *The Symbolic Species* for the third time when Aram brought Samantha home to visit. Marriage was very much a topic both in our family and in my reading. Deacon proposes that the necessity of marriage is what brought our kind over the symbolic threshold that is so very difficult for apes to cross.

Recall that those student chimpanzees who got the trick of symbols discovered the underlying regularity of the verb/object pairs by memorizing not only what worked, but what did not. Similarly, if a child were not forced to learn by rote that two plus two equals four—*and* cannot equal six or one—she would not come to understand arithmetic. What teachers of apes as well as children do is a reductio ad absurdum: they force the mind to discover the underlying pattern of what works by demonstrating that all other alternatives don't work. Samantha, a precocious three-year-old, had been taught by her parents to count the number of syllables in a word by repeatedly and with the aid of fingers matching each part of a word to a numeral until she discovered that one finger per sound was the underlying pattern that codified the number of the syllables.

Under normal circumstances, though, animals are not subjected to this kind of learning. They learn by rote any number of associations between signals and what they indicate. Signals may be the sound *mouse* indicating to Girl that there is a rodent in the cupboard, or the crouched posture and flicking tail of the cat indicating that she has located a nest of baby rabbits, or my husband's business suit indicating that he is about to leave for work. But lack of correlation between sign and signified erases the connection: now that the mice are gone, the cat dead, and my husband wears any old thing to the office, none of the previous signs signifies anything anymore. It's hard to think of a situation where memorizing what works and forgetting what no longer works wouldn't get an animal through the vicissitudes of life. The simple answer to why symbolic thought is so difficult even for very intelligent animals is that they never needed it.

In addition to Deacon's work as a neuroscientist, he is also an evolutionary anthropologist. The path he followed to the roots of language led back over two million years to the first human species, *Homo habilis*. The name, which means "handy man," refers to the ability to make stone butchering and scraping tools. The tools indicate that meat was by then a standard part of the human diet. Its provision, judging by the size of prey species—zebras, antelopes—

must have entailed considerable cooperation among the hunters both to bring down the game and to divide the carcass. An essential predicament according to Deacon's reconstruction is that the more friendship among men became critical, the more disruptive to the society was aggressive competition for mates. The turn-taking system of reproductive rights as practiced among wolves would not have worked for our larger groups of longer-lived ancestors and, since women encumbered by children could not accompany their menfolk on the demanding and dangerous hunt, jealous guarding wasn't possible either, nor was isolation from the cooperative society an option for any mated pair. Yet Handyman's very reduced canine teeth, coupled with his somewhat enlarged brain, suggest that the problem had been solved. Deacon concludes that we had by then been carried over the symbolic threshold by the necessity of the entire group enacting a promise to honor the reproductive integrity of the pair, and that this was achieved through ritual that was, he believes, the prototype of language.

Like language, ritual arranges the "words"—the symbolic objects and events—in a particular order, and the order conveys the meaning of the rite. The Easter ceremony, for example, culminates in Christ arisen, and the order of the symbolic narrative can't be changed without making nonsense of the meaning. Not only do all human societies employ ritual communication, they depend on rites to express and to share in the most critical social junctures such as coming-of-age and to communicate the most deeply felt and difficult ideas like those of patriotism and religion. Children readily formulate their own rituals, and there was in Samantha's Mommy, Daddy, Baby game all the markings of a rite. It was not intended as a rendition of the present, but as a promise for the future. It expressed a very difficult idea, and at a critical time in her life. What is more, the ritual was exactly the reductio ad absurdum that is at the root of symbolic thought: if a child is bad, and her parents don't abandon her; if the parents fight, and yet the child is cared for; if they leave home and yet remain her parents, then it must be that the relationship of mommies and daddies to their babies is reliable and permanent.

I have tried to imagine what the marriage ritual could have been when we were about as clumsy at this kind of mental representation as chimpanzees still are. Did the woman offer herself to men who ostentatiously refused? And the men in turn made advances that were refused by the woman? This is the essence of the marriage vow: "You see," such a ritual would say, "I am not copulating with any other, therefore I am mated only to this one." Perhaps the pair was marked: shorn, scarred, given some fig leaf at least to signify the married state. I can imagine too that they, in enactment of their responsibility toward future children, fed each other as today the bride and groom trade a sip of wine, a bite of cake before the treat is shared among the assembled tribe. Whatever the rite, I assume it was celebrated with a feast. There is no human rite from the naming of an infant to the laying of the dead that does not involve food sharing.

Aram's homecoming was the first since his marriage that did not coincide with a feast. We had met Samantha as an infant at her first Thanksgiving and had celebrated the next with her as well. Of all the holidays, I am most fond of Thanksgiving because it expresses so clearly the communion of feasting among kin. There are no tears of children disappointed in the presents they received nor the glut of giving that burdens the adults. The holiday is innocent too of bitter remembrance like that of Passover or mysteries like those of Easter. And there is no other holiday whose feast so suits its season with the fattened bird, the ripened fruit, and the gathered nuts.

But the two Thanksgivings that we had spent with Samantha had not been successful. The first, when she was an infant, was in Maine, where I'd never held the holiday before. The meal was the same; the place was not, and Aram's brothers weren't there to feast with us. The next Thanksgiving I served the traditional meal in Aram's communal home among housemates whom I didn't know and cooked it in an unfamiliar kitchen without the usual and wonderful confusion of all my children milling about mashing and washing and carrying heaping dishes to our old and ample table where everyone had eaten and crayoned and done their homework for a quarter of a century and more. Rituals, like Samantha's longing game, are to reaffirm the permanence of what we value most, and I found that Thanksgiving really is not a movable feast.

"Remember the time when . . . ?" begin the exchanges of boyhood stories that our sons relate when they are home for the holiday. They remember the time they parked a troublesome toddler—Aram as it happens—in our oversized mailbox to be rid of him awhile. They remember smearing their hands with peanut butter to catch gnats on the fly. They built blanket houses, raced wagons, dismembered toy robots to make monsters of them. "Remember the Neandertal campsite?" one says, and off they go, as the turkey roasts, to a childhood that is often news to me. They feel nostalgia as they share this boyhood past, and I'm aware that what has set it off is the hissing oak logs, the fragrance of rosemary, the scent of home.

Webster's dictionary gives "homesickness" as a synonym for nostalgia. The word is derived from *nostos*, Greek for "return home," plus that sad twist at the end: -*algia*, pain. I do not share the boys' nostalgia for the times they summon to memory. It is to my own childhood home that the fragrance of rosemary beckons with the pain of times gone by.

Nostalgia poses a paradox: although the emotion is not felt until childhood is over, the emotion is felt only for childhood. Interestingly too, strangers can share the longing without having shared specific memories such as those the boys bring to their group recollection. A woman whom I had never met before, but who was of my age, described in casual conversation her nostalgia for long afternoons when, home from school, the children in the neighborhood were sent out to play. She specifically recalled playing Prisoner, but it was less the games than the aura of the neighborhood she was trying to convey. She grew up in a different city, in a neighborhood I'd never seen. Yet I saw the stoop where you tightened your roller skates, the candy store, the chalk, the girls in pinafores. I was seeing the sun-hot sidewalks of my own city block, the urban side of my childhood in the 1940s. More vividly, I could smell it: a new Spalding ball, comic books, coal, dog pee on lampposts, steam from manholes, the grit scent of city. The memory recalls the scent, as the scent recalls the place, and nostalgia for it can tug as hard as a sob in the throat.

It's not surprising that scent should mediate powerful emotions. Smell is the most primitive of the senses, the one most deeply buried in time and mind, knotted hard into the brain stem, from which emanate passions as old and raw as those of sharks. The nostalgia that tugs at us must be a pale version of the passion that drives spawning salmon, in unimaginable urgency, to follow the scent of home through ocean and estuary, against falls and currents, to the upstream water of their birth.

The earliest memory that comes to me bittersweet, like Christmas morning before the gifts are opened, is the crackle and scent of varnish as I chew my wooden crib rail: there are lines of pale light through closed venetian blinds, and anticipation of being lifted from the crib. The latest childhood memory I can summon is the smell of ozone and wet sidewalk at the breaking of a thunderstorm when I was first in love. My longings for once upon a time are thus bracketed within a period of no more than twelve years, and if this is so with others too, the timing is suggestive: traditionally and universally, at the age of twelve or thirteen, societies celebrate a rite of passage from childhood to membership in the adult community. "Now I am a man," recites the beardless boy at his bar mitzvah—and goes back home to Mother. But in earlier times and other societies, the man might go to sea or war, the woman into marriage. Nostalgia may then have been, as I suspect it is with Aram now, the cultural elastic that kept the venturer oriented toward what was safe and known.

Scent (or taste) is the most basic of the senses. Even bacteria detect at their cell surface molecules of acid or sugar, and turn from the sour toward the sweet. Trees attacked by insects waft a warning odor to the breeze, and other trees receiving the chemical message arm themselves with chemical defenses. Insects themselves communicate with one another almost entirely by the scent and flavor of molecular messages. Cells within every body—a snail, a sponge, a mushroom, you—send and receive hormonal and other chemical flavors that coordinate their actions. Immune cells (white blood cells that ooze through the body like amoebas) taste their environment with receptors that stud their surface, and when they lick a substance that is not their body's self, they attack.

Self-recognition, of course, is fundamental, for if immune cells did not learn the difference between self and other, they would attack their own home body. Experience is their teacher: molecules encountered before birth are assumed to be self-markers; those encountered after birth are assumed to be alien. Curiously, the same portion of genetic material that codes for self-marking molecules also codes for odors that the body emits to the outside world, and both the self-markers within the body and those that are emitted from it are heritable: a family tends to have a familial smell.

There are many instances elsewhere in the animal kingdom of how practical a family scent can be: it helps tadpole siblings find each other and stay together in a predator-baffling school; it helps ewes within a flock of sheep to suckle only their own lambs; and in many species, it helps kin later in life avoid incestuous matings. There is strong evidence that mammals learn their mother's scent in utero: when experimenters add lemon flavor to the uterine fluid surrounding fetal mice, the offspring will refuse to nurse after birth unless their mother's belly has been rubbed with lemon oil.

The human sense of smell is dull compared to that of other animals. But it is interesting to note that children have exceptionally sensitive noses, and their later recollections of the scent of mother, father, uncle, aunt, or grandparent are very common. Taken together, this confluence of scents and sensibilities during childhood suggests to me a biological conspiracy to keep us as adults affiliated with kindred and attached to home. Aram's homesickness, Samantha's game, and the essential immobility of the Thanksgiving feast all point in the same direction:

We have to stay together, don't you see?

We have come dreadfully apart. Forty-one percent of first children are born to unmarried mothers. Fifty percent of marriages end in divorce. The majority of children do not grow to adulthood within the nuclear family of their birth. Young middle-class families move on average every five to seven years. There seem to be no statistics on the percent of individuals who remain in the vicinity of their original hometown nor any source for their distance from close kin: it is not important in our culture to track the dispersal of siblings or to account for the whereabouts of grandparents.

When our boys were little, there was an annual picnic for the "Philadelphia Steins," but that geographical entity no longer exists. Neither ethnic nor religious entities have existed in my own family for three generations now: we are Mormon, Catholic, Protestant, Hindu, Jewish, and Muslim; Chinese, Italian, Indian, Moroccan, Palestinian, and American. During our children's boyhood, we celebrated both Easter and Passover, Hanukkah and Christmas until the children grew out of Easter bunnies and I reneged on Hanukkah gelt. The home that is recalled to our sons by oak fire and roasting fowl is not the home where they reassemble now. There is no place, no people, not even a singular tradition that ties them, their mates, their elders, and their youngsters in a common bond.

In thinking about nostalgia, I have wondered what it would be like if the world were unchanged since our childhood. What if we lived in the house where we were born, among the people we'd grown up with, with everything just as it used to be and children playing as we had played back then? Can you be homesick for the home you still inhabit? Can you long for the good old days when new days are the same? Mutual reminiscing among my peers usually leads to grumbling about what's been lost, but if girls in pinafores still played hopscotch on the summer sidewalk there wouldn't seem to be much to grumble about except the weather and the inevitable aches of age.

Yet nostalgia for childhood seems a fact of life under any circumstance. When, forty years ago, we first stayed at the Maine fishing village where we summer now, men still carved the lobster buoys, women still knit the traps, and villagers still salted down cod and hung it to dry on wooden racks. Homes, not yet sold to people from "away," were called by the surname of the family that had always inhabited them. Every islander was known to every other, and all could recite their interrelated genealogies. Reading *Country of the Pointed Firs*, written by Sarah Orne Jewett about a neighboring island in Maine, it seemed to me that little had changed—including how the old folks nattered about times past.

So nostalgia may have another role besides the pull of place, and it might be this: to induce elders to reminisce so that the past may be implanted in the future. "Once upon a time," start tales from long ago, and "Tell me about when . . ." beg modern children still. The pull of nostalgia increases as we age, as does the urge to narrate, and there is no listener as avid as a child for a granny's oft-told tales. Before written history, elders embodied all that was known about the world and how to live in it. Conservation of tradition was their job.

That position isn't open anymore. I took Samantha to the American Museum of Natural History's dinosaur exhibit (where she sought, with some anxiety, evidence that they were mommy, daddy, and baby skeletons). But where once I could have shown my grandchild through silent halls among glowing rocks and iridescent butterflies, so much had changed that I could find little I had known before, and the revelation of mysteries that might once have been my prerogative had been usurped by educative audios, videos, and lengthily explanatory signs. The crowded halls were too noisy for oral narrative anyway. I bought Samantha an egg hand puppet from which hatches a baby dinosaur.

During her weeklong stay, Samantha visited her other grandparents twice, and each of Aram's three brothers in three states: New York, New Jersey, and Massachusetts. In the following weeks, she traveled with her mother and the other grandparents to Florida, then to Pennsylvania to visit a great-grandfather, and stopped again on the homeward journey to see her mother's brother in Michigan. Could it be that merely the job description has changed, that kin still can provide, but through focused "quality time," the kindred connections that children seek? I'm not at all sure. At Aram's request, Grampa Marty rode Samantha around on his tractor so that she would have some memorable adventure with her grandpa to recall in future times.

A few weeks later, I received a letter from a young naturalist recalling his boyhood: "I was a listener when I was young," he began. "I would sit in the grand rat hole of my grandfather's garage and absorb the world through the poetry and rantings of a ninety-year-old man. He would fly from German philosophy to carburetors, and I took it in."

Such taking in takes time, and the focus is that of the child on the man, not the other way around. "Cook something with her," Aram suggested as another memory that might travel back with Samantha to her California home, and we did make fudge brownies together. Once. Once is not enough for once upon a time.

Once upon a time, I used to make divinity with my aunt Aileen. She had a small apartment in the same city building where we lived, so I could visit with her easily. It now occurs to me that my idea to carve the ark might have arisen from the animals I was allowed to play with on these visits. They were made, so Aileen told me, of chewing gum—I suppose she meant of resin from the chicle tree. They were somewhat flexible, and you could dent them with your fingernail but mustn't. The animals were not toys; they were her own precious collection arranged carefully for display on the mantelpiece.

Each fall, Aileen received from Utah the crop of black walnuts from the tree in her family's yard. These she used to flavor the divinity, a white candy which is made simply of egg white and sugar syrup. Aileen made divinity as I suppose it always had been made out West: she whipped the whites on a tilted oval platter with a table fork, puffing them to a froth as though by magic.

I must have been about Samantha's age when Aileen gave me a hairbrush. You wouldn't think a hairbrush would much please a three-year-old, but this one, fashioned out of boxwood, was miraculously engraved with my name. The following birthday was at a difficult time. A "new" baby was expected—meaning to me that the old one was about to be replaced—and we were moving to another apartment. There awaited me from Aunt Aileen when I got home from school that day a basket, and in it lay two tiny babies with movable arms and legs, surrounded by all their nighties, diapers (with real safety pins), blankets, bottles, bonnets, and booties all ready for me to carry with me on the dreaded moving day. Young children's need for portable possessions must have struck a chord with Aileen, for the year I entered kindergarten, she gave me a pearl-handled pocketknife only one inch long and an equally sharp and workable tiny pair of scissors.

Then Aunt Aileen married Uncle Paul and that was that: she moved to Bronxville. Many years later, just months before her death, I told Aileen that she had been my favorite aunt. She was surprised. She recalled that she had done nothing special; never took me anywhere, never made a fuss, never planned a treat. That is true: she used to make her own greeting cards, and so I learned the secret of cutting paper lace. It was not a planned activity staged for my benefit, it was just what she did. She worked, I played, we talked. We kept each other company.

This is just how those who treasure the memory of a godmother, a grandfather, an aunt, or any elder describe the recollection of their time together: they used to do this or that, whistled tunes or weeded gardens, sharpened tools or kneaded bread, and all the while across the conversational space between the elder and the youngster flowed the secrets, the mysteries, the lore, the history that immerses us in the backward and forward sway of time.

Childhood is the story that children tell years later to explain the person they became. This, too, is a trick of the symbolic mind: we create higher orders into which to fit details, and we do so in order to make sense of what we have experienced. Our sense of self is a higher-order category in which we embed the details of our experience, selecting those that make sense to us and arranging them in an explanatory way.

Therefore, I can tell you the story of how, on walks with my father, I came to know the plants—but can it be that Susie, who does not know the plants, was never taken walking by our father? More likely, she deleted such events in formulating her story, and I magnified them in creating my own. The tale is my personal myth, a coupling of my love for my father with my love of flowers, and so by ritual compression, I link the two together to mean who I am. The truth of such narratives doesn't matter—and you will hear siblings often dispute the accuracy of each other's recollections. The richness of what is laid on the memory table for a child to pick and choose from matters very much. Samantha's visit was too short, our baking brownies too isolated an event for her to make much use of. Sitting on the couch with me, she was placing into the story of herself (the baby) her father's tales of growing up with Granny. She was trying so hard to use his stories for the construction of her own. We hold in our heads each story as we might hold in our hands a flower, peeling it to show one heart within another: yet we marvels of metaphor need to hold hands too.

The geographic and familial displacement that the suburban phenomenon hurried along can't be fixed, and if it could, the price in lost autonomy would almost certainly be more than we adults would want to pay. But we adults are responsible for Samantha, who is not prepared to float adrift from anchorage in kith and kin. (What is *kith*? I wondered, as the word arose like flotsam on my mental tide. I looked it up. The word means familiar friends, neigh-

bors, fellow countrymen: "people from the same place.") The
question that preys on me is how, given the merely symbolic, we
can keep children as grounded in place and relationship as their nature presses them to be. Nostalgia, born in the scents of place and
people of our childhood, builds bridges across time, but I fear we
are flopping like salmon who, returning to the river of their birth,
find the flow is dammed.

I knew my Utah grandmother only by her photograph, which
shows her wearing wire spectacles and a frock that reached her ankles. My father also kept photographs of his brother and sisters who
had remained in Utah, and of their children, our cousins. There
was a photograph of a formidable woman in voluminous black
clothing—a great-grandmother on my mother's side, who was
shipped to Palestine for burial dressed only in a shroud—and another of Great-uncle Joe, who is shown in formal pose with the
lovely wife he stole from a Quebecois convent when she was barely
out of childhood, and their dozen children. After my parents died,
I had all these pictures framed and hung them along with photos of
my father and mother and Marty's family on a wall of our living
room in Maine. Our sons wanted to know not only who these
people were, but in what way they were related, on which side of
the family, by what degree of kinship and order of descent, in what
frame of time and by what aspects of appearance, character, and circumstance. They needed to know themselves as a result of what
had come before them, to have significance in the present based on
the precedence of the past. The hunger of children for this blood
form of authenticity (and adopted children often suffer inconsolably
from its lack) is such that even though most of these kin were twice
removed from anyone's actual recollection, the boys sought any stories about them that had survived the years: in order to orient
themselves to the chronicle, mesh with or bend the saga to their
own persona, devise the next stanza.

    Aram was very nearly a posthumous grandchild; both grandfathers died before his birth. When my mother died—Aram was then only three—he wanted to bring her in her "box" to stay with us at home. This keeping of the ancestors is practiced in just such a concrete way by societies that bury their dead beneath the hearth or hoard the bones in the family crypt. There was something of the same "keeping" in Joshua's wish to revisit with his son the graveyard where he had last seen his grandmother in her box. Had he asked to visit Marty's parents' graves, I couldn't have complied. They are somewhere a hundred miles away, in an anonymous portion of Long Island where cemeteries are still allowed. New suburbs, unlike old villages, have no graveyards. The wall of photographs in Maine is at least similar in spirit to the household shrines that in other cultures are believed to hold the souls of ancestors. Given the little that we have to work with, we can at least keep everyone together in an album.

Together and portable: I wonder if Samantha wouldn't have liked a locket with pictures of her parents to wear around her neck? These were standard keepsakes when I was small. Mine, in simple symbolism, was shaped as a heart.

Samantha had arrived from the airport wearing a pink backpack in which she carried Mickey Mouse, Minnie Mouse, a miniature Mickey that served as their baby, and a collection of small lions. Lions once had been her protecting animals: she had lion posters, lion picture books, lion hand puppets, and stuffed lions, as well as the more portable figurines. Lately, the parental lions had begun to roar fiercely at her in her dreams, yet she was frightened to go to sleep without them. Finally, to guard against their danger, she had adopted Mickey Mouse who, in his role as St. George in the movie *Fantasia*, had slayed the fearsome dragon. Samantha was adept at choosing symbols.

Ezra, by then a one-year-old, was introduced to the whittled animals some months after Samantha's visit. He recognized a few of them. The cow was *moo*; the sheep was *baa*. I'd call that symbolic but safely so: Ezra, still innocent of stampede and rampage, had nowhere to keep them but safely in the fold. By Samantha's age, overlapping categories have let the animals loose, and children may imagine a ram to be as dangerous as a lion may be kind. It's not that the word itself has become unstable—*sheep* will always mean the same animal—but by virtue of its symbolic nature, *sheep* can take part in any narrative, and the bleating *baa* can turn from plea to threat.

This inherent danger of symbolic imagination may be one reason young children take to toys in miniature. Regardless of the narrative, and even if a wolf appears in sheep's clothing, the size relationship between child and toy remains stable: what harm, really, can a handheld predator do? The fact that Aileen, like a fairy godmother, mind read my wish to have babies of my own was certainly part of the bond between us. My mother read the same wish, and so do many parents who, at the birth of a new baby, present the older sibling with a baby doll. In those days, pediatricians made routine neonatal house calls, and during these visits when Dr. Craig measured my infant sister's length, I would have him measure as well the life-size baby my mother had given me. My baby failed to grow; I never played with her again. She was too big for pretense.

I have looked in the granny catalogs I receive for miniatures the grandchildren might enjoy. There is no lack of sturdy dollhouses and barns with families, animals, and all accoutrements. I bought a dollhouse for Samantha; Aram made her a barn. The buildings serve as stages on which she and her friends manage in miniature their frightened, wishful, or perplexing dramas. And, at night when bad things threaten, all the people and all the animals can be safe inside together.

At first I kept the animals on an old wooden tray with rails around three sides. As the months passed, the tray grew crowded. The flock of sheep, sometimes followed by the wolf and sometimes not, edged up against gorillas, trailed into zebras, nudged the ducks. When the animals numbered over a hundred, it became clear they could never fit aboard any ark that I could build. In an attempt to solve this vexing problem, I considered plans for a flotilla—a variety of floating outbuildings and the leading ark. Still, I was dissatisfied. The idea lacked authenticity—Noah's Flotilla, for heaven's sake!

At last I hit on a solution: boxes.

Now each group of animals is kept in its own Bahia-brand cigar box, well made of aromatic cedar, dovetailed at the corners, and fitted with a sliding lid. Cigars, I discovered, have different names depending on dimension. Great beasts and gorillas are in a Torpedos box. The cattle, sheep, and swine are in Robustus, and birds in Panchos. Triceratops fits into nothing short of Corona Gigante.

The scent of the boxes sends me: sends me back to the cedar closet where, as a child, I hid for solace among stored woolens and silk quilts. The quilts were made by my Utah grandmother from scraps of her best dresses. We were allowed to use them only when we were sick, and in their scent and softness, in their seeming sympathy, I knew the far-off grandma that I never met.

I ordered from a woodworker's supply catalog small brass hooks to hold the lids of the boxes so they won't slide open when children carry them to and from the ark—or wherever in the future they may go. Yet then, vexed again at their compartmentalization—uncertain still as to their groupings—I pasted into a sketchbook the paper patterns I had drawn, in the chronological order of their making, with penciled notes as narrative of who they were and how they had come to be.

Children do not come with automatic anchors. They come equipped only with the need and the capacity to become embedded in whatever firm ground their culture offers. By the time children can speak fluently, we take for granted that their perception of reality is as stable as our own, but that is not at all the case. Children routinely become "lost" in stores or parks when they are merely feet away from their parent. I was six years old when I made the astonishing discovery that the road to the farm, with its passing features, was the same as the road back from the farm, with its different passing features. "Are we there yet?" children ask when the car has barely left the driveway. Aram, after a seven-hour drive to Maine when he was four, wailed to go back for the hat he had forgotten.

One day Aram and I brought Samantha to visit my friend Alma and her next-door neighbor's child, Sam (a name that confused Samantha since she, too, is often called Sam). Aram suggested a game of Hide-and-Seek. Sam and Sam shut their eyes while Aram hid in full sight on the couch by placing a small cushion on his face and another on his chest. The children opened their eyes and couldn't find him. When Sam the boy finally did notice Aram's protruding limbs, he had yet to convince himself that the face was there by peering beneath the cushion. Next it was Alma's turn to hide (bulging behind a curtain right in front of them) while Sam and Sam, hand in hand and slightly scared, searched in vain for her.

Samantha could count in three languages—English, Spanish, Mandarin—and also recite the days of the week, but it was impossible to explain to her how long until she could fly back to Mommy. Joshua, when he was about the same age, traveled with us on an airplane. We looked at planes taking off and landing. We looked at the airplane we were about to board. We boarded: he asked, "Where's the airplane?" Even the regularities of kinship, so obvious to us, can be mysterious to children: Joshua assumed that his teacher at nursery school was the mother of all the children except himself, whose mother was me. I proudly wrote on the label of my father's brand-new toolbox the name that would identify him among all others: "Daddy."

Psychologist Jean Piaget thoroughly explored how children construct reality over the years of early childhood, and child psychoanalyst Selma Fraiberg further revealed the workings of young minds in her classic *The Magic Years*. I recommend reading both authors (Piaget is difficult) if anecdotes aren't sufficient evidence of how strange and slippery time, space, quantity, kinship, and lan-

guage itself are to the average preschooler. As a child, I was horri-
fied to learn that my father was going to "fire" a secretary—that is,
burn her up.

I can't figure out whether it was good or bad for Samantha to
discover, on her Disney trip to Florida, that Mickey Mouse really is
"bigger than my mommy!" Symbolic thought is inherently magical; ritual, far more than wordy reasoning, has been the way our
species has subdued and reassured its scarily imaginative mind.

I hadn't realized until Aram's visit how much a child's passage
through time and space is made certain and stable through the rituals of everyday life. A reason he gave for his visit was that home—
his California home—was in chaos. Mealtimes were whenever;
food might be eaten anywhere, by anyone, and while doing whatever else the person wished to do. There was no bedtime. The parents had been unable to settle even on a morning ritual that might
reliably get Samantha to school in time to join the morning circle—and in her day-care group a child late for circle was sent
home.

Thinking about dinner as an example, I saw that the stability of
family—the mental representation of relationship—depends on regularities of time and space. "Dinner's ready," my father would call
in days long ago; "I'm coming," I'd reply. "So's Christmas," he
would tease, acknowledging my customary preoccupation with
whatever I was doing at the time. Dinner was at seven: the meal
began when everyone was seated and our mother had taken the
first bite; the meal ended when everyone had finished and our father rose from his chair. Our mother and father sat at opposite ends
of the table with we three girls between, each in her place. The
structure of family was in this way daily reenacted through the
grammar of our synchronized performance.

Mealtimes also resonated with the surrounding culture. Businesses had shut down and shops had closed by suppertime. The
hour of the day's main meal varied little among families: in early
evening in the city, at midday in rural areas, where even the post

office closed for the noontime dinner hour. One could assume
with reasonable surety that throughout the neighborhood every
family simultaneously was sitting down to eat.

Even the days of the week were culturally defined. Saturday was
the double-feature matinee at a special price for children at the
neighborhood movie house. All commercial enterprises (except the
movies) were closed on Sunday. Monday remained wash day in
many families, including ours. For some reason unaccountable to
me now, village stores were closed on Wednesday afternoons. If one
employed a cook, Thursday was her night out. Friday was the
meatless meal—among Catholics traditionally but for everyone
during the war.

Menus marked the seasons. In winter we often ate boiled dinner
comprised of beef (fresh or corned) cooked with cabbage, carrots,
and potatoes. Few other than these storage vegetables were available
except in cans at that time of year. Fresh asparagus appeared briefly
in early spring and sweet corn in August. June was strawberry-
shortcake time; you couldn't get strawberries either earlier or later
in the season. Strawberry festivals are still held in June in some rural areas, but they are a relic of a much broader "festival" when
everybody everywhere around was sure to be enjoying shortcake in
the strawberry season. (Suddenly I remember my white pinafore
with red strawberries bordering the bib.)

Aram showed his daughter where each of the brothers had sat at
table when they were boys, but mealtime customs were rapidly un-
raveling in our sons' generation. During the single decade of the
1950s, TV dinners were invented, take-out pizza became available,
and the first enclosed shopping mall, near Minneapolis, Minnesota,
opened its doors. By the 1960s, blue laws that had forbidden commerce on the Sabbath were struck down in state after state. By the
time Aram was in high school, markets routinely stayed open after
commuter hours, and often seven days a week. Now there are groceries that run around the clock, regardless of day of week or season. And now it's impossible to tell the time of year by which

vegetables are on display, nor can one guess when one's neighbors sit down to table, or whether they do, or what they eat, or if they eat together or separately. Meals are idiosyncratic: they are no longer a ritual by cultural consent nor are menus constrained anymore by the cycle of the seasons.

I don't regret in terms of my personal convenience that I don't have to eat fish on Friday and can if I wish shop for groceries on Sunday: I am pointing out that a family unshackled from cultural convention finds it that much harder to choose the conventions by which to lead its family life. I like that I can have strawberries whenever I want, but their run-on season has deleted still another of the punctuation points that used to make us pause long enough at least to gather together for our cake.

I forgot to say that my aunt Aileen broke the egg against the platter, spilled out the white, and cupped the yolk in the half shell all in the motion of one hand. I'd like to pass along that trick, but I never mastered it. I used to make divinity for Christmas; it was a family joke: the first batch always failed to crystallize and had to be thrown out. By then there were no black walnuts to be had anyway. The oily nuts turn rancid quickly and therefore have dropped out of our culturally commercial landscape despite the fact that the tree, native to America, ranges from the Great Lakes nearly to the Gulf Coast, and from the Atlantic across much of the Great Plains. From there the trees grew wherever they could be cultivated by those bound to preserve tradition, even if they had to carry nuts or saplings, as my great-great-grandparents did, by foot across the nation to the Continental Divide.

I forgot to mention also that in those early years it was my aunt Aileen who made Thanksgiving, and when she moved away, my mother carried on the tradition until she died, and then I picked it up. That feast at least I can preserve down to the last giblet.

It is my earthbound job to keep things pinned this way, and I'm more than a little aggravated that things have drifted so far from anchorage. A song I recall from childhood keeps playing in my mind: "Here we go gathering nuts in May," begin the lyrics, but who is left to see the joke when nuts that actually can be harvested only in the fall are now available at any time of year?

Thinking along these grandmotherly and grouchy lines, you can imagine my astonishment to learn that Thanksgiving is not an old holiday at all. Or rather, the first Thanksgiving over three hundred years ago was not repeated as an American tradition for the following two centuries.

The first Thanksgiving was held in the fall of 1621 in Plymouth Colony, and continued for three days. One Edward Winslow's account of it that December begins, "Our corn did prove well," and, after some remarks on the "indifferent good" barley crop and "peas not worth gathering," continues:

> Our Harvest being gotten in, our governor sent four men on fowling, that so we might after a special manner rejoice together after we had gathered the fruit of our labors. They four, in one day killed as much fowl as, with a little help beside, served the company almost a week.

The "company" included, besides the colony itself and the helpful Squanto, Chief Massasoit and ninety of his male kin. "A little help beside" included five deer the Indians provided.

After that first Thanksgiving feast, there were no others until 1863, when President Lincoln proclaimed a day of national celebration to be held annually on the last Thursday of November in honor of the Pilgrims. (There had been many other, one-time and local thanksgivings held in gratitude for good fortune of various sorts, including military victory, but those generally were days of fasting, not feasting.) That long gap between the first American harvest festival and its present counterpart doesn't mean that the tradition is modern, however. The ancient Jewish festival of Succoth celebrates the harvest, and I had thought that Halloween, judging by its autumn date, must once have been a harvest festival too. And so it was but in a way more interesting than I had imagined.

Under the Celtic name Samhain ("summer end"), the festival was one of food sharing, right enough, but with the dead. Animals were sacrificed to ancestral spirits, and fall crops of hazelnuts and apples were offered to propitiate souls whose anger at the ungrateful living might otherwise lead them to destroy the fertility of the land.

Christianity reinterpreted Samhain as All Saints' (or All Souls' or All Hallows') Day in honor of church-sanctioned spirits, and eventually Halloween—a corrupted pronunciation of All Hallows' Evening—became the secular and specifically children's celebration that we know today. Now children dressed as ghosts enact the dead and threaten "trick or treat" to adults who propitiate them with candy.

Forgotten by adults in this seemingly pointless ritual is the very real fear that once was aroused as days darkened into winter, but consider Samantha and other children her age: they are scared of the dark and of ghosts and scared too of abandonment by parents angry at their naughtiness. If Thanksgiving preempts and reshapes a very ancient sigh of relief that there is food put by for winter, Halloween dives deeper still below the surface of our minds to express in ritual an assurance that our worst fears won't come true. *If*, said the adults' original ritual, *we share food with ancestors, they won't be bad to us. If*, says the child's inverted ritual, *we aren't bad to grownups, they will share food with us.* To light the grinning jack-o'-lantern through the dark and chilling night is a symbolic act but not an empty gesture. Or it wasn't once but may be now when children party safely within doors on All Hallows' Eve. Symbols can be stretched only so far from their original meaning before losing their efficacy.

When families actually gathered in their crops, no symbolism was necessary to understand a feast that celebrates the fruit of human labor. The groaning board was matched by laden shelves of applesauce and relish, pantries strung with onion braids and drying herbs, bins filled with meal and flour, sheds hung with meats smoked and dried and salted, and cellars stacked with crates of roots stored to last the winter. My father used to say (rather often) that you can't appreciate a chicken until you've raised and killed one yourself. There was a grumpy man!

No doubt he was right, but here we are, chickenless, and we must make the best of it. I used to buy a twenty-five-pound turkey for the feast. The bird was far too large (we ate hash and sand- wiches for days thereafter), but I wanted the boys to gasp when the great fowl was brought to table. I wanted a bird too heavy for me to lift from the oven, too big to fit any ordinary platter. My mother, when she took up where Aileen had left off, served the turkey on a platter that depicted the wild and living bird. Or so it seemed to me then; I now think the picture was of a breast-heavy domesticated bird.

One year, after Thanksgiving was mine to manage in my turn, there happened to be few enough of us assembled that I was able to set the table with old pewter plates (I had just eight of them) and even older staghorn-handled, two-pronged forks and knives (only six of each). These primitive utensils were hard to handle—try spearing mashed potatoes with a two-pronged fork!—but by the light of bayberry candles one could summon a bond with Pilgrim kith. Not bayberry-*scented* candles: the real thing. Or candles made of beeswax, which authentically comes from bees (a beekeeper friend molds them in a hexagonal shape, as bees shape their waxen combs). For the most part, the best I can do is cook up tradition by duplicating each year what was served the year before. The stuffing must be fragrant with rosemary, sweet with chestnuts, and there must be wild rice as well as mashed potatoes, and cranberries both as sauce and jelly, and giblets in the gravy certainly, and pies, dried fruits, and nuts still in their shells, and always much too much of everything for anyone to eat.

For the rest, I rely on the underlying authenticity of the Thanksgiving holiday. Communality is in our blood; sharing food is fundamental to our kind; joy in glutting is primitively human. Long, long before grain was ever planted or cattle tamed, our kind apportioned meat among kin and fellow hunters. We can't learn from stone tools and fossil bones whether there was ritual meaning to meat feasts: whether, as is suggested by chimpanzees, the apportioning of prey among the hunters affirmed group affiliation or, as is suggested by contemporary tribal societies, acknowledged the social standing of the hunters by the quality of the portions each received. My father certainly took his role as pater familias and turkey carver very seriously, and I like to think that his adroit performance—his division of the carcass by light and dark, breast or thigh, with skin or without—carried forth an authentic tradition more ancient even than the marriage ritual may be.

Our mother always received the choicest cut.

Sam moved away from the house next door to Alma. So did Samantha move with her mother from the only home she'd known. They were the same age as I had been when I moved with my basket of babies to the new apartment, so I know well their fear that they would be left behind, or lost, or their possessions go astray. Even we adults, closing the door on the broom-clean empty home, experience a loss of self as though we were a turtle forced to leave its shell.

This difficulty of moving to another place seems strange for a migratory animal. Moving ought to be in our blood, for we followed our food as hunters and gatherers throughout prehistory. And I think moving is in our blood but not in the sense that it is practiced now. We move *away*, while as foragers we had always moved *with*: moved with one another, moved with the seasons, moved with the ripening fruit and the running caribou, moved with our customs in our minds and our possessions on our backs.

There is a common fantasy that may express the sort of moving humans used to do. The fantasy takes different forms, but it is basically a wish to have all that is precious and necessary—minimal but sufficient—packed and portable, ready to go. I played out the fantasy as a child by accoutring my bike with a headlight, a speedometer, and saddlebags to carry sandwiches, jackknife, wrench, and the compass I never learned to use. Backpackers and campers play out the fantasy as well, with their compact and folding tents, utensils, sleeping bags, and stoves. My father's family, so the story goes (but now I wonder if the story isn't embroidered with fantasy), walked from New Hampshire to Utah with their possessions in a handcart. Men load their pockets, women their pocketbooks. The Iceman found frozen in the Alps where he died five thousand years ago exemplified to perfection the basis of the fantasy: he carried on his person everything necessary to obtain food, treat illness, even mend his clothes.

So I think Aram was right in what seemed at the time a vagabond decision. He moved into a recreational vehicle ready to go with, not away from, his wife and child. Samantha's room in this small RV is a bunk above the cab lined with pockets to hold storybooks, clothing, her lions, and Mickey Mouse. Aram culled his own possessions to a minimum: the clothes he wore the most; the music he loved the best; the few utensils necessary to lead his daily life. There was no room for anything but essentials and no option but to keep what there was in order: dishes washed and stashed, paperwork done and stowed, toys picked up and put away in wooden boxes that he built and custom fitted for their storage. He minimized, even miniaturized, his home world, and on this reduced stage, rituals of mealtime, playtime, and bedtime were magnified as though in a dollhouse.

We are, when we can be, acquisitive and greedy, but those traits evolved under circumstances that made their satisfaction rare. We traveled light, physically limited by what we could carry in our bellies and on our backs, and yet possessed of great riches borne in that most commodious container, the mind. Samantha's strippeddown plight was a reminder of what little, really, a child wants of us, but of how great the want is and how heavy the burden when parents alone are asked to bear it.

The Vegetable Plot

"It's broccoli, dear," says the mother in a classic *New Yorker* cartoon. "I say it's spinach," replies her daughter, "and I say to Hell with it." The picture shows a little girl at a large dinner table defying her concerned parent.

The cartoon was published before my birth but was shared with me by my concerned parent when I, too, was a little girl and fellow spinach hater. I also did not eat broccoli, cabbage, or any other member of the Brassicaceae. In fact, I ate hardly any vegetables at all. They tasted poisonous. Now, having outlived the early death from malnutrition that our family doctor predicted, I appreciate why: vegetables really do contain toxins, and children, because they are more sensitive than adults, detect the warning flavors that plants formulate to discourage herbivory.

Not that spinach or broccoli could have harmed me: selection in the course of domestication favored mild versions of the wild crop. You'd have to eat an awful lot of broccoli, and eat it raw, for it to make you sick. The herbivores that have occasioned plants' chemical defenses are mostly insects: that we, whose greed for leaves is hardly comparable to that of caterpillars, can be sickened or killed by vegetable insecticides is entirely accidental. Spinach never had it in for me. But it was in me to be wary of its bite.

As was often pointed out to me, I ate like a bird. Birds actually

have large appetites for their small size, but it would have been fair
to say that my preferred diet resembled that of robins: they eat meat
(in worm and insect form) during the breeding season; sweet
berries in summer when there is leisure for dessert; oily and starchy
fruits to fatten for the rigors of migration. My mother, hoping to
stimulate my appetite, played Baby Robin with me, but she offered
to my gaping mouth vegetables that no robin would have eaten.

I've read that tomatoes, when they were first cultivated by Eu-
ropeans, were thought to be poisonous if eaten raw. They may well
have been. Our oldest son acts as though they still are: he won't eat
a fresh tomato, although he likes them cooked. Cooking destroys
toxins that otherwise would make many plants inedible, and I have
often wondered whether cooking originated in medical necessity.
Nibbling the root of wild carrot (also called Queen Anne's lace)
makes me doubt that early humans could have enjoyed the vegetable untamed and uncooked: the harsh flavor is decidedly unpleasant. "It's good for you," my New Yorker parents used to say of
stinging spinach, as though it were medicine, not food. Maybe
spinach was a medicine once upon a time.

Among the reference books in my library are a field guide to
edible wild plants and a volume of medical botany; some North
American species are discussed in both. I could use young sweet-
flag shoots to spice a salad, or I could candy the roots or brew them
for cough medicine. Or, I could confuse blue flag with sweet flag
and poison myself: this eating from the wild is tricky.

Wild-parsnip root is "excellent eaten raw, sauteed in butter, or
boiled until tender," says the field-guide author Lee Allen Peterson,
who claims that angelica and water-parsnip roots are good food too
but that water hemlock, another member of the carrot family that
could be mistaken for Queen Anne's lace or any of these carrot kin,
is the most poisonous plant on the continent. A single mouthful
kills. About even the innocent wild parsnip, parent of our cultivated
crop, Peterson warns that contact of wet or sweaty skin with the
leaves, coupled with exposure to sunlight, may cause a nasty and
persistent case of phytophotodermatitis.

In some cases only one portion of a wild plant can be eaten: the ripe fruit of mayapple is safe to eat in moderation; unripe fruit, the seeds, and every other part of the plant cause diarrhea. Poke sprouts are delicious early in the spring: older stems and leaves, flowers, roots, and fruit contain deadly toxins. Birds, though, gorge on pokeweed fruit without ill effect: the plant depends on them to disperse its seeds. Box turtles perform the same service for mayapples; the fruit hangs under the leaves for their convenience.

Perusing the book of wild edibles, I get the impression that none gives a fig for our convenience. Many of the compounds that deter insects are so strong that the plant can be used only by the pinch: you couldn't eat a mint or tansy salad. You have to quickly pick dandelion leaves before they're old enough to make their bitter chemical deterrence. "Handle only with gloves," warns the entry for stinging nettle, omitting mention of long pants and sleeves. Preparation is often daunting: three changes of boiling water are necessary to make the edible parts of many species palatable, and others must be thoroughly dried before they are safe to use. With few exceptions—cattail is one—the effort expended in gathering and preparing wild vegetables would seem to exceed the caloric reward.

Neither my book on medical botany nor the herbals I consulted give recipes, probably for the sound reason that there is often scant difference between a therapeutic and a toxic dose of the active chemical in even an herbal tea. Imagine the hazard of brewing or nibbling your way to knowledge of digitalis, opium, curare, aspirin, vincristine, and quinine! Whether for medicine or nourishment, the miracle is that we learned to consume vegetables at all.

So no wonder children are dubious about them. They were, to this child anyway, an acquired taste, and the acquisition did not come early, easily, or naturally to me.

And yet:

If you could try ramp soup! If you could dare eat the poke shoot steamed with butter! If you could savor, as I do now, sorrel leaves and tips of lamb's-quarters in your lettuce salad!

I acquired a taste for vegetables late, not in my own, but in my children's childhood, and it was exactly our shared adventures in the wild that sharpened my appetite. But I intend to approach the subject slowly and with deliberation because of the ambivalence that vegetables so easily arouse. I don't want you to think, as little Artie Bacon did, that I'm some kind of witch.

I apologize in retrospect to Artie, a childhood friend of Joshua's, who suspected me, at least, of purposely serving bad food, if not of meaning to poison him outright with the fungi, crustaceans, and thistles I brewed for supper. To children, good food is traditional food endorsed within the family, and Artie's family apparently did not eat mushrooms, shrimp, or artichokes. I think that part of my own eating problem as a child was that during my earliest years, we children were served separately in the nursery a diet more or less of chicken fricassee with dumplings. My belated encounter with broccoli came as something of a shock. Our species, though, is quite ready to distrust food—and the hand that serves it.

One of my reference books declares that the ancient Egyptians considered food to be the cause of all disease and so practiced thrice-monthly purging with a mixture of castor oil and beer. Oil pressed from the seeds of *Ricinus communis* was still a medicine-cabinet staple in my childhood several millennia later, and the notion that the body needs regular cleansing through catharsis hadn't changed much either. The older meaning of the word *catharsis* refers to spiritual purification, as in emptying out bad feelings, not bad food. An herbal expert I met in Florida pointed out to me a certain violently cathartic plant that Indians took to purify themselves both in body and in soul before going into battle.

Vomiting and diarrhea are, of course, the body's routine mechanism for ridding itself of toxic substances, and the spasms are followed by a sense of emptiness and relief distributed in equal measure in the gut and in the mind. To make the point with other words, we have a "gut feeling" that purging does us good. Many food notions similarly are gut feelings, and they tend to be immune to reason.

My daughter-in-law Jean, who is Chinese born but American raised, upsets her father by not correctly balancing the "hot" and "cold" principles in the food she prepares. He's upset on all counts: the food isn't good, it isn't good for him, and it isn't good of his daughter to serve it to him. To Mr. Siao, preparing "balanced" meals is a moral and cultural, as well as a nutritional and culinary, obligation. Wouldn't you agree? The cook, whose responsibility it is to ensure good food, is in a delicate position, and has been ever since Eve poisoned the future with her preferred apple.

The worst fright I can remember from childhood was the yellow poison that my sister Susie told me was rising toward me through the branches of an apple tree where I sat, helpless and terrified, literally out on a limb. There was no way to escape it: the aura was rising higher, higher, higher to engulf and kill me. The essence of our fear of poison is exactly its insubstantiality: like germs, like pollution—like evil spirits too—it creeps into us undetected by sight or scent or flavor. And, like the aura that Susie so convincingly evoked, poison seems to us to arise in the malice of the poisoner: Snow White's deadly apple, an Alar-sprayed Delicious.

Jean, nostalgic for the foods recalled from her early childhood in Taiwan, took me to a Taiwanese restaurant in New York. Much as I thought myself by this time in life sophisticated when it comes to novel foods, I caught myself acting much as my younger sister did when sampling her first morsel of raw oyster. She looked and sniffed I suppose, but I don't remember that, and the scent of an oyster is simply sea. She was only five. She held the tender mollusk on a fork, took it into her mouth, and closed her lips but not her teeth. Then came that look—that brow-drawn, throat-clenched concentration, that long moment of tasting at the front of the tongue, the morsel not yet chewed, the choice not yet made whether to spit or swallow. That courage! The subject of my similar performance, urged on by Jean, was sliced pig gut with cubed congealed pig blood in broth, and I wouldn't have taken that soup from the hand of strangers.

When you think about the actual dangers of indiscriminate eating, biology unsupported by traditional knowledge couldn't possibly provide enough information for an individual to choose foods wisely. The fruits of yews, which are commonly used in home landscapes, accord with our visual bias, for they are plump and red when ripe. The fruits have no warning scent; they indicate by their sweetness to the tongue that they are edible. However, the seeds within the sweet pulp contain a cardiac glycoside that causes sudden death. Only culture can warn of that insidious and fatal danger: historically, the strong tendency of children to eat conservatively, according to family knowledge and tradition, saved each new generation from lethally relearning what previous deaths had taught.

In former times, everything served at home, at friends', in the streets, or at a restaurant was traditional food, and this is still so in many parts of the world. If you want to sample the cuisines of Italy, you have to travel: each region has its specialties, and among the rural inhabitants, those specialties are everybody's daily fare. My brother-in-law Mohammed, who grew up in a family compound in Morocco with enough male cousins to form opposing soccer teams, didn't have to face even a strange grain until he left for college. The staple carbohydrates were whole-wheat bread and couscous; that's what everybody ate. Everyone ate artichokes and lamb, squash, chickpeas, and lemons preserved in salt. There were no Arties there, scared of thistles.

I rather teased Artie for his fear to venture much past macaroni; I should have taken his malaise more seriously. His was a case of what has become, by now, an epidemic of food anxiety that began to spread during his generation. Americans may enjoy dipping into the melting pot for ethnic foods from sushi to burritos, yet we are scared of the basic ingredients. They have become strange to us.

What heavy metals contaminate our fish? What bacteria infect our eggs? What hormones pollute our meat? What residues toxify our fruits and vegetables? And what about irradiation? Transgenic crops? We no longer know what lurks in food or who to blame. Diet has become our daily dread.

I keep a snapshot of granddaughter Emma sitting in the grass holding a big bouquet of yellow flowers. People ask me what the flowers are; no one has yet been able to identify them. They are broccoli in bloom.

Broccoli in bud, before the flowers have opened, is the vegetable we eat, and what with all the fuss that's been made about its healthy properties, you'd think any schoolchild would recognize it in that state. Not so, according to an art teacher who brought in a bag of fresh produce for a lesson in still life only to find that the subjects were mostly alien to her class. Few recognized the head of broccoli, or whole peppers either, or peas in the pod. I wouldn't have believed this story if I hadn't witnessed the education of a young woman from California who had never seen a carrot in the raw.

From California!

The woman had been raised on frozen vegetables. In her slender experience, carrots were orange cubes, rounds, or slivers. She was surprised to discover that they were roots. I'm not sure how you spend a childhood in California without bumping into fresh produce, but after examining the loaded carts of supermarket shoppers in my own neighborhood, I can see that carrot blindness could be common: many families do not prepare vegetables from scratch.

The Korean greengrocery where I buy produce has changed considerably in the last few years. A good portion of the space once given over to whole vegetables with pods and leaves and dirt still clinging from the fields is now given over to prepared salads, carrot sticks, sliced mushrooms, shelled peas. A similar change in fish display occurred years before. I can remember when fish were laid out whole. How else could you check their eyes for that telling clarity?

Fish are now disembodied: skinless, boneless slabs that seem never to have lived. Only a decade or so ago, it was still popular for the butcher department to mount a poster showing from where on the steer each cut of beef was carved. Now I suspect that even the meat cutter (they're not called butchers anymore) doesn't really know for sure. Meat is no longer delivered to stores by the carcass. Only one meat department I know of in my area sells such recognizable parts as pigs' trotters and oxtails or such innards as cow stomach, lamb kidney, and calf liver. They all carry shish kebab, preskewered.

The trend toward precut and packaged foods is generally thought to arise in convenience: working families these days just don't have time to spend in basic food preparation. That may be so, but I suspect there's more to the sanitized phenomenon. Whether as the cause or the effect of disconnection from the living food, we have become squeamish. Few people really want to know that a skirt steak is a steer's diaphragm.

My California friend, raised on fish sticks and chicken nuggets as well as frozen vegetables, was definitely squeamish. She couldn't eat "mixed up" dishes: stews, soups, or casseroles in which the ingredients were hard to distinguish and therefore might get into her body by mistake. She was uncomfortable with animal anatomy as revealed by a whole chicken or a fish. She distrusted strong flavors and stuck mostly to lemon and butter to enliven her meals. Nouvelle cuisine, with its emphasis on few and fresh ingredients, simple flavors, small portions, and lucid presentation, suited her well. It was the 1970s, and the growing popularity of the nouvelle-cooking style was perhaps due to increasing distrust of food during those years.

I can almost put my finger on when the fear began. Our oldest son, Lincoln, at about the age of eight—that would have been the late 1960s—came home from school one day and threw out all the boxes of cereal in the pantry. They contained the food preservative BHT. From then on, this avid reader and would-be scientist tortured my marketing with minute examination of every label on all packaged foods. BHT, he sternly warned, caused mutations; so had said the science teacher to his young charges. Smart as Lincoln was, he didn't understand about mutations. He thought that if he ate BHT, he would mutate into a monster. I imagine his classmates thought so too.

Another child I know of wouldn't taste lobster because he had misheard its name as *monster*: he literally believed "You are what you eat." My California friend once confided to me that her aversion to peas dated from when she had been informed as a child that they were seeds: she feared a vegetable pregnancy. Aversions to brown and messy foods—kidney beans, gravy—often begin as children struggle with toilet training: they are trying so hard to keep "clean." When to these primitive but common, even normal "dangers" are added invisible pollutants, you can see how the problem might escalate. And when, in addition, dyes, preservatives, insecticides, hormones, antibiotics—*chemicals!*—are put into our food by strangers whose motives we have no reason to trust, you can see how food anxiety can reach unreasonable heights. We defensively buy "organic" produce, "health" foods, and the "pure," "fat-free," "low-sodium," "no-caffeine," "all-natural" packaged goods that burden grocery shelves. There's a rise in eating disorders, food phobias, children who turn vegetarian at the age of twelve. There can hardly be anything more unnerving than to distrust the food one eats.

A problem with this mounting fear is that it feeds on itself. The more we favor prepared foods, the more distant we become from their origins. The more we inform ourselves of what can harm us, the more we suspect intentional harm. One of the ironies of our anxiety is how we have found comfort in fast-food chains like McDonald's, where—and no matter where—the fries and hamburgers are always what we have been accustomed to eating away from home: they are our tradition.

To most Americans today, growing, harvesting, and even preparing food is a mystery performed by strangers whose names we don't know, in places we have never been, for motives detached from the social significance of food sharing. Until about midway through this century, we'd never been separated from the living plants and animals we eat, never been divorced from cutting and cooking (if not killing) them, never eaten food whose ingredients were not familiar staples in our homes. Prepared and packaged foods—pickles, sausages, jams, bread, pasta—had their counterparts in homemade goods, and I can't think of any that I had not watched being made by somebody I knew. Knew the person, knew the ingredients, knew the process, and so knew my grandmother's calves'-foot jelly straight from the hoof.

I was stupefied to read at the butcher's the other day a poster advertising free-range chickens: it claimed the birds were 100 percent vegetarian. I've known a few free-range chickens in my time. They all ate bugs. How would a chicken farmer keep insects out of the chickens' free range? At least I wish the people who run Truth in Advertising, whoever those folks are, would clarify the meaning of "organic." A substance is organic if it contains carbon atoms, and the additives and residues people fear are nearly all organic chemicals. What really is meant is *not synthetic*: made by real plants or animals rather than by us unnatural people. I'd certainly agree that man-made vanilla flavoring lacks the subtlety of the vanilla bean's oil; we aren't, for sure, as chemically adept. But the emotional leap from synthetic to sinister doesn't make sense. Pyrethrin, a "natural" insecticide that a grower may use and still be allowed to label the produce "organic," is no less poisonous for coming from a daisy. But whom are we to believe?

Nearly one whole issue of the *New York Times* weekly science section was devoted to dieting recently. It seems that ever since "the big push to limit fat took off in the 1970's," obesity in America has *risen* by 50 percent. People believed what they were told, and the proportion of calories derived from fat in the national diet decreased from the typical 44 percent then to 34 percent now. However, a low-fat diet leaves people hungry, so they fill up on carbohydrates that add up to even more calories and they get fatter than they would if they ate more fat.

The trick, the article advised, is to eat fats but the right kind and in the right proportions: a total of 30 percent of calories as fat, divided about equally among saturated, polyunsaturated, and mono-unsaturated fats but with special avoidance of trans fatty acids and special attention to omega-3 fatty acids, especially alpha-linolenic acid, which protects against sudden death. "Fat has been perceived as the enemy, but that's not true," claimed Dr. Hu, quoted in the summation. "Some fats are good, some fats are bad. We should be worrying about substituting good fats for bad ones . . ."

Good. Bad. Worrying: What if the worry is worse for our health than what we are worrying about?

Well, I don't know, and I don't think anyone else does either, and having lived in apparent health through lack of broccoli and love of butter, I'm more inclined to address the fears than to adjust the fats.

As Voltaire said, "Il faut cultiver notre jardin."

It was my job during the summer weeks when my parents were in the city to cultivate our garden at the farm. I may not have liked broccoli, but I was taught how to grow it. I knew how to hoe the shallow furrow, space the seeds, thin the seedlings, water the row, and harvest the budding plants before the heads unfurled their yellow flowers. I knew how to peel and cook the vegetable too. It was during World War II, when even city families who had access to vacant land kept victory gardens. Most of the children I grew up with also knew these things; planting, picking, and processing were how food got from field to table. The garden and the kitchen were everybody's business.

I'm not with Wendell Berry, who seems to want modern society to disintegrate and recongregate back on the family farm. Nor can I use reason to dispel the gut feeling that "they," the nameless agribusinesses, aren't to be trusted with the public health. I do think that some experience of homegrown produce can alleviate children's malaise or at least make more comfortable the fit between spinach leaves and boil-in-the-bag green mush.

A suburban school where a friend's children are enrolled did try to forge a link between undressed vegetables and processed ones by taking my friend's daughter, Katie, and her prekindergarten class on an outing to Fresh Fields. Sounds like a farm, doesn't it? Fresh Fields is an organic-produce store where the children were assured that spinach leaves sold there had not been sprayed with poison. What did that mean for vegetables sold elsewhere?

What did it mean at all? To children's sensitive palates, spinach stings the tongue, dries the mouth, and leaves a bitter aftertaste. The effects are due to the species' chemical attempts to make itself inedible. Like humans' own defenses, these take time to mature. Baby spinach is innocent, delicious, succulent, and sweet. So you grow it from seed, harvest it in infancy, and eat it right away, raw or cooked. Or, if you want, blanch the baby leaves, stow them in freezer bags, and later serve them up. I don't mean always: just once. Just once to restore some meaning to fresh leaves and fields.

Thinking back on my father's vegetable garden, I realize that there were few species that I enjoyed and that the care of them wasn't all that pleasant either. What child really wants to hoe a straight row, especially if most of the rows yield still another member of the numerous cabbage family? There was no adventure in being asked to harvest (ugh!) kohlrabi. You just walked to the row, leaned down, and pulled them up, that's all. The sun beats hot in a vegetable garden. The soil turns dusty.

Ah, but a corn patch! My father planted corn in hills, the way the Indians did, and the clumps of stalks grew tall within the block where, in their shade, I wandered cool and undiscovered. The whole corn plant is sweetly fragrant, as many other grasses are, and the blades rustle nicely in the breeze. A certain judgment is required to choose which ears to pick. The fullest, fattest ones, with silk drying well below the tips, are chewy and starchy; my older sister liked her corn that way. I liked my corn young and sweet and tender, when the silk had barely begun to dry. Either way, the ears break nicely from the stalk with a neat cracking sound, and there is no grit the picker has to rinse.

Indians didn't plant the vegetables that I didn't like. All those cabbagy sorts (spinach and carrots too) are from the other side of the globe. What the Indians planted happened to be vegetables I did like: winter squash, its pumpkin kin, and beans harvested and cooked like Indian corn when the seed is dry and starchy.

I imagine that Indians didn't like hoeing any more than I did, nor the tedious chore of watering. They planted pumpkin and squash to scramble among the corn hills and let the bean vines twine the stalks. I've read that they cultivated the garden plot twice during its early growth. As the foliage covered the ground, the shade helped to retain moisture and discouraged weeds: there was no more work to do until harvest time. And harvest time was just when harvest should be: in the pumpkin season. I like that. I like, too, that these species are planted when the soil has warmed to about sixty-five degrees, which, in the Northeast, happens to coincide with the Memorial Day weekend.

I remember, but not by name, the speckled beans my father planted. We harvested them when the pods were dry and brittle, heaped them on a sheet, and whacked them with sticks to break the pods. Then we each took a corner of the sheet and tossed the harvest in the autumn wind until the chaff had blown away. Such beautiful shiny, speckled beans! The Vermont Bean Seed Company lists in its catalog the original rose-blotched buff bean that Indians let twine around their corn and left as a gift to the Amish. It is ungratefully called Mayflower. Another pole bean, Tongues of Fire, has pink flowers and large red-splashed beans. You can eat that one young in the pod as a snap bean or ripe but still tender as a shelled bean, or leave the beans on the vine to harden for winter storage.

The corn my father planted was an old-fashioned sweet variety. The seed came in a burlap sack and probably was nameless too. The

stalks were tall; the ears ripened in late August. You can get old varieties—and truly ancient popcorn—through Vermont Bean or
from Seeds of Change. Seeds of Change offers a corn called Rainbow Inca that sounds quite wonderful. The kernels range from
cream and maize to pink, wine, and purple, and the variety is supposed to be excellent when eaten as sweet corn while the kernels
are in the "milk stage," or it may be used for Thanksgiving decoration after the colorful cobs have dried on the stalk.

I've been moseying among the cucurbits: which to choose? The
vines crawl pretty far over the summer. Say you plant nine hills of
corn, spaced three feet from one another, six seeds to a hill: that's a
block about ten feet by ten feet. What with the beans growing up
the stalks from the edges of the hills, there's not enough space left
for more than a couple of squash or pumpkin vines plunked down
in the middle of the patch to creep out toward the sun. I guess I'd
lean toward Vermont Bean's classic Small Sugar-Pie pumpkin,
which would be more exciting food than old Hubbard squash and
would make good jack-o'-lanterns too.

I like that such a garden would be a memorial to Indians who,
as much as any soldiers since, died for the country that was theirs. I
like its practicality as well: an Indian vegetable plot is compact,
largely self-sufficient, and nutritionally complete—except for green-
ies. As far as I know, Indians didn't cultivate leafy greens: they gathered them.

I spent the summers when I was ten and eleven at camp in Maine.
These were the last years of the war. We knitted blankets; we were
sent to the bean fields to harvest the crop for canning. Beans and
blankets were shipped to our boys overseas, but once a week we
were treated on the home front to blueberry ice cream from fruit
we had picked ourselves. Everyone made their own ice cream in
those days.

Some products, though, you couldn't get and couldn't make:
rubber balls and bubble gum, for instance. My favorite flavor of

gum before it vanished from the shelves had been "teaberry." The package showed a sprig with rounded leaves and bright red fruit. Now think of the wonder when, in the Maine woods, I came upon that very picture in actuality in the wild and nibbled a leaf and found it was the very same flavor: *Gaultheria procumbens*, otherwise known as wintergreen. As though that weren't thrill enough, an older camper introduced me to spruce pitch, a lump of which, harvested when dry and chewed past the bitter, stick-to-the-teeth stage, was a passable chewing gum. For the gathering! For free! Like wild strawberries shy beneath their leaves ripening in the orchard at the farm.

There was a rest period after lunch when those of us too old for naps were allowed unsupervised time. I used to wander the camp trails during that hour, looking for whatever. I thought I had found one day a much more plentiful source of wild strawberries than grew back home. The plant spread in large colonies, had strawberrylike leaves, and bore abundant and apparently identical red fruit. But it was barren strawberry, a *Waldstenia*, not a *Fragaria*, species. The fruit is not poisonous, but it is not edible either. I was disappointed. The flowers, I observed for future reference, were yellow, not white like those of strawberries.

Blackberries grew bigger than my thumb at camp, and there were sweet-birch twigs as well as wintergreen leaves to chew for their spicy flavor. So I wandered and nibbled and knit and picked my way through two summers, and then I was twelve, and the war was over, and so, within the year, was childhood. It was not to return until I had children of my own.

Motherhood is a regression: you feel, in one sense, grown up for the first time in your life, and yet childhood overtakes the years in between. By 1970 Lincoln was ten, Rafael eight, Joshua five, and Aram three. We had bought an old farmhouse at the dead end of a village street on an island off the coast of Maine. Wintergreen grew in the woods. The spruces oozed pitch. The older boys, like their mother before them, found barren strawberry. We bought at the

newsstand downstreet Euell Gibbons's *Stalking the Wild Asparagus*. I
reentered kindergarten.

But let me pause in my story for a word of warning: Sam and
Sam, who couldn't see the man for the pillows, also couldn't be
trusted to tell the wild strawberry from the barren sort, and I
wouldn't want them to find out by tasting. Most accidental poison-
ings from plants and other substances happen to children between
the ages of one and five. Prior to kindergarten, children don't have
the capacity for rote learning or the eye for detail that both alpha-
betical and botanical recognition require. And they are notoriously
rash about what they put in their mouths. Perhaps this is because, in
these earliest years, they have to be open-minded about food which
might, by cultural tradition, be insect grubs, swallow saliva, seal
blubber, seaweed, snake meat, or any number of other items that
wouldn't seem the least disgusting if you'd been weaned on them.
Presumably, adults have always had to keep a close eye on young
children lest they sample the luscious fruit of wild yews or, these
days, the candy-colored pills, gaily labeled cleansers, and attractive
houseplants that parents keep or cultivate. Aram was still in nursery
school when I resumed my interrupted foraging education; he ate
what we gathered but was left in his father's care during our expeditions.

We started easy, with clams and mussels, and raspberries, blackberries, and huckleberries: ordinary meats and fruits that lots of
people know. We got a little more adventurous: whelks and peri-
winkles steamed and winkled from their shells with toothpicks, sea
urchins gathered at low tide for their delicate roe, and chanterelles—orange, vase-shaped mushrooms that are hard to mistake for
any poisonous sort. Then foods that required more preparation:
wild apples, gooseberries, and cranberries for jellies, jams, and relish. Some vegetables were a one-time experience that it seemed
good to know, but hardly what one would wish as daily fare. Beach
peas were edible but starchy and beany, not to mention tedious to
shell. Various salt-marsh plants we sampled are still on my sampling

list—I nibble orache and sea rocket when I find them—but I wouldn't want to have to live off such puny prey. We never found wild asparagus, but I have since, right in a friend's disused horse pasture, all three stalks of it.

And yet:

These wild edibles, which hardly stick to the ribs, stuck to my brain like no other food. There is something indelible in the concentration required, in the careful tasting. Leaf palatability depends on where on the plant the leaves grow and in what season. Rose petals gathered in the morning are more heavily scented than they will be at noon. Seemingly luscious berries from one patch of brambles may be sour, whereas from another they are sweet. To gather a salad is to taste in your mouth and balance in your mind perhaps a dozen ingredients. I was thought by my kohlrabi-loving father to lack a "palate"; it was the necessity of focusing on flavor during foraging that developed my taste for vegetables and brought me even—oh horrors!—to a love of spinach.

Some of the crops we garnered in the wild are incomparable: there is no cultivated counterpart to the resin-scented chanterelles that grow in spruce woods and no domesticated vegetable with so haunting a flavor as wild poke. I dare not give you in print the recipe for potentially poisonous pokeweed pizza (my own husband, Marty, eats it with reluctance), but in summer I gather rose petals, and in spring I gather ramp (wild leek) leaves; the clear pink jelly from the one and the rich green soup from the other are treats that can't be gotten in any other way.

ROSE PETAL JELLY

I've used only *Rosa rugosa* for this jelly, but other very fragrant roses should work as well. I try to remove spiders and such from the gathered petals, not for my own sake, but for theirs (since the petals are strained and only the liquid is

used, bugs can't get into the finished product). The recipe
makes two pint or four half-pint jars of jelly. Consult any basic cookbook like *Fannie Farmer* or *Joy of Cooking* to prepare
the jars before you start to cook.

    2 cups fresh rose petals
    2 cups water
    3½ cups sugar
    2 tablespoons fresh lime juice
    1 pouch liquid fruit pectin

Bring the water, a little of the sugar, and the rose petals to a
boil. Turn off the heat, cover the pan, and let the petals in-
fuse like tea for 15 minutes. Then strain the liquid into another saucepan, add the rest of the sugar and the lime juice,
and cook over high heat, stirring until the sugar dissolves
and the mixture has come to a rolling boil. Add the pectin
(keep stirring!), and boil hard for one minute. Pour into the
jelly jars, seal, and let cool at room temperature.

RAMP SOUP

Ramps are wild leeks, *Allium tricoccum*. The broad leaves resemble those of lily of the valley but have a strong onion
scent. They appear midspring in moist woods, often with
skunk cabbage. The season is short: the leaves wither by the
time hot weather sets in. Some cooks dig the white bulbs,
but I harvest just the tender leaves.

    1 bunch ramp leaves, just as much as you can hold in
      one hand
    3 medium baking potatoes, peeled and sliced
    4 tablespoons butter

8 cups chicken stock (or more)
1 pint half-and-half
Salt and lots of white pepper
Sour cream

Roughly chop the ramps. Sauté the sliced potatoes in butter for a few minutes, then add the ramps and cook a little longer until they are wilted. Add half the chicken stock and simmer, covered, for 20 minutes or until the potatoes are very soft. Puree the mixture in a blender or food processor, adding more broth as necessary. Stir in the half-and-half, and thin with the rest of the broth. Season to taste with salt and white pepper. Chill and serve with dollops of sour cream.

I hope you're intrigued, but you are right to be annoyed as well. Usually an exotic recipe is followed by a commercial source for unusual ingredients, but who sells ramps? Where have all the roses gone? Even if I had given a recipe for the more traditional wild huckleberry pie, which is naturally spicy and so needs no additional flavoring, you'd have reason to complain that the necessary ingredient isn't to be found locally. Foods that once were common along farm paths and roadsides are scarce now. The possibility of finding wild asparagus, and therefore the pleasure in the find and in its eating, is largely gone. I tempt you with wild dishes because I want you to realize how distant the urge has become from its potential satisfaction, how disappointing to wish to eat off the fat of an anorexic land.

So let us grow our garden in another way. The Indian corn patch, for all that a child would like it as a thing to plant and a place to be, isn't edible during the summer salad season. What I have in mind is a forage garden based on one my friend Alma and I came upon in the mountains of Virginia.

We were visiting our friend Carol. She asked us to go into the garden and gather greens for salad. Alma's vegetable garden at home in Connecticut is planted like my father's was, in straight rows with paths between; so had mine been in former years before that piece of ground became a nursery for other kinds of plants. Perhaps Carol's garden was once in straight rows too, but if one can apply a highfalutin term to mountainous expedience, her gardening "philosophy" is to let plants go about their business as best they can.

Carol's home sits perched above the oldest river on the continent (which, in an irony of nomenclature, is called New River), and her garden stumbles down the steep terrain. Over the years, the garden grew wherever it could be grown, until now it is a mosaic of narrow walkways meandering along courses of least resistance among patches of vegetation that change in location and composition from year to year. Here is an exquisite iris—frosty, crystalline, edged delicately in mauve—tendriled with young pea vines clinging for support. A mulberry sapling pushes up past feathers of bronze fennel, and purple pansies grow interspersed with chard. Whatever goes to seed, Carol leaves to seed, and if next season's offspring are edible, she leaves them to seed in turn.

So when we were sent for salad, we were less on a harvesting, than on a foraging, expedition, for we didn't know what we might find, or where to find it, or often even the identity of the greens. It is one thing to recognize parsley growing in a row, but to differentiate parsley from cilantro when both grow together, and when both grow also among young spinach and assorted Brassicaceae, and all are interspersed with species that might possibly be weeds, and the whole green, leafy, flowery mass of vegetation is spilling confusedly downslope over nearly invisible foot trails—and when, as Carol told us, we ought not to stick only to lettuces—the hunt becomes an altogether different thing from plucking a head of Bibb or Boston. We were compelled to nibble: we had to taste and thereby judge the quality of our prey.

What Alma and I brought back for our supper salad was amaz-

ing in its variety, its succulence and savor: tender leek sprouts; tips
of lamb's-quarters; some cilantro leaves, more parsley; pink rose
petals and blue violets; bits of fennel; robust young spinach, chard,
and mustard leaves; and lettuces, of course. This was no ordinary
salad compiled of texture dressed to taste. Each leaf was distinctive.
Lamb's-quarters have a rich and nutty flavor; mustards bite while
roses soften; the flavor of parsley is a synesthesia of green; cilantro
commands attention whether you like it or not (it tastes, to some,
like soap). The bland lettuces, I found, provided background for
the sharp surprise of these other greens.

Although the gathering was easier than foraging on the island
had been, and safe for preschoolers since there were no toxic
species in the garden, there was the same delight in not knowing,
and then discovering, what in the lush and tumbling vegetation was
there for us to eat. There might have been more in Carol's garden
that we didn't find that day: certainly more herbs to lend licorice,
lemon, or mint tones to salad, and sour sorrel and peppery nasturtium. Back home again, I went out onto my as yet unweeded terrace to taste the banes of my garden: wood sorrel, which is sour but
leaves a sweet taste in the mouth, and purslane, a weed that has, in
fact, been cultivated as a similarly sour-sweet salad green. I nibbled
dwarf dandelion, a species related to the common lawn weed but of
a different genus: *Krigia*, not *Taraxacum*. The pale, blue-green leaves
of this little native American were rich in flavor and not bitter at all,
though the plants were in full flower.

Dwarf dandelion can't be bought because it is inconsequential,
unvalued for either food or decor, merely a trod-on commoner not
aggressive enough even to be a weed. I had found a *Krigia* colony
on a cliff above the Hudson River, pried two plants from a crevice
with a jackknife, and took them home in a plastic sandwich bag to
plant and populate the terrace. They have been more than satisfac-
tory: their blowballs have distributed seed all over, and wherever
there is a blank space between the paving stones and light sufficient
for their germination, the tiny plants fill in. I never know where

they'll be. I never knew I could eat them. I hadn't had the adventure of foraging elsewhere than in the wild.

And so, on the weekend after my return from Carol's precarious garden gone its own way on the steeps above New River, I moved out the young pawpaws and virgin's bower that were ready to be transplanted anyhow and raked out a patch where I could sow salad with abandon—without rows or paths or any consideration for the individual needs and horticultural particularities of each species—just all mixed up together. The patch was small, not much bigger in area than a kitchen table, and the species were only those few I had intended for the herb garden: spinach and basil, parsley, cilantro, dill, a couple of lettuces. Wild lamb's-quarters usually finds its way into any salad garden, and I trust it will; I can move some dandelions from the terrace. Going through seed catalogs—alas, too late for planting—I planned what to add in following summers.

Edible flowers certainly, especially nasturtium. Leeks and chives to represent the onion family; some milder Asian mustards; and lemon- and anise-scented herbs. In one catalog, I found cultivated varieties of both sorrel and purslane. Seeds of Change offers "beetberry," a *Chenopodium* species that must be related to lamb's-quarters since it's in the same genus. You eat the scarlet fruit as well as the leafy stems. The same catalog offers "ruby orache," *Atriplix hortensis*, which, although it is also called "mountain spinach," lasts through the summer heat when spinach bolts to bloom. A wild orache that I eat in Maine is green; the leaves of this one are magenta. Who could resist it? And could a child?

Well, probably.

This is not a serious garden. If it were, it wouldn't be much fun. I think it is a mistake to be too serious with children about vegetables, especially to emphasize why they must eat them for their health—why, that is, they should appreciate their medicinal qualities. (You might wish to know that in the course of their growing reliance on vegetation, our originally insectivorous primate ancestors lost the ability to make certain enzymes called vitamins, which change the shapes of other molecules so that they can fall apart or join together in the continual renewal of our bodies. So we, their human descendants, do need vitamins—carnivores like dogs do not—but in such small quantities that even veg-averse children like I was remain healthy because vitamins in the body last a long time.) I doubt that children would eat many of the leaves or flowers from my forage garden, but I wouldn't, for that reason, sow it only in the butter lettuces they might find most palatable. There is more to be learned from vegetables than the healthiness of spinach: that they are plants; that they grow from seeds; that they are rooted in the ground; that they bloom. And that pumpkins are fruit; corn is seeds; turnip is roots; asparagus is stems; lettuce is leaves; broccoli is flowers.

And that each has a name and flavor. And that someone somewhere has sown and raised and harvested every vegetable we eat.

(Or don't eat, as the case may be.)

I forgot sunflowers. There should be room for a few in the Indian corn patch. I also forgot gourds, which are about as magical a crop as any child could wish to glean (and needn't eat). And we have yet to have dessert.

The Penobscot Indians used to summer on the island for the very reason that made foraging there so gratifying to us: unlike the developed area where we have our permanent home, the still sparsely inhabited island is chock full of things to eat. Lobsters ply the waters there more numerously than anywhere along the coast, mussels cluster on the rocks like grapes on vines, and marshes fill with cattails whose roots, shoots, stems, and flowers yield, according to season, wild versions of flour, pickles, potatoes, salads, and cooked vegetables. You couldn't wish for more fruitful ground for foraging dessert: strawberry, Juneberry, blueberry, huckleberry, raspberry, blackberry, elderberry, cranberry, crowberry, bearberry, gooseberry, and chokeberry. And wild cherry, grape, sumac, currant, wintergreen, and rose. And four species of tasty-fruited viburnums whose common names are hobblebush, cranberry bush, nannyberry, and wild raisin. And apples!

There may be among this list some species you haven't heard of, and there must be many elsewhere in the country that I haven't heard of either. Many of those I do know I haven't yet learned to prepare, for those that can't be eaten out of hand have to be pressed or cooked or steeped or dried before they are of much use. Because Juneberries are used like huckleberries, I surely could manage that wild pie, but as for where I might find enough of them to heap into the crust or when I'd have a chance of harvesting the ripe fruit before the robins ate them up, I remain in helpless ignorance. And, as my parents quite rightly insisted, one can't anyway live by dessert alone. Those foraging summers forced me to realize the tremendous cultural knowledge humans had to have to live "naturally" off the land.

Indian tribes typically used several hundred plant species in their region, for medical and manufacturing purposes as well as for food. Each was known in multiple ways: by name and use, by where to find it and when and how to harvest it, by the methods of its preparation and storage, and by the myth and lore that embedded the species' value in tribal heritage. A valued plant for which Penobscot Indians continued to visit the island into the twentieth century was "sweet grass," used to weave strong but pliable baskets. A lobsterman in his eighties told me he'd heard as a child that it grew somewhere along the shore of the saltwater pond where we live, but he had never found it. Neither he nor anyone I questioned knew the grass by botanical name or description.

The boys had all grown up, and I'd forayed often by foot to the library and by canoe along the shore, before I found and identified by name the apparently last remaining island stand of the grass, *Hierchloe odorata*. A hank of it still hangs on the sun porch where I dried it, for there are no elders in my tribe to show me how to weave it. But I bet, I just bet, the supple blades would weave a light carryall, and how could one gather Juneberries without something to carry them in? This eating from the wild is tricky, as I said: it must also have taken all the years of childhood to learn the tricks of it.

In our and other cultures, formal education begins at age six. During the following six years, roughly corresponding to elementary school, sons and daughters were traditionally expected to learn not only what in the environment was there to be used, but also how to use it. At the age of twelve, they were expected to be ready to pass from childhood to membership in the adult culture. Although we still mark that passage ritually in the ceremonies of bar mitzvah and confirmation, I say these are empty passages now, and I am being very serious:

Children who can't obtain, produce, nourish, maintain, earn, or in any other way be of use to their family remain juvenile compared to their peers in other cultures and in former times. They don't deserve to be kept useless, and they don't like it, and they show by their behavior toward their elders that they blame us for swaddling them in childish ignorance.

Dessert can wait. It comes at the end of the day, and there is work yet to do.

The Working Child

In one of the heritage-vegetable catalogs, I came on an antique illustration of a bean house. The unspecified variety was one of the vining pole beans, and the slender poles, spaced in a wide circle at their base and drawn together at the top, formed a tepee. Foliage completely covered the frame except where an opening had been left for a doorway. I wanted to move in, but the drawing showed a child had gotten there before me.

I could easily make a bean house using bamboo poles and twine (plus the beans, of course) and so could anybody except the nearly everybody who says they can't make anything. Can't build, can't sew, can't draw, can't carve: really, this is incomprehensible for a species descended from Handyman.

After I'd been whittling for a while, someone loaned me a book on how to whittle. The author mentioned how his four-year-old son demurred, after a slipup with the blade, "I didn't cut myself *berry* badly." The remark was only to show his child's cute mispronunciation. He assumed there was nothing remarkable about preschoolers wielding knives. The book was written in the 1930s; a whole era has passed between its publication and that of another of those catalogs that I love to throw away.

This one featured plastic sandwich ingredients: yellow cheese, red tomatoes, green lettuce. There was a subplot to the toy: square bread was shown matched with square ham and cheese; round roll with round hamburger and tomato. The lettuce was square (guess which sandwich it belonged to). The toy was one among a large collection that conveyed the extent to which we think children should pretend their way through the preschool years.

The plastic sandwich was designed for three-year-olds who, to my mind anyway, ought to be able to put a real hamburger on a real bun. Of course, these representational fake foods are safe, washable, and good for playing house, but I'd rather see children at that catalog-recommended age able to safely cut a real sandwich with a real knife than to invalidate their very genuine effort by giving them a set of polyethylene cutlery that can't cut a thing. The cutlery was in the catalog too, along with a set of polyethylene carpenter's tools.

There seems an urge in our present culture to keep children childish. Instead of introducing them to actual tools and the skills to use them, we encourage them to make believe what's real. We emphasize arid tasks over genuine competence and play over work, the fantasy of a bean house over its actual construction.

Most tellingly, we think it more important that children play with children than that they work with us, as they have been trying to do since they were toddlers and from the age of three can begin to do effectively. Plastic knives and hollow hammers are serious insults to a preschooler's capability. More than that, our neglect to teach children useful handiness insults our kind, whose hands preceded our heads in the evolution of a unique intelligence.

For another reconstruction, besides Deacon's, of how human intelligence evolved, I read *The Hand* by neurologist Frank Wilson. That work, too, traces the evolution of our symbol-minded brain back to the beginning of our genus, *Homo habilis*. But Wilson, noting that the slight trend toward a larger brain was accompanied by notably improved anatomy of the hands, looks to dexterity as the engine that first drove the evolution of the brain.

This is hardly a new thought: the coincidence of stone implements and larger brains has led others to hypothesize that increasing reliance on tools favored increasing expansion of the brain. Unfortunately, the evidence doesn't support the view, or at least not stated in so raw a form: throughout the period of about seven hundred thousand years between *Homo habilis* and nearly modern *Homo erectus*, tools remained "little more than sharp flakes or lumpish rocks with an edge whacked away." The brain, however, nearly doubled in size. Suddenly, with the first *H. erectus* fossils, there appears the Acheulean tool kit with its greater variety of more carefully shaped implements typified by symmetrically carved hand axes described as "beautiful teardrops of quartz or flint." And then this advanced species, who built enclosures and used fire and whose brain capacity continued to expand to nearly modern human capacity, went right on using the same tool kit without further innovation for the next million years. Though tool technology and brain expansion must in some way be related, they didn't exactly go hand in hand.

Brain capacity alone, even the more pertinent size of the neocortex, isn't strictly correlated with intelligence, and whatever it is we think IQ tests measure, those numbers, too, have little to say about how competent we are. As Wilson points out, there may have been more subtle rearrangements of the brain that can't be detected in a fossil skull but that advanced the efficiency of thought. He made me notice, for example, something counterintuitive about the workings of my hands as I whittle.

Our everyday experience is that the right hand (or the left in left-handed people) is dexterous, precise, and rapid in motion, while the other hand is slow and clumsy. In whittling, though, the right hand merely performs repetitive motions—precise and rapid to be sure but on the order of peeling a potato. Meanwhile, the left hand continually orients the piece of wood, turning it this way and that, adjusting the grip, altering the angle; the right hand just keeps on chipping. It's not that one hand is inferior to the other, but that they perform contrasting and complementary tasks. The dominant hand seems specialized for fast, accurate, and rhythmical work: chip, chip, chip, chip, and forceful CHIP to rough the body and, to shape the snout, very careful little gentle chips. The smart hand attends to details: the grain of the wood, the shape of the ear, the hold on the knife, the speed of the cuts, the pressure to apply. The dumb hand, the left one in my case, handles the choreography, the ongoing flow of the work as it moves through space and time.

Each hand is controlled by its own (but opposite) side of the brain, and the division of labor implied by handedness is reflected in a marked division of labor between the right and left sides of the brain for many kinds of tasks. Flaking an edge on a stone tool is similar to whittling: the two hands coordinate activities, the one orienting the flint and the other striking it with the hammer stone. Our vaunted laterality—the specialization of one side of the brain or the other for such tasks as judging distance or recognizing shapes—might well have been driven by a tool-making culture in which coordinated differentiation of left and right was more useful than ambidexterity.

This is only a matter of degree: other primates have somewhat lateralized brains. Language, though, depends heavily on lateralization—not crudely, as in the dichotomies claimed by popular psychology, but in terms of subtle processes such as computing speed. The left brain specializes in the fast work necessary to perceive or produce the rapid-fire sounds of words. The right brain, working with this information but at a slower rate, tracks the flow of sounds and scans the phrase to find the meaning in it. It also is more adept at interpreting the emotional context of what is said: the tone of voice, the facial expression and accompanying gestures. It orients the meaning of the words.

Watching films of Australian Aborigines and Yanomamo peoples of the Amazon, I've been impressed by the vigor and drama with which they enliven ritual and narrative with exaggerated facial expressions, body postures, and especially the motions of their hands. Sam and Sam, and our granddaughter Phoebe, too, when she was younger, used their hands more vividly the more words failed the intention of their speech. Some gestures have universal meaning, as in the waved greeting or the begging palm. The pointing of a finger to indicate an object emerges spontaneously in the first year of life.

Based on such ubiquitous and meaningful use of hands, I had hoped that Wilson might have found a way to move from gestures to gestural language, but he had not. If gestures ever were linguistic, that isn't evident in how they are used now. At best, they emphasize or demonstrate what is being said, as in a chopping motion when speaking of "axing" an employee or describing how to cut a tree; or they indicate an object, an intention, or a state of mind. As expressive as hands may be, their movements do not constitute a symbolic system of mental representation.

An exception is "sign" language used by the deaf. However, that system is not a relic of some earlier form of communication, but a true language, with its own syntax, grammar, and inflection. The movements are not translations, like the hand position that mimics a V for victory, nor are they indicative like the flung arm that might stand for "away," but in their trajectories, destinations, speeds, and forms are as arbitrary—as truly symbolic—as sounded speech. Like spoken Creole languages which arise spontaneously among children whose pidgin-speaking parents have only a crippled mix of phrases with which to communicate, the silent one known as American Sign Language—Ameslan for short—arose spontaneously in modern times among deaf children whose fully evolved linguistic capacity created the silent form of its expression. This was not realized until only a few decades ago, when teachers of the deaf realized that the signage they were "teaching"—to their minds a translation of spoken English—bore little resemblance to the language their students used with one another. They were teaching in pidgin, like an old-fashioned Western in which a native might say by sound or sign, "Me, food, you have," whereas the children were saying, "Gee, am I hungry! Can I have one of those sandwiches you made?" Apparently, the capacity to produce sounded language preceded the rare incidence of its silent form, and children, hearing or deaf, can linguistically invent ways of communicating the symbolic relationships by which they perceive reality even with incomplete models on which to base their invention. (A footnote on this propensity is that identical twins have been known to invent a private language between them that no one else comprehends.)

The less direct connection between hand and speech that Wilson explores is based on a concept that has come to the fore only recently in evolutionary thought. It is that evolution favored by one sort of behavior can be co-opted in the service of quite another sort of behavior. If the shaping of a stone to make however crude a tool was more efficient the more an individual's brain happened to be lateralized, and if making such tools more easily, quickly, or in greater quantity enhanced the individual's ability to raise offspring to maturity, and if descendants with that sort of brain found it useful in symbolic communication, *then* there is a connection between dexterity and language.

There is not a purposeful connection; there never is in evolution. But the concept, misleadingly called *pre*adaptation (as though the organism knew ahead of time that it was getting ready for the real thing), helps with a shocking difficulty in any reconstruction of how speech came about: we couldn't speak. I mean we hadn't the apparatus for it: the mobile tongue, the molding lips, the modulating throat, the control of vocal cords and of the flow of air that spoken language requires. Very extensive anatomical reorganization and innovation evolved *after* our brains seem to have had the wherewithal for symbolic thought (leaving us, as it happens, the only animal whose gullet and windpipe cross in such a fashion that we can choke on a lump of meat). Symbolic communication in some form, perhaps ritual enactment aided by sound in the same way that speech is now aided by gesture, drove the reshaping of our vocal apparatus until we could tell as well as show.

Wilson, following the serendipity of how toolmaking and language might be connected, remarks on another human peculiarity. Although other animals use tools, and some modify the tool to increase its efficiency, we are the only toolmakers who combine different parts to fashion an implement. A spear, for example, requires that the head and shaft be bound together, a form of manufacture that requires not only the cooperation of the two hands, but also an understanding of the manufacturing sequence: you can't wrap the binding around the shaft until you've inserted the spearhead, and first the head must be shaped, the shaft prepared, and the binding processed. Language in ritual or lexical form similarly depends on stepwise preparation: choosing the actions or words, then assembling them in the correct order to implement the meaning.

I have a bad habit when I'm whittling (I have the same bad habit when I'm making anything): I tell an invisible but interested audience what I'm doing and why I'm doing it. "See," I pedantically explain, "first you draw the profile, then you saw the shape. You have to cut this way, diagonally through the grain, not straight along it, or your blade will split the wood, and you must round the belly before you shape the legs. The paint goes on in layers, base coat, then patterns or shading, and last of all, the eyes." I choose as a particular target of this silent monologue adults who claim incompetence or children who might cut very well if shown how to do so. I have in this way shown imaginary people how to quilt, how to make clam chowder, and how to refinish a chair.

Theorizing comes as free as pine scraps from a lumberyard, and my theory of the ultimate connection between dexterity and language is that from the showing came the telling, and we found our tongue just so.

Rudyard Kipling's *Just So Stories* were the best yarns I ever read when I was little. They were addressed to "Best Beloved," and best beloved is what any child wants to be. They were stories of efficacy; physical explanations of how things came to be the way they are. The leopard got his five-fingered spots from human pigment in the days before political correctness; the rhinoceros rubbed his skin to folds in trying to relieve himself of itchy crumbs; the Elephant Child got his trunk in a tug with a crocodile on the banks of the great green greasy Limpopo River (and so I painted the elephant on the ark in what I thought to be that color). Best—oh, best of all!—was the story of the cavegirl Taffimai's invention of "The First Letter" in a hilarious tale of symbolic misunderstanding among those who misread her pictograph.

Taffi, as she was nicknamed, was fishing with her father when he stabbed his spear at a carp but missed and hit the river bottom hard. The blow broke the shaft; it would take most of the day to fix it. A stranger-man came along, and Taffi had the idea of getting him to carry to her mother in their cave a picture explaining that her mother should give the stranger-man another spear to bring back to Taffi's daddy.

However, her mother interpreted the drawing to mean that the stranger-man had broken her husband's "arm" (the old spear), stuck a spear (the new one) into his back, terrified her daughter (Taffi had drawn herself as young children do, with her hair on end), and now had come to gloat over his wickedness. The stranger-man ends up thumped, rolled, and sat on by a bunch of outraged cavewomen, who, in addition, smear his head with mud.

To avoid in the future the potential ambiguities of pictographs, Taffimai, in the following story, goes on to invent the phonetic alphabet—a carp's gaping mouth for the sound *ah*, a snake for the hissing *s*. This was perfectly credible to me; I might have invented the alphabet myself, just so. I, too, could have scratched my efforts on birch bark with a shark's tooth. My daddy, like Taffimai's, could certainly have made a fishing spear from a wooden shaft fitted with shark-tooth barbs. And if the spear had broken, he, too, would have taken out his mendy bag to fix it with reindeer sinews, beeswax, and resin. Of course, not being Neolithic ourselves, we did not live in a cave.

In fact, we lived for several summers in a barn, for Tony was obstinate about dying, and my parents had promised not to build their
own house on the farm until he did. The barn was not the original
three-tiered affair, but a smaller one built by my father, with a box
stall for Roosevelt the horse. Roosevelt did die, and his stall became
the only private quarters in the otherwise open barn. We had an
icebox (cooled by the block of ice cut to size at the icehouse), a
kerosene stove and lamps, and mosquito netting that shrouded our
beds, our caves against the night. We drew our water with a dipper
from a spring and stored it in a milk can. Water for bathing and
washing dishes was heated over elm logs that burned on the stone
hearth outside the barn door. Some of the cooking and all the
garbage disposal was done by fire as well. I've already mentioned
the privy. And my cherry-trunk horse (but let me add that he had
a burlap saddle and rope reins).

My daddy could make just about anything. He expected that I
should too.

He showed me how to tie the sash on my bathrobe—this was a
sober and formal session that ended not with a full bow, which was
too difficult, but with a half one—and later he demonstrated square
knots as opposed to grannies and eventually the more complicated
knot for my clothesline lariat. Knotting is a valuable and enjoyable
skill, good for lashing a kayak to the car, making a harness for the
cat, or making yourself a belt. My father didn't teach me the craft
of macramé or anything as complicated as a Turk's-head knot. He
showed me that different knots function in different ways and that
my hands could tie them.

The details of how he taught me to handle a pocketknife have
vanished, but he might logically have started with a marshmallow
stick, which needs only to be shaved to a point. Arrows, made from
straight lilac suckers, are a little trickier. Besides the point, they
need, at the other end, two cuts, one opposite the other, with a
notch between where the arrow will be fitted to the string. The
bark should be peeled too and the shaft sanded.

The bow is more complicated still: first, the green length of sapling has to be shaped into an arc, which is done by bending it slightly and wedging it under the edge of a clapboard or a windowsill so that it holds its shape while it dries. Then, when it is dry, you taper both ends, cut notches for the string, prepare the string with loops to fit, and, bending the bow against the ground with one hand, string it tautly with the other.

Not that such bows and arrows shoot either hard or straight, but they work. You're maybe five or six years old, and you've made something that works. Or you've worked together with a grown-up to make a pair of stilts, a slingshot, or a wooden boat with nails hammered into the deck to wind a string around for the railing. Now you're doing the deeply human thing, combining knotting with cutting, using wood and string, attaching one thing to another to make an object that you have imagined in your mind. And, since you really are, somewhere inside, a Neolithic child, you learn to build a fire and keep it burning, catch a fish and clean and fry it, and, because your mother really is not so much a caveman type, you learn to sew as well.

But perhaps you've never lived in a barn; perhaps your dad never split the kindling or your mom never stitched a hem. The descent of manual skills from adult to child through umpteen generations has come nearly to a halt. Many parents now are of the can't-do generation, so how are they to show their children that they can?

Kipling's *Just So* story has the answer. Taffi and her daddy worked together to invent the letters that neither of them knew beforehand and, ever since, those who know something have written, for those who don't, how to do just about anything at all.

The picture book *A Hole Is to Dig*, written by Ruth Krauss and illustrated by Maurice Sendak, captures a turn of mind toward efficacy that begins where toddlerhood leaves off. The text of the book is simply word definitions supplied by children. The words

the author asked children to define were all nouns; the definitions
the children supplied were all verbs. Grass is to cut. Dogs are to kiss
people. Mashed potatoes are to give everyone enough.

The book was prescribed reading in a child-psychology course I
took in college, when I also studied Piaget. But whereas I lost
somewhere along the way to motherhood *The Construction of Reality in the Child*, I held dear the very small and utterly charming picture book to read to my own children someday.

They were totally nonplussed. Of course, snow is to roll in, and
buttons are to keep people warm. There was no charm to them in
the obvious: hands are to hold; hands are to eat with; hands are to
make things. If it is somewhat difficult for adults to grasp the pur-
poselessness of evolution, it is impossible for young children to see
anything but purpose in everything. "The leaves make the wind
when they move," remarked four-year-old Joshua one breezy day,
unaware that he was exactly quoting one of Piaget's examples.

Nursery schools are prone to ask students to define their parents' work, as in "My mommy is a doctor." So far so good: doctors
are to give shots; doctors are to look in your ears. So might a carpenter be to hammer—but an accountant is to what? My nephew
Marco, whose father is a lawyer, created for himself, during his
early years, a desk with pads and pencils, erasers, envelopes, and paper clips: desks are to arrange; lawyers are to arrange them. One of
our sons explained in nursery school that his architect father's work
was to build "teeny-tiny houses." In his concrete perception, archi-
tectural models were something; plans for buildings were not.
Children can understand making birthday cards but not being an
executive for Hallmark. They can understand fixing broken cars but
not being an auto-insurance agent. Another of the boys took a
great liking to the nice man at the cash register in the grocery store
who gave us money when we bought our food. In terms of action
and purpose, my work was certainly the easiest to understand: "My
mommy drives the car," one young son ingenuously explained.

Children's separation from the grown-ups' workplace, and the immaterial nature of many parents' work, is another of those difficulties that has been thrust upon children in this modern age. They wish to do what grown-ups do, but for the most part, they are clueless as to what that might be. Their scope of work has been diminished.

Think of the home economy that prevailed in the walking city described by Kenneth Jackson in *Crabgrass Frontier*. There could have been no mystery when Dad the tailor cut the cloth and stitched the seams right there before your eyes, nor any doubts as to the purpose of his work, and opportunity to participate—to unbolt the cloth or pull the basting threads—and the whole procedure from fabric to finished coat was open, transparent, and comprehensible to any kindergartener. Potter, Tinker, Taylor, Sawyer, Carter, Carpenter, Weaver, Baker, Brewer, Smith: all trades of the home workplace, the only school there used to be for children under six.

Imagine, too, when every object a child encountered—housewares, furniture, clothing, vehicles, toys, and all the tools of manufacture—was made by hand. Think of the items commonly made by any householder at the time of the first Thanksgiving or in the days of the American frontier: preserves and pickles, soap and candles, socks and shirts, ax handles, fishing bobs, quilts, and dolls. In this milieu—this workaday nursery school and kindergarten—the transition from a toddler's handling of materials and utensils to a child's handiness in using materials and utensils was a matter of course. Little Ezras banging spoons became bigger Ezras hammering nails. Our second son, Rafael, working alongside his father building our first house, hammered the plywood subfloor to the joists below. He was not yet three.

Then he went to nursery school and learned to glue pasta to a piece of cardboard.

A subject of great concern to parents nowadays is their children's self-esteem. We didn't used to have self-esteem. The term existed but not as something adults were to build in their children. The first I heard of self-esteem in that sense was when our oldest child, Lincoln, was in nursery school, and I was told by his teachers to say of his inept drips and smearings that he'd sure used a lot of paint or must have worked very hard to cover the whole paper. Here was a boy who wanted to draw the pictures he saw in his mind but couldn't, so to build his self-esteem, we were supposed to praise his failures, but in such a way as not to reveal how failed we knew (he knew) they were.

Self-esteem arises in the match between intention and result. Praising a result that falls short of the intention forces on children a sense of fraudulence, a secret knowledge that they are not as advertised. The sort of praise that was suggested to us was appropriate to a toddler, who may very well intend to use a lot of paint, but by the age of efficacy, a brush, like the shark tooth Taffi used to write the alphabet, is to limn something recognizable to others. Or, like Rafael with his hammer, to do something useful.

Shelling peas is useful. I was shelling peas one day with a five-year-old named Alex. He and his father had harvested the pods; the peas were overdue for plucking, no longer sweet, but still usable for soup. We sat on a bench under a tree. The father stood by beaming (though not helping) and, in the "progressive" manner, praised his son: what a hard worker he was; how quickly he was shelling and how few peas he spilled. Unthinkingly, I fell into step—said something about how good the boy was at popping open the pods. We thought we had finished when someone remembered another large bag of peas harvested the day before. I figured Alex had had enough of this tedious occupation and started to finish up the job myself. He came and leaned against my thigh, and said, "Can I help?"

The job wasn't finished, and he knew it. What if I had said, No thank you, Alex, go and play? He wasn't really good at shelling either, and he knew that: what if I had said, Look how many peas you've shelled!—when there before us, as any kindergartener could see, was his little bowl half-filled and my big one brimming.

The job was finished when all the peas were shelled, when

spilled pods and peas (in fact, there were many) were picked up and bagged for the compost heap, when we carried our product into the kitchen to blanch and freeze the crop. Nothing needed to be said but, Thank you, Alex, and soon we'll make the soup.

I stayed overnight with Joshua on my way to Maine last summer. I arrived close to dinnertime. The parents were home from work, and one-and-a-half-year-old Ezra home from day care, and they were all three in the kitchen preparing the meal. I watched as Ezra rinsed tomatoes. He was naked, fresh from his bath, standing tiptoe on a chair to reach the kitchen sink. He had picked the tomatoes himself and was rinsing them under the tap, placing them in a bowl, and dumping them out to rinse again. His performance was not pretend and it was not creative: it was a semblance of adult endeavor. Aping the activities of adults precedes the ability to pretend them and precedes, too, any differentiation between work and play.

Laura was chopping the tomatoes for salsa. Joshua was at the stove sautéing vegetables. Ezra wanted to do that too. Joshua held him in his arms, let him hold the wooden spoon, then started his hand in the circular motion of stirring until Ezra took over for himself.

There hung on the refrigerator a finger painting by the boy—or rather, a single jagged finger line through the paint his teacher had spread. Apparently the work had not engrossed him, not the way rinsing and stirring did, although I'm sure it would have if we all had been finger painting the kitchen floor together that evening. Ezra was well short of the age of efficacy but nevertheless on the track of definition: water is to rinse; pots are to stir. He was in developmental apprenticeship for doing such things effectively and to a purpose. It is this urge to apprenticeship in family endeavor that we interrupt during the preschool years, when children are to play.

Certainly children do play, and their play is to many purposes but not to ours. We may treasure our little boys and girls, but we have little use for them. We don't need a kindergartener to rock the baby, gather the eggs, pick the peas, herd the geese, or check the rising dough, yet work participation is what children seem to be preparing for, and in the past have done, and have earned more self-esteem from their competence than our compliments can give. Although Ezra won't be able to join Joshua's research in molecular biology (he grows teeny-tiny plants) or help Laura to practice medicine, the scene in their kitchen that evening suggests the direction we might go. However narrowed our home activities have become, we should let our children help us do them.

Probably you don't grow peas, so they can't pick them. And you don't have time to shell them from the pod, so they can't do that either. You buy peas already shelled or frozen. Your child certainly can put them in the pot. But the pot is already on the stove, and the water is boiling! Then you should have a sturdy kitchen stool to reach the stove, and show your child how to put vegetables into pots of boiling water without splashing (with a small colander or a slotted spoon, for instance).

And who carried in the groceries? Every bag? Children like to lug the heaviest burden they can manage. The feat proves their muscular strength—not to you, to themselves. Long before children read, they recognize products by brand and can lift box or can from shelf to cart, unload the bags, and—by symbolic category, wet soup with sauce, dry rice with flour—put groceries away.

Where is the safest place for a child's hand when you are chopping herbs or slicing fruit with a sharp knife on a cutting board? On the knife handle, underneath your own hand, getting the feel of the motion to learn how safely to do such jobs alone. Fear of injury prevents many parents from letting children handle implements and appliances, and I can't claim that your young apprentice won't suffer an occasional cut or burn. I'm adept at kitchen work and still I keep Band-Aids in a drawer and a potted aloe on the windowsill. They stop the bleeding; they kill the pain. Minor injuries are no big deal. Serious ones are far more likely to happen as a result of forbidding children to use knives, stoves, and food processors than from teaching them how to use these tools properly.

Something other than fear of injury, though, must explain our reluctance to have children work. It isn't dangerous to load laundry into the dryer or to unload the dryer into a basket. That's clean and warm, and soft, smell-good sort of work. Children aren't going to cut themselves with knives or pierce themselves with forks by setting the table or unloading the dishwasher. Yet we feel guilty in asking for such help, as though household work were the equivalent of child labor in factories and coal mines. I think the reluctance goes back to the suburban ideal of childhood, which was to be as innocent of economic contribution as was the recreational lawn.

Alex's father could remark that this son was "the worker of the family"—meaning that he had the moral quality of persistence—without conceptualizing the boy as part of a production unit that got pea soup to the table. If he had, he would not have stood by beaming while we two did the work, and he might have expressed some interest, too, in the ultimate soup. That detachment was not his fault. He has been led to believe that parenting is a form of cheerleading, a keeping up of spirits regardless of results. He is captive to a culture that hopes shelling peas is "fun"—and the reason we did not go on from seed to soup is that he held out to Alex a Rocky and Bullwinkle movie, followed by dinner out at a Japanese restaurant where the chefs do stunts with shrimp.

That the ideal of fun childhood doesn't really sit well with us adults is the resentment that ultimately hits. Finally, but belatedly, we want results—good grades, real work: chores.

Chores are usually sprung on children when they are years beyond kindergarten, when parents feel it is time they take some responsibility for the work that must be done. There is often something punitive in the assignment, like a tax the child must pay, and an assumption that the work—walking the dog, doing the dishes, mowing the lawn—is intrinsically unpleasant. And so it is by then, to eight- or ten-year-olds who have never rinsed a glass and now are told to wash the dishes all alone. That's what parents have done, all alone while the children had fun; now it is their turn to labor, ours to relax. In keeping with the suburban ideal that assigns to each activity its separate space, we retire to the living room having missed altogether the coupling of noun with verb that preschoolers naturally conceive: work is to do together.

Joshua's family was assembled in the kitchen. All of them; all working to the purpose of getting dinner on the table. No one was off somewhere watching television or amusing the baby while someone else did the work. The work was conversational; the family was sociably sharing chips with salsa and keeping an eye on Ezra and helping him and one another, all joined in the making of the meal.

All four of our boys can cook a meal, sew a button, iron a shirt, tile a floor, build a shed, plant a tree, clean a toilet, and diaper a baby. I think this general can-do competence came about because there never was a break in our working together: no assigned chores, no rotating tasks, no one required to work in isolation. What needed doing we did together, each boy helping to what extent he could and without discussion of who had made what mess. Maybe one picked up clothes and another sorted them, and when the wash was done and dried, we all folded too. The youngest could do no more than pair the socks and the next fold nothing more complicated than a towel, but there we were around the big table, all hands busy with the work. It was the same with putting toys away, preparing vegetables, wiping up the bathroom, and the once-a-week thorough cleaning of the house. After Saturday cleanup, we all together did the grocery shopping for the week.

This sharing of the work is probably similar to how things were done when the family economy was centered in the home, and it seemed to suit the boys, to please them. It was also similar to the way children play house, joining together yet parceling out roles, and talking all the while. When the house was clean, the clothes washed, the groceries stashed, the meal in preparation—and the dripping faucet fixed, the broken pane replaced—there was no question of *self*-esteem. The family was competent and all the children in it.

I listened to a tape of G. K. Chesterton's autobiography on my way to Joshua's house and thence to Maine. Chesterton was recalling his father, whose most intense interest in life was not his work (he was a land agent, what we would call a realtor), but his hobby: making miniature theaters with intricately constructed and painted scenery and delicate cardboard figures. Chesterton dwelled on the centrality of crafts in the Victorian household, the number of things adults and children made themselves, their pleasure in family projects. The taffy you have pulled yourself, he claimed, tastes better than any you can buy.

I participated in a taffy pull once at a birthday party. It was not just fun to pull and fold with buttered hands the warm candy until it was light and stiff; it was magic to discover that what is bought can be made. Ice cream! Beanbags! Kites! Envelopes! Looking for favors to give children at my husband's annual office picnic, I came upon a humming toy (it cost $5) that worked on the same principle as the humming buttons we used to make. You thread a length of string through the two holes of a big button, then tie the ends of the string to make a loop with the button in the middle. You hold the two ends of the loop and spin it until the string is tightly wound. Then you pull the ends to make the button sing.

A beanbag can be made out of a sock half-filled with small white beans, then knotted at the top. A handkerchief becomes a rabbit (tie two adjacent corners, then gather the fabric together with a rubber band just below the tie) or a baby (put a lump of cotton in the middle, twist the cloth into a neck below it, and secure the neck with string tied in a bow). A mitten becomes a hand puppet with a pair of button eyes. Newspaper, rolled and fringed at the top, pulls open like a telescope into a giant corn stalk.

I learned that particular trick from a magician at another birth-day party, where we also folded our own party hats from sheets of newspaper. All grown-ups are magicians when they perform such amazing transformations; all children wish to learn the secret from them. The list of paper transformations is by itself amazing: boats as well as hats, all sorts of airplanes that twirl or loop through the air or fly fast and straight; accordion-folded springs, pleated fans, wo-ven baskets, looped chains, masks, Möbius strips, "cootie catchers," pinwheels, paper lace and snowflakes, dolls that unfold hand in hand in hand in hand, all identical to one another.

We decorated the Christmas tree with metallic paper chains, stars made of paper straws, and animal origami. We made Valentine cards as I once upon a time used to do with Aunt Aileen, and we learned to fold envelopes as well. These are playful pastimes but se-rious in the expectations they meet: that materials are to be trans-formed into objects, that grown-ups are to show children the secrets of manufacture; that children are to master the skills that are required.

Young children, I learned in Child Psychology 101, think phenom-enalistically. That is, they accept phenomena such as lights coming on without wondering what it is about a switch that makes light happen. Supposedly, preschool children outgrow that incurious ac-ceptance and begin to ask Why? Why is the sky blue? they ask, as if we knew the answer. Does the air ever sleep? I had once to write a book of science for young children and found out very quickly how few answers I had. What is fire? stumped me for weeks. Elec-tricity was only slightly easier. I also came to appreciate that my own thinking wasn't much less phenomenalistic than that of young children. What are marshmallows made of? Well, out of marshmal-low, says the lame and limp adult.

The alchemy of cooking has been lost to us and with that loss, the gratification of transforming substances from one thing to an-other. No, more than gratification: *power!*

Marshmallows are sugar, corn syrup, cornstarch, water, and gelatin beaten to a froth and flavored with vanilla. What is vanilla? A bean. Vanilla extract is the bean's fragrant oil dissolved in alcohol (you can use vodka). And gelatin? Gelatin is elastic proteins extracted from hooves and bones by boiling them in water, like my grandmother's calves'-foot jelly (but the original gelatin in marshmallows was a plant elastic extracted from the roots of marsh mallow flowers). Probably you know from label reading that noodles are wheat flour and eggs, but noodle is noodle to kids. Have you ever made soup from scratch?

We don't do these things anymore because the manual labor involved deters us from the task. It's easier just to buy the stuff and not ask questions: to remain as phenomenalistic as a three-year-old and as disempowered by minds as ignorant of bread as our hands are innocent of kneading.

I don't think it's critical to rise before dawn to bake the daily bread or make the pasta, but I do think it's important to experience dough. A few times, anyway: otherwise, questions can't arise. Why knead? Why yeast? Kneading distributes the elastic starch–fiber gluten throughout the mass so that when you roll the noodle dough, it doesn't fall to pieces. The packet of yeast you add to bread dough is fungi that digest carbohydrates and excrete carbon dioxide; their breathed bubbles are what puffs the dough. Or maybe it's not important to know bread in even such a mildly technical way but just to know that yeasts are alive, eating and excreting until you bake them to death. Or just to know about noodles that the dough had to be rolled and then cut into strips and dried. Noodles don't make themselves. The wheat starch they're made of is what the plant supplied its embryos, its own offspring; the starch in the seed was for their consumption, not ours. The peas I shelled with Alex had just about used up the resources provided through the umbilical stem that connected each to its aging, shriveling pod. Some embryos, having taken what they needed from their parent, were sprouting—using the accumulated sugar-turned-to-starch to grow the roots and leaves of the next generation. Just let's realize.

Prescientific peoples could not make these connections. They knew what happened, how to make it happen, but not *why*. Now we can go from manipulation to cognition, but Wonder bread without the experience of baking will not lead children to wonder about the holes in bread any more than noodles without the experience of making and cutting them will lead children to wonder why the stuff is in strips.

I remember well the pain of cutting paper with the dreadful scissors we used in school. They were blunt nosed for safety but dull bladed for economy, and the pin that held the halves together was either too loose for cutting or too tight for squeezing. Tools of torture, I'd call them, for the paper and for the hands.

The memory of the dent they made in my thumb remained so vivid that as soon as I had a child old enough for scissors, I went to Hoffritz for Cutlery in New York City to buy him a proper pair. Now, thinking to do the same for the following generation, I called the 800 mail-order number (the world has changed). O Best Beloved, Hoffritz still carried children's scissors! Four months later, though, the world had changed again: a friend, encouraged by me to buy good scissors for her children, found Hoffritz subsumed under a company on the Internet whose Web site was nonfunctional. She bought instead child-size Fiskars, those orange-plastic-handled scissors that are widely available, and reported them to be comfortably usable by children and cheap as well.

I was chastened and chagrined: why didn't I think of Fiskars, which, after all, I keep in my own kitchen drawer? Because I'm tool obsessed; because I wanted you to shell out $12 for the all-steel, last-a-lifetime, best-of-all scissors for children. I'll settle for Fiskars but not for cheap imitation tools like those cutely made in child-size versions of a carpenter's toolbox or a lineman's belt. I'm serious about calling them imitations. A tool that doesn't work is not the real thing.

There are all sorts of small tasks that children like to do: retightening screws, rewiring plugs, removing nails, installing cup hooks, hanging pictures. When my friend Alma found her small home in

Vermont, she inadvisedly bought a set of bargain tools for just such household uses. They were unusable. The hammer was poorly balanced and too light, the screwdriver blades too thick, the pliers clumsy, and the adjustable wrench got stuck at every turn. She had to replace them all and add the necessary awl, wire snips, and needle-nosed pliers that had not been included in the set.

A hole is to dig, says the book, and hardware companies think they do children a favor by offering child-size sets of rake, hoe, and spade. Naturally, for the child's safety, the rake has blunt tines and the hoe and spade dull blades; they are cheaply made; the metal bends and breaks. Such imitations might work on the beach but not in the yard. You can find in garden stores small-bladed spades, narrow rakes, and cultivating hoes, which are shaped like a triangle instead of a wedge. Just cut the handle to the child's size. Skinny trowels are easier to dig holes with than fat ones. For years I was dissatisfied with my cutting tools: pruners, even those designed for women, were too large for my stubby hands; shears were too heavy; saws too dull. The solution was Japanese tools.

We Americans have a he-man attitude: tools are to wield. The Japanese must have a different concept, that tools are to do your work for you. Also, they are a smaller people: the shears, pruners, and saws are diminutive, light, and very sharp. You manipulate the handle; the blade cuts the wood. The Japan Woodworker, where I got my whittling blades, sells the wood-handled shears and saw by mail order (800-537-7820). The best little Japanese snub-nosed pruners in the world, made by a company called ARS, can be ordered from Orchard's Edge (orchardsedge.com). I'd certainly let an eight-year-old use these tools, once I'd taught her how and told her why and showed her which twigs and branches should be cut, just like my dad taught me to prune his apple trees. I still have his old wooden loppers.

Good tools are an investment in the future, and not only the future of your temper when trying to accomplish everyday tasks, but the future of your child's developing brain.

Here is a pencil and paper experiment: take any sort of paper and any pencil, close your eyes, and scribble. The paper may be rough or smooth, the pencil sharp or dull, the lead soft or hard, and you don't need to see to feel what either one is like. But where do you feel these qualities? Not in the fingers that are holding the pencil and that are the only possible source of sensory impressions that reach the brain. You feel the rough paper or the soft lead *at the pencil point*. The tool has been incorporated into a schematic map within your brain as though it were a living extension of your fingers.

So it is also that the knitter feels the tension of the yarn in the needles, the carpenter the sharpness of the saw where blade meets wood, and the musician the instrument as a living part of him. I questioned an expert backhoe operator as to where he feels the give of soil and the heft of a rock: at the very teeth of the bucket.

These mental phenomena are a continuation of a neuronal mapping that begins in infancy. Babies are born with an area in the brain that roughly coincides with their body plan: sensory impressions from the tongue, thumb, or toes arrive to the brain in the same top-to-bottom pattern in which they actually occur. But if a mosquito had bitten Ezra in that sultry southern climate where I first came to know him, he would not have known exactly where he itched. As with other sorts of knowledge, the brain must construct from experience the details of body image. Fantastically and wonderfully, that image comes to include the tools we learn to use. The self we come to know—the self that is to have esteem—extends beyond the fingertips into those implements, instruments, and equipment that we become skilled at using. It seems unwise to give our children blunt and clumsy fingers when, with excellent tools, we can refine and make them deft instead.

As a child, I puzzled over the adage that one's reach should be beyond one's grasp. Now that I understand the figurative meaning, I also see that those who literally haven't grasped very much fail to reach very far. This is as true of the physical use of hands as it is of the abstract use of symbols. If you learn to cut a marshmallow stick, you have some intellectual basis to suppose that you can use a knife for more demanding tasks, and as blades become integrated with your body image, you may conceive one day that you can whittle. But if you were not allowed to use a knife, or the knife you were allowed to use was too dull to cut, then you might not come to recognize the connection between competence and creativity, between imagining and manufacturing, between play and work.

Skill learning is of a different nature altogether than the learning of an abstract subject. At first, as you practice a new skill, you're aware of your motions; you know what you're doing but must concentrate to do it. When you learned to tie your shoes, you had to look at your hands and perform the sequence of motions by rote. Ultimately, the skill became automatic: you lost the awareness of how to tie the bow. Now you can show someone how, but it takes enormous effort to reconstruct the sequence in your own mind or to translate it into words. And yet you can't forget how to tie a shoelace. The knowledge appears to have left your head and moved into your hands. I can explain to my invisible audience the gross sequence of activities in whittling an animal, but how do I draw an elephant? How do I get its shape out of the wood? I have no idea. The drawing and the shaping are in my hands.

It is only once the necessary skills are automatic that the mind is free to be creative. The barrier between imagining and doing is lifted: You think the elephant, and the pencil enacts the thought. You think the tusks, and the blade finds them in the wood. So is the difference between work and play erased: the effort has eased; you are free to play at the work. This is true also of the knitter who no longer needs a pattern, or the cook who no longer uses recipes, or the pianist who improvises, or the watercolorist who catches clouds as they run across the sky. They can be playful and inventive, engrossed at the same time that their mind floats with the relaxed and delicious detachment that mine does when I carve.

I like to show people the animals, and I like them to praise my work. But I know that when I paint the elephant the color of the great green greasy Limpopo River, and he looks just like the Elephant Child as I had imagined him to be, I have cause to be proud without the need to be hung on the refrigerator door.

Back in the bean house, children are playing. They are pretending for the most part to be grown up. We can't imagine them as grownups; neither can they, not really. They also don't believe they *are* growing up. Their idea of becoming adult is not developmental; it is transformational: someday, like the frog who became a prince, they will *turn into* adults.

I was working in a nursery school at the time that I was reading Piaget and also preparing to write a thesis on fairy tales. It was an interesting combination, the tales of Cinderlad and Cinderlass and the dramas the children were performing as they played house and school and store. In fairy tales, the hero or heroine—who is often merely ordinary and none too smart—is given a set of tasks to perform or challenges to meet or instructions to obey. The protagonists do what they are told. Then adulthood—the state of "happily ever after"—is conferred on them as the reward for being good.

I began to realize that the children's dramas were often moral plays that explored themes of obedience and disobedience, competence and clumsiness, violence and control, reward and punishment. I began to see also that the roles (the superhero, the fancy lady) were a trying on of the magical reward (the Power! the Beauty!) that would be theirs if they were good. If they were good *children*; if they were good at *being* children.

And now, having raised a few myself and known many more, I understand that action and enaction are two sides of the same coin. Being good at being a child means being good at doing things: at following instructions, at carrying heavy groceries, at stacking the cans, at pouring without spilling, at cutting a sandwich in half. The accuracy that children aim for as they become able to balance towers or crayon within the lines is gratifying to them but pointless if their domain remains confined to unit blocks and coloring books.

Adults are to give meaning to the skills: heap logs, bricks, or towels so they do not topple; ice cupcakes, color lips, or paint steps within the given space. I wouldn't for the world deny preschoolers the props and dress-up clothes that support enactment, but when the play is over and the props are put away, the fairy tale turns real: the coach is a pumpkin after all, and the child can't cut it if she can't wield a knife.

Handsoff.edu

Fifty children sat imprisoned in their school bus while a park naturalist climbed aboard to "bring them under control." He had told me that this had to be done on the bus because once the children spilled out onto the parking lot, there was no way to get their attention or bring them to order.

He explained the rules. The students were to walk in pairs and never leave the trail. They were to keep their hands at their sides, not to pick any flowers, and not to touch so much as a leaf. They could ask questions when the group stopped to listen to what the naturalist explained but should not talk among themselves. "If I can hear you," said the naturalist, "so can the animals."

The children were two fifth-grade classes from an urban school in Michigan, and this field trip was an adjunct to their study of glacial geology. They were certainly in the right place: the park occupies two hundred acres of land that, during the Ice Age's Wisconsin Stage, which ended about thirteen thousand years ago, lay between two lobes of a glacier. Although blocks of ice toppled from the melting mass onto the land—and these huge blocks accounted for the park's sand and gravel soil, its steep kames and boggy kettles—the interlobal area had never been scoured clean of life by the glacier itself. Its biodiversity was therefore astounding: five hundred species of plants, including over a dozen orchids and a number of endangered species, two of which were the only remnants of their kind in the state. The composition of the forest ranged from southern trees like tulip poplar to boreal ones like larch, so I knew what a treasure of diversity I was about to see.

The children trooped off the bus and, after some milling around to partner with friends, lined up facing the naturalist for his introductory lecture. The descent from kame to kettle would be eight hundred feet—and the climb back the same. Groan. The children's home city lies as level as water in the bed of an ancient lake: few of them had ever climbed a hill.

"Ernest," said one of the class teachers, "you remember that: *thirteen thousand years ago*." "Janice," she added, "you remember this: *ice one-mile thick*." Harry was having trouble with his arms: they kept flailing around, jostling other children. A teacher moved to his side. By prior arrangement with the naturalist, wise guys were to walk with teachers.

So we all set off along the gritty trail to our next lecture stop in an old field where one student, posing as a block of ice, was used to demonstrate how the weight of the ice block forms a kettle hole, while the dirty water melting from the top and running down the sides deposits a rim of raised sand and gravel kames. "These are vocabulary words," warned a teacher. "Remember *kame* and *kettle*."

The next stop was the poison-ivy lesson. "How many leaves?" asked the naturalist, holding a sample by its stem, which he had wrapped carefully in a spicebush leaf. "Three," ventured several voices, but the naturalist was expecting that wrong answer and so enjoyed the planned opportunity to explain that it was a single, *compound* leaf made up of three *leaflets*. It was late September; the poison ivy was beginning to turn a stunning scarlet. Classes are not allowed to use the park for collecting fall leaves because poison ivy breaks into those three leaflets that are hard to identify and therefore might be picked up by mistake. I plucked a spicebush leaf to crush and sniff—but secretly, not wanting to be caught.

We descended, stop by stop, to wetland, accompanied by a

growing vocabulary: *muck, marsh, bog, fen, meadow, karr.* The naturalist pointed out a rare poison sumac growing twenty feet off the trail in the wet, shrubby karr but not the equally rare fringed gentian blooming brilliantly and by the score at our very feet.

My own partner on this walk was an avid amateur naturalist, about my age, named Maryann. The sight of the gentians moved us simultaneously to nearly identical reveries. As a child, I once, and never again, had found fringed gentians blooming in the orchard. Maryann also, and only once, had come upon the flower in her youthful wanderings. Both of us, stricken by the purity of its color and the delicate perfection of its form, had held that moment of discovery in a halo of wonder for decades.

None of the fifty eleven-year-olds asked what they were.

By the end of the next climb, to pristine oak savanna, and faced now with the continuing uphill trek back to the parking lot, the children were tiring. Harry's restless arms swung back to tease the boy behind him, who began what soon became a chorus, "Are we almost there?" This was against the rules: the children had been told they would be "there" when they could see the school bus, and not before.

We saw the school bus through the trees; we reached the asphalt. And, for the first time, the children came to life: they were to have a picnic in the park.

Read this sentence carefully; it's from *The New York Times*: "Outside, summer beckons, with bikes to be ridden, video games to be played, cartoons to be watched, Barbies to be pampered for hours on end."

Now, I know some errors slip past editors, and this certainly was one of those, but some errors also point to a truth, and this was one of those as well: the author apparently couldn't think of just what the "teasing afternoon breeze wafting through the windows" was tempting third-grade students to do outdoors, once they were released from remedial summer classes in a city public school. What *do* children do when they are outside and out of sight? The middle years of childhood are largely played out behind our backs. There's no telling where children might wander from the academic grounding we think we give to them.

I gave the boys field lenses so they could examine the stomata on the underside of leaves, the geometry of pollen grains, the anatomy of bees' legs, the garnet gems in grains of sand. They set leaves afire with the lenses. They crisped ants. I duly took them to the American Museum of Natural History when they were in elementary school to show them an exhibit on human evolution that featured sculptured reconstructions of the facial features of various species based on fossil evidence. I didn't find out until they were men that as a result of that lesson they had been able to identify in the woods a Neandertal campsite strewn with ancient hammer stones and streaked with blood evidence of human sacrifice.

The afternoon of the day I walked the park with that paired line of fifty children, I was taken to an altogether different and highly unusual demonstration of childhood education. The teacher ran a preschool at her suburban home whose modest play yard bordered on a municipal park. Her home also served as a day-care center for former students, who were dropped off by the school bus and stayed until picked up by their parents at the end of the working day.

We arrived after the preschoolers had gone home but just as the school bus arrived with five ex-students: four girls and a boy, ranging from seven to twelve. A few years before, the same children, then aged from four to nine, had participated with their teacher in researching flood control and water quality in the local river. With their mentor, they had petitioned the town to allow them to plan a retention basin in the park, applied for and gotten funding for the project, hired a backhoe to excavate the basin, and planted the catchment area with plugs and seeds of wetland prairie species. Several of the children had given formal presentations to the municipal government (one standing before an audience of 250 people) and

conducted interviews with the press. All the children, in mud
above their ankles, had planted the prairie.

During that portion of my Michigan visit, I was staying with
my neice Leila, who teaches heat exchange and fluid dynamics to
sophomore physics students at the state university. She is one of
those gifted teachers who makes every effort to inspire students to
really grasp the subject, to think it through, to make it theirs in so
deep and comfortable a way that they can use their knowledge cre-
atively in the same way that one can whittle any figure once the
hands know wood and blade. But Leila was finding the going
rough: her students aspired to know no more than how to reach the
answer, which formula to use, how to score well on what would be
the physics equivalent of a kame-and-kettle test.

Naturally, I compared the children of the morning with the
children of the afternoon, and it would be belaboring the point to
explicate at length the obvious differences between those who walk
a trail with hands at sides and minds on tests and those who best recall squishing plugs of switchgrass into gooey mud. Both may learn
vocabulary (or they may not), but the trendy term "hands-on education" hardly begins to convey the contrast between memorizing
the fact that muck soil is made by decaying plants, and planting the
makers of muck soil.

Yet after the mud-loving children had finished impressing this
adult with the considerable depth of their knowledge and passion
for water purity, they ran off, as if by common consent, on a tide
of ebullience, dodging the undertow of their educational duties.
Or so it seemed to me: they surged as a unit toward the "Porcupine
Trees."

This was a stand of spruces, closely spaced but enclosing a dark
circle of prickly-needled ground, and entered through a single
opening among the trunks. I wasn't invited. I followed anyway but
not far, because, as I emerged out of the hot sun into the cool
opening, they were already way beyond me, high up in the trees. I
leaned my back against a tree trunk, bemused by this generational

reversal, remembering my own pine hideaway from which, as a girl, I spied on the mundane doings of adults, at roof level, listening to their terrace talk below. I tried to catch some shred of these children's privacy, but they knew my eyes and ears were turned on them, and they grew shy.

Like animals.

I see two strands of childhood entwining. One is linear; it grows straight up among adults who all along the way tell and show children what they are to be and how, from rinsing tomatoes straight through to the history of exploration in the New World, where the tomato plant evolved and was domesticated. These are formal connections, the schooling that only adults can give. The lessons are informative and explanatory, narrations as anciently human as myths that explain anything a child might notice, like wind (blown by zephyrs or the laws of physics) or mountains (raised by gods or plate tectonics).

All the while, though, as children year by year grow in disciplined understanding, they are sprouting along another strand that curls around the first, sometimes looping off from it, spiraling away, sometimes twining so close that the two strands fuse together. This is the wild vine, growing tendrils rampantly, experiencing wind, water, dirt, hills, bugs, flowers, snow, stones, leaves, toads, smells, sidewalks, hamburgers, stars, storekeepers, teachers, and the occasional naturalist.

Vines are interesting things. One, of the *Monstera* genus that you might meet near Tortuguero, may sprout on the forest floor, in the middle of nowhere. It grows toward the dark, the shade of trees, absorbing nutrients as it goes but not rooting, instead dying at the tail end while sprouting at the front, and in that strange way moving along the ground. It roots only when it arrives at the darkest spot, the base of a tree. Then it changes its strategy entirely, growing upward now, clinging to the tree for support, reaching for light way up in the canopy where it can finally bloom and fruit. I think

of babies who, as they become able to engage adults in more articulate ways, leave behind them infantile traits that were crucial to
their survival at first—the automatic smile, dimpled baby fat, and
suckling, which weaned children soon forget how to do.

Most vines—grapes are an example—have a less intricate strategy: they germinate, grow tendrils, and wave about (clockwise
or counterclockwise, depending on the species) until they engage support. Then, like *Monstera*, they climb upward toward
the light where, in sunlit maturity, they are able to bloom and
fruit. The support that will enable the plant's maturational program is there all the time, with its great height and sturdy branches,
but the vine has to reach for it and continue to feel its way up bark
and branches to the top. Random exploration is essential to fulfill-
ment of the vine's biological program. So are the wanderings of
children.

I have given you a lesson in botany, and if you have found
metaphorical seeds for thought in it, that is because you have experienced the wanderings of a child, and how it feels when what
you have come upon suddenly makes sense. First, you wander the
kames and kettles, kick sand and sink in mud, climb up and down
the abruptly steep terrain, find fringed gentians, suffer poison ivy:
then you reach for the fabulous coherence of glacial geography.
Nothing is wrong with formal education except that we have got it
backward. Children need experiences to make sense of before what
we teach them can make sense. In this view, education is not something imposed from outside, but arises in children's need for adults
to arrange coherently the chaos of their perceptions.

An example is classic storybooks, such as *Goodnight Moon* or
Where the Wild Things Are. Each gives narrative form to internal experiences that children suffer—the loneliness of being put to bed at
night, the rage of a tantrum. The authors of such books are adults
at their best, formalizing and clarifying in narrative what the child
already but inchoately knows and feels.

The children of the Porcupine Trees had, since kindergarten, been given the run of the park that verged their play yard. They had already made it theirs—the ground of their adventuring, their perch up in the trees. They knew the low spot in the grass where water collected after rain, the grate over the storm drain along the curb, and the close-by river too. Maybe they had sailed Popsicle sticks in the gutter, dropped pebbles through the grating to hear them splash. We don't know exactly what children do when they just muck about, pretending this, poking that. If you look back over your own childhood, though, you'll find that it is made up of numerous stories and that often you can see yourself in the pictures, even though at the time you were behind your eyes, seeing but unseen to yourself. You have made yourself into a character, the protagonist of the scenes you recollect. You have told yourself the story of who you are.

So had the tree climbers, in their many hours of freedom, begun to place themselves within the landscape of their experience. To put that identity in very general terms (for we cannot know what fantasies each had in the privacy of their minds), they at least knew themselves to be splashers in the water, lovers of the park. *Then* they were eager to be schooled in drainage basins, soil filtration, catchment areas, water purity, and community action. And *then*, much more than merely being a player in the story, each could emerge as hero or heroine in his or her narrative of self.

For most people, the story begins when they were five or six. The earlier years often are lost, like the vine's tail as it creeps forward for support. Maybe a certain linguistic sophistication must be reached before experience can be encoded in narrative. And, too, only by five or six years old are children given both the freedom to explore without supervision and the schooling by which private experience can be formally expressed and fit within the surrounding culture. That makes sense to me, but if it is so that children are to bring to school the raw material of their experience, and teaching is to give form to what they already in some sense know, then it is critical to their education that they discover on their own.

We no longer give children freedom, privacy, place, or time to do that.

My fourth-grade teacher was Miss Moore. She was feared for her reputation of shaking students by the shoulders when displeased with them, and rightly so: Miss Moore—tall and bony, with black hair parted in the middle and pulled hard into a knot—was impatient with stupidity, untamed by curriculum, and independent to the point of delicious wickedness. Her passion was ancient Egypt.

Miss Moore taught history, as I recall, without a textbook. Egyptian tombs depicted acrobats, so she had us learn back bends, cartwheels, and how to stand on our heads. She vigorously shoved desks aside to make way for a roll of brown wrapping paper on which, kneeling, we painted a scrolled mural in stereotypical Egyptian style: parallel zigzags for the water of the river Nile, fans of papyrus, stiff lotus flowers, fish, and fowl, and people with head and limbs in profile but chest full front. We practiced posing in that unnatural but compelling position and learned to clothe ourselves in rectangles of fabric tucked and folded into skirts and tunics. We visited the Metropolitan Museum of Art, where I met necklace-decked Queen Nefertiti, lapis scarab amulets, flesh-and-bone mummies, whittled-wood models of bakeries, potteries, and shops that now would be toys but were then supplied to the important dead for the continuance of their comfortable daily lives. We put on a play for the rest of the school, using our mural as backdrop and our acrobatics as inter-act entertainment (I don't remember what the acts were all about). Everything about ancient Egypt made perfect sense to me. Now, having traveled there as an adult, I understand why.

Egypt is a narrow land, a ribbon of green snaked like a stretched oasis through the desert. The Nile River runs from south to north, no wider through much of its length than an average swimmer could easily cross in less than a lazy hour. A ten-minute walk takes you from lush riverbank, through a perched village, to Saharan sand: the land is that circumscribed. You can't be disoriented as you might be in a cornfield in Iowa or a forest in Oregon. The river is always in sight: as you face downstream, the sun rises to your right and sets to your left. Egypt is a legible landscape, terse but expressive, pared to essentials but lucid in meaning. Any eight-year-old could grasp what it was to live there in ancient days.

You were born where the sun rises and died where the sun sets. In between was the river that fed fish and fowl and that watered the land that grew the grain and cattle. The river was banked with clay—earth colors of ocher, umber, and sienna—and the banks were planted with oil palms and dates. You slept within walls of sun-baked mud, under a roof of rushes, and your baskets were rushes too, as your pots were clay. Clothes were linen woven of flax—but you ran naked until you came of age: summer was all year. There are no rainy days in the land of Egypt.

Your fears were real: the dark jackal stalks the night and eats the dead. Your reverence was shared: the giant scarab beetles roll their ball of dung across the ground like the sun across the sky. The gods are animals. You believed in magic, amulets, omens, and incantations. So did everybody else.

And what you wished to do as a child converged with what you had to do as an adult: mud pies to mud bricks, string games to string hammocks, hiding to stalking, chasing to herding, throwing to spearing, climbing to harvesting the sweet ripe dates from the shinnied palms. Hardly any children went to school: the stories that you loved to hear explained the world.

The Egyptians depicted children as miniature adults. I think one would not have felt, as a child then and there, the discontinuity between childhood and adulthood that children experience here and now. The material culture was handmade: true, a child had to grow into the skill to turn a pot or the strength to haul bricks, but that was a difference in degree of dexterity and muscle, not child's play in contrast to grown-up work. The spiritual culture was similar to how children naturally imagine, only more elaborate and formalized, the fear of jackals expressed as the jackal god Anubis, who took the dead. I fiercely wished to wear a scarab amulet.

And yet my excitement about ancient Egypt was not only because the subject accorded with my own ways of thinking: it was because Miss Moore told and showed the culture to us in our own terms, through spun cartwheels and painted water, and by appealing to our girlish attraction to glittery jewelry, our awe of the mummified dead, our quivery feeling when entering the museum's mock tombs, like caves. She seemed to read my child mind and then read back to me the picture book that put it all in order.

From then on, schooling often seemed to veer away from me. The next year was Greek and Roman history. The naked infant Cupid and the boyish goat-bottomed Pan peeled off from the grown-up gods, as though adults were no longer allowed to be primitive like children. This was the dawn of modern civilization, and I was not quite ready to be civilized. At times in following years, my wild vining found support again—the barbarians, the Dark Ages, and anything to do with natural science—but for the most part, I divorced the grown-up world to live a secret life like Phoebe fluffing her private bower with milkweed out of sight of parents who had given her that name unaware that a phoebe is a bird.

The Peter Pan I knew as a child was not the one made famous in the Broadway play, with Mary Martin as the eternal prepubertal boy. The Peter I knew was from J. M. Barrie's novel *Peter Pan in Kensington Gardens*, published in 1906, two years after the play was first presented. In this version, Peter is an infant who, not yet realizing that he is no longer the bird that all infants are before they are born, flies from the nursery window to the Gardens and lives on an island in the Serpentine. He has flown from the nursery to escape being human and, as Barrie says, "If you think he was the only baby who ever wanted to escape, it shows how completely you have forgotten your own young days."

True to his surname, Peter makes himself a pipe of reeds, and he "used to sit by the shore of the island of an evening, practicing the sough of the wind and the ripple of the water, and catching handfuls of the shine of the moon, and he put them all in his pipe and played them so beautifully that even the birds were deceived, and they would say to each other, 'Was that a fish leaping in the water or was it Peter playing leaping fish on his pipe?' "

The yellowed volume I have was published in 1938, when I was three years old. It was read aloud to me; I can still hear my mother's voice as the Chrysanthemum, saying of a child left behind in the Garden after lock-out time, "Hoity toity, what is this?" What made me reach for the book was a brief return to being a bird child myself.

I was at a conference in Florida, at a session exploring the relationship between art and natural science. The group of some fifty people was led to play the sound of rain on the instruments of our fingers, hands, and feet. The rain started quietly, with snapping fingers, drop by drop, slowly picking up speed. Then, palms patting thighs, the drops fell more heavily until—feet tapping now as well—the rain became a downpour. A hand clap of thunder struck, and another. Then the storm passed: feet stopped; hands relaxed; snapping fingers sounded the final drops, and stilled.

We *were* the rain, and then, the session finished, I retired to the hotel bar with two fellow rainers who wanted to see how to whittle. Afterward, we went to supper on a lawn where the woman who had led the rain-play sang through the warm moonlit evening. There was one child, a toddler, among us hundreds of adults. He felt happy or, as the fairies in the Gardens say instead, he felt *dancy*. So he danced. He danced to every melody, to any rhythm, alone and oblivious to all but the happy sound going in and dancing out.

Alone because no one else got up to dance.

In the book, Peter is not a human; neither is he a bird. The birds call him a Betwixt-and-Between, and although Barrie depicts him as an infant through Arthur Rackham's illustrations, the text suggests the middle years of childhood, betwixt and between first grade and puberty. Peter tries to fly off the island on a kite and finally adventures over the water in a thrush's nest, which he learns to paddle with a child's left-behind spade. The boy very much wishes to be grand things, like *afraid* and *brave*.

"It is all rather sad," reads the last line of *Peter Pan in Kensington Gardens*, and that is how I felt as I watched the boy dancing alone in the moonlight on the grass, unlikely ever to be joined by adults in his human primitivity nor in the years to come ever again let free to be the young animal he was.

The conference session attempting to weave connections between the creative arts and the natural sciences was strained, I thought, and at times embarrassing. The audience, largely people responsible for public education in municipal, county, state, and national parks, was technically trained, ecology minded, passionately preservationist but hardly the artsy-craftsy sort that feels comfy with songs to greet the morning sun.

The session was structured as an open discussion between the audience and a panel comprised of the singer, a poet, an artist, a "festivalist" (he arranged celebrations, processions, and similar happenings to emotionally engage people in the natural world), and me. Me with my animals: I had flown with them in their boxes to Florida for the conference.

By then I had gotten pretty good at whittling. I'd just finished a small group of truly tiny mammals—gopher, wood rat, vole, two mice, one shrew—and had started on an ambitious group of fishes. I was happy to show them off but couldn't for the life of me see how the craft of carving could get anybody interested in nature. Interested in whittling, yes, and maybe greedy to collect, but I did not believe that figurines, poems, songs, or paintings bring people out of their shelters into the wild woods. Quite the opposite: I was sure that what inspired the panelists' creativity was their experience of nature and that it cannot work the other way around. Creativity is the result, not the wellspring, of experience.

I was as right as I was wrong.

The artist showed slides—not of her own work, but that of others, and most of it as temporary as Phoebe's milkweed bower. One took place on a pebble beach. The artist had built a cobble cairn with white stones at the base grading to pale salmon, then a deeper hue, then a top of richly ruddy stones. Any child could have done it. Just sort the colors; just pile them.

The poet recited two of her works. One was about a crazy man who waded deep into the Okefenokee to rant and pray, and was rescued by the police. A newspaper story: sucked by and succored in the swamp. The other was about bird banders with mist nets capturing birds to record technical data: breed, size, weight, sex. Living birds, banded. She recited these poems from memory, and they had the force of incantation.

The festivalist hinted at something about procession—an image of hands joined, feet in unison, communality—but he said it, didn't do it, and his art remained a hint. The singer was too tree-huggy for me by a whole lot until she let us make rain, and then the storm came pouring down on me: the point was not getting people to come to nature, but to be their nature—processing, incanting, sorting out and piling up, forming, hoarding, narrating. The creativity that we suppose is spiritual and cultural as opposed to physical and scientific is what Peter did with his reed pipe: let the stuff in and play it out. The nature we must come to grips with is our own.

But that, as Barrie suggests, is what we have forgotten.

In the long ago at the school I went to as a girl, we processed into the auditorium in the hour before we recessed for winter vacation. The hour would have been toward four o'clock, the end of our school day and, in the time of the winter solstice, the daylight was already darkening toward night. The folding chairs were put away; the floor was clear. Each older girl held the hand of a younger girl—classes were from kindergarten to twelfth grade, all in the same building. We linked with one another throughout the school, along corridors and stairways, hands held with teachers too, and the school secretary, headmistress, janitor, and kitchen staff. We called what then occurred "the snail," for the line moved step by step, hall by hall, and floor after floor, hand in hand into the auditorium, those in front winding into a small circle in the middle, and the others as they entered coiling around them to form at last a spiral that filled the whole room. Then we sang—two hundred of us, small hands in big ones, piping voices with maturing altos—songs that we all knew.

The odd thing is, I remember the snail in candlelight, although I know that can't be so. How could candles have been held, since every hand was in another? And what school would have allowed such a perilous gathering of children carrying flames? The false memory must have been evoked by other processions that I witnessed later or simply by the archaic expectation that humans make light to hold against the dark.

We loaned our house in Maine to friends, the Wordens, for a week one summer. When we arrived for our vacation, I found on my worktable a display of gifts. From Alicia, age eleven, a still life of dried seaweed, beach glass, crab claws, and pebbles arranged on sand in an empty wine carafe. From Lila, age ten, a similar assortment of beachcombings glued to a slab of driftwood. From Charlie, age six, a fist-size bait bag also found among the strewings that the sea brings in and containing the sea's tossed treasures. A card from the parents said that they had never seen their children as happy as they had been during that week.

I have to state right off that these were happy kids. They lived in a small city on a block of Victorian houses where neighbors knew each other and the gardens were overgrown with age. Their parents worked at home; they had a dog, a cat, and varying numbers of gerbils. They were not diffident or bored; they were fond of cooking, drawing, and putting on elaborate and ridiculous performances for an audience of two. I emphasize this general security and ease in order to extract from it the particular delirium they experienced for a week on an island in Maine.

What had the children done? Nothing much. They searched for

things rare and curious. They explored strange shores. They picked flowers. They hunted for small creatures at low tide in salty pools. They climbed a pitch pine. They hid among giant slabs of granite in a quarry. They ate wild berries. The two girls paddled a canoe up the long inlet that runs beside the house and then had quite an adventure paddling back against the wind and tide. They slept in the barn. They made those gifts for us of the things they had collected. They did, in short, what children do when they are wild and free.

According to the children's mother, their delight was surpassed only by that of the family dog who, leashless at last in redolent wildness, spent a week in ecstasy.

No one is surprised when a leashed dog let loose shows wild happiness. No one is surprised when people of my generation reminisce about the wild adventures of our childhoods when even city kids had access to those uncared-for places where we led our private lives. I'm surprised, though, that so few people have noticed the *necessity* of wildness for children's happiness. Give them a ditch, a vacant lot, a fallen tree: that's where their wings unfold.

We summered on the island for two months every year from the time Aram, the youngest, was three. At the time we bought the old house, the ferry from the mainland held only a few cars; cargo was limited to what could be stashed on the small deck remaining, or goods were carried to the island on the fishermen's own boats. Much that was needed on the island was made there: nets, traps, buoys, the boats themselves. A farmer supplied milk and eggs. Electricity was from a patched-up town generator that often broke down, leaving us in candlelight. We found in the sagging barn a blacksmith's forge, a shoemaker's iron lasts, and handmade spindles, cod hooks, and quarrying equipment. The attic was entered by a trap door; one of the children came upon a dead rat there, mummified in the heat. And best of all, the whole place was an island— a treasure island of brimstone and seal skulls, boulders and crashing waves.

We did some things together. We gathered dye plants to color hanks of yarn. We picked huckleberries for pie. Most of the time, though, I did not know where my children were or what they were doing. As in my own childhood, they left in the morning, wandered back when they got hungry, were required to sit down for supper, than disappeared again in the long evening light to return only at bedtime.

Things have changed now on the island. "In the old days," warned the island doctor recently in his weekly health column, "you could go out all day and get a nice tan. Now one hour of sun can cause a burn! A single severe sunburn episode for a child increases the risk of melanoma later in life." He advised using a minimum SPF-30 sunblock (PABA free), a hat to shade face and ears, and cotton clothing to cover the rest of the body. The doctor failed to deal with the problem of how to protect the face from sunburn while wearing a bicycle helmet or with how to avoid getting long pants legs caught in the bicycle chain. Ticks that carry Lyme disease weren't yet a threat on the island, so he didn't need to mention that pants legs should be tucked into socks to discourage their entry. But what about poison ivy? Bees? And the neighbor's pesticided lawn?

A reason the *New York Times* writer might have reached for video games and Barbie dolls as summertime adventure is that she hadn't seen many children out-of-doors lately. It's gotten too dangerous out there.

Laura keeps me informed on the parenting scene in the Boston area: the latest is summer camps that promise air conditioning. Or do children go outdoors at camp anymore? The advertisements in the newspaper's parenting supplement that she sent to me were for foreign-language camps, computer camps, music camps. Not a one mentioned *camping*: under the stars, through the rain, around a bonfire, outdoors *overnight*, for heaven's sake! The same section advertised after-school classes, many of them open to children as young as four, for the same sorts of specialties offered by the camps. I was struck particularly, though, with ads for "body movement" classes. Doesn't it seem strange that children should be taught to move? Naturally, in these parlous times, camps and classes emphasized adult supervision.

It has become very difficult to be an animal child.

Risk assessment is not among humans' greatest intellectual talents. Being weak in the mathematical department myself, I bought some years back the book *Innumeracy*, by mathematician John Allen Paulos. It didn't improve my ability to calculate, but it did increase my awareness of how vulnerable we are to statistics that we don't really understand. Paulos cites, for example, the headline, "Holiday Carnage Kills 500 Over Four-Day Weekend." Careful parents reading this bad news might decide to forego in the future their usual Fourth of July drive to visit Grandma. However, the number of people killed in automobile accidents is about 500 in *any* four-day period.

Another example was a furor some years back over the danger of Dungeons and Dragons, since in a single year, 28 adolescents who played the game committed suicide. Missing from such reports was that the estimated number of teenage Dungeons and Dragons players at the time was 3 million and the separate fact that the annual suicide rate among that age group was 12 per 100,000. There are 30 one hundred thousands in three million, so the expected number of suicides (12 x 30) among teenage players would be 360—about thirteen times the actual number of deaths. One might claim—but just as wrongly—that the game had a protective effect on depressed adolescents.

Sometimes we even seem to prefer fear to facts. Fear of ticks has become almost a disease in its own right: I overhead one mother explain that she can't let her children play among the dunes at their beach home because they would certainly be bitten by ticks in the grass. Certainly they would. However, at the time an infected tick first sinks its jaws into flesh, the bacteria that cause Lyme disease are in the creature's gut; they have to migrate from there to the salivary glands—quite a distance for a microscopic germ—and from gland to mouth, before they can gain entry into the wound. The process is very slow—two days at least, sometimes longer. The fact is that a daily tick check at bath or bedtime is precaution enough to prevent infection.

But we seem to have to worry about something, and children are naturally worrisome. When most childhood deaths and disabilities were from infectious diseases like tuberculosis and polio, parents were saturated enough with germ anxiety that they hadn't the worry left for sunburn and rashes. We were bundled up in winter lest we "catch our death" and tucked into bed for even common colds. Scarlet fever, a streptococcal illness that not infrequently resulted in heart-valve damage and kidney disease, was cause for quarantine. I'm not sure that parental anxiety has actually increased, just that it is aimed now at different targets—and many of the targets are outdoors.

I must say I was a little nervous with those children monkeying about so high up in the trees. That may reflect a fundamental change: parents are older now than they used to be. My mother-in-law was nineteen when she had her first child; I was twenty-four. Laura was thirty-two when Ezra was born. Caution does grow with age.

And also, Laura knows much more about potential dangers to children than I know even now. Today's parents have access through television and the Internet to every possible worry about their children's health and welfare, leaving the larger picture lost in a welter of often conflicting, exaggerated, or unfounded detail. The larger picture is of American children who are increasingly anxious, inactive, obese, and indoors.

Peter Pan wanted to be afraid and brave. The girl left in the park after lock-out time (her name was Maimie) thought he could never be afraid because he was already ever so brave, the bravest boy she ever knew, what with his paddling to-and-fro across the Serpentine and living all alone on the island with no mother. And in fact, were it not for the permanence of that leave-taking, Maimie would have squeezed close to Peter in his thrush's nest and gone to live with him as a Betwixt-and-Between forever.

I think that is what is happening to our children. They don't intend, when they venture off, to take leave of us forever, but rather to attain the skill and courage that their nature tells them they must have to become one of us. It is we who, like Peter's mother (she had a "new" baby by then), bar the window to their return, for we neither grant them the freedom to explore the garden in their own way nor give them the knowledge of how we use its resources. We have created a new kind of Betwixt-and-Between that never quite grows up and that is not altogether human.

It is all a little sad, but let us not blame it on computers.

I've played some of the computer games that children play and parents complain about. They are compelling.

You enter a new landscape; it is strange and scary. Traps are hidden in your path; beasts lie in ambush; evil and malice lurk and spring, but you are all alone. If you are not brave enough to leap the chasm, not quick enough to zap the lunging beast, not sharp enough to detect what snares are set for your demise, you lose, often bloodily.

Adults, when they think of landscapes, may picture vistas along a scenic highway—postcard views, serenely distant and comprehensible in their entirety. Virtual landscapes in computer games are narrower, can't be taken in at a glance, are more as children see their surroundings: large scale, close up, episodic, and kinetic. They are like boulder-strewn shores where the scene unfolds underfoot because leaping is the only way to move and a stone may tilt or a wave rise frothing through a rift in the rock. Or the scene is like a forest in which the way must be learned detail by detail, through pathless trial and error, without knowing the lay of the land or what lies beyond the trees. Or, again, the way is obstacled by cliffs that cut the view or opens past the sudden rounding of a bend to a hole that leads into a cave, to a drop, a flood, a maze of creepy vegetation. You don't know what will happen if you touch the proffered food, push the loose stone, choose this turn or another—or fail to notice the coiled rope, the odd stick, the objects that might hold the secret of your endeavor or your life.

You ought to try playing just once to see how hard it is to stop. I like the Pokémon ones for their lack of bloodiness; Submarine Titans, though, sounds intriguing in an e-mail review I received: "It happened to the dinosaurs, and in the year 2047, or Y2K47, it's humankind's turn to deal with a massive celestial body that slams into the Earth and ravages the surface, sending the survivors to the bottom of the sea. Instead of working together toward a peaceful underwater kingdom, they start scavenging for resources and destroying each other. Stupid humans. Oh well, their loss is our gain. Submarine Titans takes us to that underwater place of the future for a unique twist on real-time strategy. Features a fully 3-D underwater universe, three unique civilizations, massive maps, and a powerful scenario editor . . ."

I was about to obey the reviewer's command, "Click below to preorder," only not being a child myself, I couldn't figure out if the game would work on my Mac. Better get some help from someone under thirty. But really, immerse yourself, then look out the window (provided it's not already midnight when you drag your eyes from the screen) and compare the two landscapes.

No place to hide. No trees to climb. No feathers to find. No trails to follow. No streams to wade. No fruits to gather. No flowers to pick. No stones to heap. No shells to hoard. No animals to chase or stalk or catch or fear. Nowhere to go and nothing to do, not on that boring, adult-exposed, and insidiously forbidding lawn.

Forbidding because, by its lack of privacy, mystery, risk, adventure, and treasure, we might as well have outright forbidden children to explore outdoors. And dangerous, too, because if we can't join them in their primitivity, and they can't join us in our sophistication, and they can't create for themselves and we won't create for them some common ground where the urges of childhood and the usages of adulthood converge, our flown sons and daughters may well remain enisled and estranged.

I don't like using the word *vision* as a verb; I'd rather *en*vision. But in Michigan I was asked to vision what the Rouge River might be

like if homeowners within its watershed replanted their land as natural habitat. The concern of the conference was water purity and
water conservation: the Rouge, which runs smack through Detroit,
is a seriously degraded river. But although it suffers from pollution
by industrial waste and farm runoff, the larger issue at the conference was exactly the one the children had addressed by planting a
retention basin. The Rouge, ravaging in spring, tears cruelly at its
banks. The river, drying in the summer, sinks into the mud.

Where is the Rouge? I rhetorically asked to open this visioning
exercise. Following its course on a map or scanning the flow from
its banks, a river appears to be confined to its basin. Actually, a river
extends throughout its watershed, sheeting off roofs, pouring down
rainspouts, streaming over lawns and under streets downhill to its
bed. A river is the rain that feeds it. Its quality depends on what
happens to the rain on the way to bed.

Now envision the strange and dangerous suburban terrain that
rainwater travels over on its way to the river: rain, pattering, then
pelting against the ground, runs down clipped blades of grass to
shallow roots, hits hard dirt and flows on, over impenetrable paving,
through iron grates, and into storm drains that lurk with gaping
maws. It has no chance to sink, to rest, to trickle deeply through
the lazy days of summer. (I could put this technically: as much as 95
percent of rainfall is immediately lost as runoff on a lawn.)

Now, vision! The rain falls on softer land. There are prairie
grasses with roots not inches deep but two *feet* deep, *six* feet deep,
and flowers that root three *yards* below the surface. The trees grow
in woods, and under the tall canopy grow layer after layer of smaller
trees, and shrubs, ferns, and forbs all slowing the rain in its descent,
all softening its blow against the ground, all rooting through the soil
to act like a sponge, cushioning and holding the water for a while.
(I can put this technically, too. There is zero runoff in natural habitat: the rain just sinks.)

And then down, and down, and down, slowly among webbed
roots, past fungal threads, filtered through silky clay, cleansed by
microorganisms, the water trickles over weeks and months, relaxed

in spring, still flowing through the summer, toward that bed you see—but clean and gentle now—the river.

I offer this narrative not asking that you cleanse any particular watershed where you may happen to reside—not that which feeds the Rouge or Nile or Serpentine or the Mianus where I live—but so that you may see that however you approach our present predicament, whether in educational or psychological parlance, following fact or metaphor, through science or art, you come upon, at every turn, the necessity of envisioning ecologically the land where we grow up.

"When I grow up," announced a lawn-bound girl in Michigan, "I want to dig holes in the dirt."

And, from another child in Florida a few weeks later, "When birds talk to one another, why do they always say the same thing?"

I have imagined what I would do if I were a science teacher. The fantasy is usually cut short, very short, by my being fired. I can't be fired from writing as I would from teaching, though, so I can indulge here.

The school year would start with a field trip, a scary one. I would take the little children out into the dark before the dawn, and we would huddle in the cold to see the separating of the sky from the land as the sun came up. Then I would start, "Once upon a time, the world was formless, and darkness lay upon the deep." Sound familiar? More gripping than "you remember that: *thirteen thousand years ago*"? And believable, too, if you have waited in the dark for dawn.

Science is strange tales of animalcules too small for eyes to see: a child must see them through a microscope to believe them; and see them alive, swimming in water from the pond where he, too, swims; and smell the bottom muck to know such things as *stink* and *rot* before it makes sense to teach how soil is a massive digestive system, what with all those animalcules eating the leavings of all creatures that die. Remember that, Ernest: *decay*.

I'd scramble eggs with peas for lunch: See that little stringy thing atop the raw yolk? See the tiny stem that holds the pea to its pod? See your belly button? We've all been fed, chicks and peas and children, through our umbilical cord once upon a time (here the principal walks in, sees the class half-undressed, and I am fired). But wouldn't the children be spellbound (they would love to go to school!), just as I was when listening to tales of Egypt past.

I remember being incredulous as a child that there had been a world before me: My mother once a child? No airplanes in the sky! There is no difference to a child's mind between history and natural history: to all children, creation begins anew at their own birth, awaits their discovery, unfolds to them through stories of how the present has come to be.

I remet Miss Moore by chance at an art exhibit one day when my oldest child was about the age that I had been when she was my teacher. Twenty-four years had passed. We recognized each other right away, which was no feat for me since she had changed little but in the graying of her hair, but I was startled that she could see in a middle-aged woman the child she had known so long ago. She said she never could forget my intense and absolute absorption in what she intended to convey. I asked her if she was still at work. She had retired from teaching school. Instead, Miss Moore was teaching terminally ill children to whom, in the brief time left to them, she could impart that joyful and passionate growth of comprehension that happens only when the tendriled child grips true bark.

Now I am torn between birds and beetles. Having finished the group of fishes (had you any idea that there are over eleven hundred species along the East Coast alone?), I feel that I have slighted the birds.

Mostly, I've whittled waterfowl, because I felt I could honorably defend dispensing with their feet. Peter anyway found ducks and such particularly stupid, for when he begged them to teach him how to swim, they told him to sit on the water and paddle his feet, not seeing that it was the sitting on the water that was the problem for him. Crows and thrushes are more sensible, each in its own way, but, without legs, they would look like amputees, and their legs are too skinny for me to manage. On top of that, my dipping back into the Nile during the writing of this chapter has reignited my early passion for beetles. In addition, I've discovered through Joshua and Laura a type of varnish that, when applied over dull paint, creates an iridescent sheen.

Think of it! A box of opalescent beetles!

And yet, the birds.

What if Ezra were to read *Peter Pan in Kensington Gardens* and discover that Solomon Caw, Peter's sage advisor, was not among the animals on the ark? This bothers me very much, that I should appear to have forgotten. Adults are forgetful, grandmas especially, but having solemnly sworn in my own youth that I would not grow up, I must certainly prove to him that I have not, not quite. Not enough to leave him stranded anyway.

But oh! How clever I have become in my old-crow days! I shall make eggs, freckled and speckled, spotted and blotched, in warm shades to rival the cobbles on the beach, as earthy as the clays of the Nile, and in goose green and robin's-egg blue besides, sized from hummer to emu, spherical to ovoid, or plain as a chicken egg.

Vision for yourself, Ezra, what may hatch from them.

(And don't ask me why, in the Deluge, it was necessary to save the fish.)

An Animal Past

I had tried several times to draw the Noah family. Each time I was dissatisfied. Their bipedal posture was difficult enough; worse were the australopithecine skulls: the chinless jaw, the lipless mouth, the lack of forehead. The drawings were without charm; the apish faces had no personality. Hominidae they may have been, but my attempts did not convey that they were people.

Then one night quite late, they came to me, the whole Noah tribe, thirteen of them in all. Seth the sober: a responsible but unamusing youth, holding a pike in the crook of his elbow and accompanied by his sweet, small wife who is pregnant, I believe, with Aram. Ham the sturdy: a likable lad, stockily built and of a mediating, placating temper, but capable of delivering the killing blow with his bludgeon. Ham's wife is a more wayward sort; her red-headed twins, just toddlers now, will be a handful to raise. Japheth is still a boy, going on twelve perhaps, whose interest is more in keeping than in killing animals. Perhaps Japheth most resembles his father, Noah, a farmer at heart, though stern with his children and not above smiting an unruly child with the staff he holds. Noah's wife is one of those quiet, patient women whose personality is most clearly expressed in her actions toward the children when they need protection. She carries an infant, a new grandchild, and there are two other children, both girls, whose parentage I am unsure of.

The carving was frustrating. I needed what is called "five-quarter" pine shelving (the extra width was necessary to accommodate the shoulders), but every board I examined at the lumberyard was sawed from the outer sapwood of the tree, not the much stronger heartwood that I had used for the other animals. Blades crunched and chewed the wood instead of cutting clean. Slight mishaps slumped shoulders, flattened faces, elongated necks. I had to make the best of such slips by following through with some consistency of posture and gesture. In this way, the images that I had drawn grew differently in the shaping and developed more uniquely than they had been born on the flat graph paper of my design.

Belatedly, for the figures were carved and awaiting paint by then, I reread the Noah story in Genesis and discovered that most of the children had not yet been born at the time the ark was built. But God's plan for the future of the family He had saved was interesting: when the flood was over, God gave Noah the rainbow sign with accompanying instructions. Noah and his sons were to go out into the dry land and multiply, each to generate his own nation, and his children's children also were to found separate peoples. I painted the family, therefore, in a rainbow of flesh tones, from blackest Noah to fairest twins.

God's second instruction to Noah concerned the animals that had been saved aboard the ark: "And the fear of you and the dread of you shall be upon every beast of the earth, and upon every fowl of the air, upon all that moveth upon the earth, and upon all the fishes of the sea; into your hands they are delivered. Every moving thing that liveth shall be food for you; even as the green herb that I have given you."

Except for one caveat—that the lifeblood of man and beast were to be offered to God as His due for creating all life—no further moral guidance regarding the relationships between humans and others of God's creatures was forthcoming.

Genesis still lay open to the Deluge when the newspaper reported what seemed a parallel story. It had been known for some time that the first migration of anatomically modern man out of Africa about one hundred thousand years ago had gotten no farther than today's Israel, presumably because the attempt was thwarted either by the cold of the Ice Age or by those experts at Ice Age survival, the Neandertals.

Neandertals, *Homo sapiens neanderthalensis*, then occupied the eastern Mediterranean, and from there had spread westward and northward over much of Europe. They were truly "giants in the earth": thick boned, barrel chested, with arms and hands far stronger than modern humans, and sometimes tall as well. One whopping male stood five feet, ten inches and had the largest cranial capacity of any hominid fossil yet found. The Neandertal brain lay behind the eyes, not atop them as in modern man: they were bony browed, with receding chin and sloping skull, but we can't assume they were less brainy than other *Homo* kin. Through most of their history, Neandertal tools and weaponry (there is evidence that they used spears) were as advanced as those of contemporary *Homo sapiens sapiens*, who evolved (depending on who is interpreting which fossils) somewhere between one hundred thousand and two hundred thousand years ago. Neandertals lived in caves, built hearths, and cooked over the fire. Peas parched on oak coals were uncovered at a Mediterranean site.

One fossil find shows that Neandertals lived in groups as large as eighty people; others suggest ritual burial: the corpse positioned with arms laid across the chest and belly or encircled by inward-pointing pairs of wild-ibex horns. Some remains show distinctive signs of cannibalism: the marrow-rich ends of upper arm bones, along with meaty thighs, are missing from the skeletons, and other bones bear cut marks made by human tools, not carnivore teeth. The most complete Neandertal skeleton, dating to sixty thousand years ago, includes the hyoid bone which, embedded in the throat, anchors the muscles necessary for speech.

So one can see why, adventuring again out of Africa some fifty thousand years after the first attempt, *H. sapiens* would have been wise to avoid so formidable an opponent, but if not overland across Suez into Israel, then how? Every other route is over water.

Noah built a boat, and the estimated population of about two thousand individuals who successfully dispersed from Africa also must have built boats or rafts, though we do not know what kind. The newspaper reported the discovery of the route they took and the course of their dispersal. They left East Africa from what is now Ethiopia, crossed the Red Sea at its narrow southern neck, continued along a coastal route around the Arabian peninsula, and then boated the Strait of Hormuz to a landing on the Indian subcontinent. The course was traced through genetic comparisons among populations of modern Ethiopians, Indians, and Saudi Arabians, all of whom show similarities of DNA that are not found in any Mediterranean peoples. Further comparisons showed that the route continued into Southeast Asia, island hopped through Oceania, and reached Australia by forty thousand years ago. That feat would have required some form of navigation. At about the same time, *H. sapiens* doubled back toward the Mediterranean and moved onward into Europe. The Noah story is, in a sense, a second creation, for the flood destroys every descendant of Adam and Eve save Noah and his immediate family. So, too, by thirty thousand years ago, the tide of modern man overcame the Neandertals, and they became extinct.

Two other pieces of evidence, both dating to the time of the dispersal, suggest that something new was happening in the human mind: the invention of an elaborate and specialized set of tools, and the first appearance of art. Perhaps Neandertals communicated by ritual, perhaps by muscular speech, but that postdispersal humans drew pictures and carved images, navigated by sun or stars, and invented tools as they were needed for novel jobs, supposes detailed and articulate communication, very possibly language in as sophisticated a form as ours has today. Anatomically modern humans had been around for ages; behaviorly modern humans were a second creation, borne across the waters through all the world.

But, says Genesis, God was fed up with the whole human thing: "I will not again curse the ground any more for man's sake; for the imagination of man's heart is evil from his youth."

I do think He was hasty in coming to that conclusion, but from the point of view of other species, we certainly are cause for fear and dread: our record regarding the animals delivered into our hands is outstandingly bad.

The megafauna that survived the Ice Age, including the cave bears, mammoths, mastodons, sabre-toothed cats, and several species of giant ground sloth that were prey or predator of Neandertals, in short order were hunted to extinction throughout the northern regions as the glaciers receded. Once-upon-a-timers like to think that the respect and reverence tribal peoples showed toward prey animals evidences a conservation ethic, but more careful attention to ritual significance suggests the intention was appeasement to encourage the prey's continued deliverance into the hunters' hands. There have been times of apparent harmony of humankind with nature, but over the long run, these have proved to be transient states of ecological equilibrium that have existed only until the population outgrows its natural resources.

When this occurs, we have historically exercised one of two options, neither of them morally driven: invent a new technology to exploit the homeland more efficiently or invade a neighboring land to increase the economic base. (A third alternative, which is to retreat from a materially advanced culture to a less consumptive way of life, has often happened, but not by choice.) Thus, bones in the burying grounds of people in the throes of agricultural invention show that starving preceded planting at every location where farming first began. Bison barely escaped extinction during the nineteenth-century slaughter for commerce in their tongues and hides but, contrary to notions of the noble savage, Native Americans were heavily involved in that trade: the surviving herd happened to inhabit a no-man's-land where neither of two warring tribes dared to hunt them.

We are all descended from warring tribes of hunters; our legacy is genocide and extinction.

How can it be that Noah's family, chosen for their goodness, were so bad that the Lord himself gave up on them before they even had dispersed over the flood-ravaged land?

Emma was ten when she got a dog of her own. I thought the gift overdue for a child so capable as she, who knitted cotton pot holders when she was in kindergarten and who, by the time she got her dog, could have cooked a whole meal while tending to her sister, Phoebe, as well. But Rafael and his wife, Jennifer, were awaiting some special act of responsibility to indicate Emma's readiness for dog care, and this is how that happened:

The family had gone to a fair with some of Emma's and Phoebe's friends. The children had been told they could go on a hayride but would have to be back at that spot to meet the parents at a certain time. The hayride was delayed, and Emma, realizing that the children would not be back at the appointed time but not wanting the others to miss the ride, stayed behind to explain to her parents what had happened.

Emma is a good child.

Of all human traits that appear to set humans apart from animals, morality is the one most exclusively claimed and also most exclusively attributed to culture. That notion is captured succinctly when, in the face of amoral acts, we accuse the perpetrator of being an "animal." Animals, by definition, cannot be *humane*.

Yet many have been convinced that our inborn nature also is bestial—greedy, selfish, and violent. Rules of behavior, the knowledge of right and wrong, and the practice of altruism must be imposed on children from the outside by their native culture and maintained throughout life by the force of law, the pressure of religion, or the condemnation of society. Where, though, could culture come from if not from within ourselves?

Good Natured, the book that first stimulated my thoughts along this line, was written by leading primatologist Frans de Waal, who has devoted his life to studying primate societies both in captive colonies and in the wild. He and other workers in the field have noted incipient morality in several primate species, most notably the apes. Altruism itself—the sacrifice of one's own interests for the sake of others—goes back much further in evolutionary history, for it is the hallmark of motherhood.

Mothering animals necessarily behave altruistically toward their infants. They risk their own welfare in defense of their young and share their own resources in their nurturance. Parental interests are served in the long run by the greater survivorship of the nurtured young who carry their genes into descending generations, so in an evolutionary sense, a wren or mouse can be said to have a selfish "motive." Or so the biologist realizes, but the animal does not. Its emotional attachment to its young and its urge to care for them are no less real for having been selected by the disinterested workings of nature. Jays who postpone their own reproduction in order to help their mother raise a new batch of sisters and brothers have an interest in the survival of siblings who share their genes, but we cannot deny the fact of their family tie.

Self-interest may also lurk in the genes of the vampire bat who, returning with a full belly, regurgitates blood not only to its own young, but also to unrelated members of the group who have gone hungry. The "motive" is reciprocity: a vampire bat can't survive more than two nights without food, so any individual might find itself in dire circumstances if others did not come to its rescue when in need. Although generosity can't arise in the course of evolution if it is more likely to harm than to advantage its practitioner, feeding the hungry can hardly be called an act of selfishness. Crows have been observed vying with one another for the dangerous honor of attacking an owl, and female crows have been observed choosing the heroes for their bravery. We may calculate the reproductive advantage to both—the male by winning the opportunity to mate, the female by choosing a strong and brave partner to help rear their offspring—but the ensuing bond between the mated pair is nonetheless solicitous.

All these behaviors—self-sacrifice on behalf of kin, granting fa-

vors in expectation that they will be returned, and bravery itself—
are embedded in human nature, but they do not constitute morality. Morality is the internalization of a code of conduct, an inner
sense of right and wrong: a conscience.

Some highly intelligent and social species show behaviors so
strikingly "human" that it is tempting to think they act out of conscience. Dolphins will hold an injured companion at the surface of
the water to save it from drowning. Elephants will attempt to raise
a sick companion from the ground, tenderly stroke her with their
trunk and feet, and may place food into her mouth as well. Apes
and monkeys comfort each other when one is in distress, and chimpanzees assiduously attend to one another's wounds. Such acts of
succor presuppose affection for members of the group similar to
that of parents for their offspring but extending to friends as well as
kin and, in the case of dogs, even to members of another species.
But does a dolphin who puts less effort than the others into raising
his companion feel ashamed of his failure? Does the elephant who
has not helped her friend suffer guilt? Aid and comfort to those in
distress may be simply conduct that the animals have been taught to
do, not what they feel they *ought* to do. (I have taught Girl to keep
out of the garbage; she gets into it anyway if I am not at home.)

Emma's behavior was not selfless. Quite the opposite, moral decisions require a firm sense of self. Emma had to imagine, through
her own responses, the other children's incipient disappointment as
well as her parents' potential distress. She had to consider her own
position as eldest child and the effect of her action on her reputation in the eyes of others. She had to recognize herself not only as
the person in the mirror—children can do that at a very early age—
but in the social mirror held up to her by the reactions of others:
the self as it is reflected from outside itself.

Chimpanzees are among the few animals who can recognize
themselves in a mirror (as often evidenced by their turning and
looking over their shoulder to view their own behind!) and also
among the few who can resolve difficulties in a manner that approaches Emma's feat.

De Waal points out the many similarities between chimp societies and ours. The young remain dependent for many years and, in fact, never do outgrow dependence on the group to locate and share food, defend against predators and enemies, and provide emotional support. Males (and, to a lesser extent, females) are ranked in dominance from the acknowledged leader of the group, through a "middle-management" level that is more shifting and fluid, to the lowest-ranking individuals. Rank confers advantages: the deference of others, their defense against harrassment, more affectionate grooming, greater shares of food, and increased access to mates. Political power, though, is not achieved by brute force alone; the dominant male may have won his position through alliance with another male, and the social positions of both sexes at every level are supported by friends at the same time that they are threatened by rivals.

Social tension is inherent in this vying for position, and yet de Waal emphasizes that for an emotionally volatile animal, and one that is also aggressive and armed with dangerous fangs, relations are remarkably stable and peaceful most of the time. The leader, though challenged, may hold his position for a decade or more. Squabbles may be broken up by the intervention of a mediator and ruffled tempers soothed by others in the group. Sometimes a chimpanzee will remove a weapon, such as a stick or rock, from the hand of a would-be aggressor. And after a fight, the combatants reconcile with kisses, hugs, and grooming (as well as care of any wounds inflicted) to the evident relief and even celebration of the onlookers.

De Waal describes chimpanzee life as being lived within a social cage. Every individual is known to every other, kinship is recognized too, and all are aware of the shifting social structure of rivalry and affiliation within the group. Note is taken of transgressions— the ally who fails to come to a friend's defense, the hunter who is reluctant to share his prey—and lack of generosity is reflected in a decrease of reciprocity as well as loss of social status. Sometimes a chimpanzee who is slow to make peace after a quarrel is punished by bystanders for his or her failure to mend the breach in the community.

This is not to say that chimps are conscientious: their deficiency in symbolic representation precludes the formation of ideals and, though possibly embarrassed when caught in a transgression, chimps show no evidence of lasting guilt. But whether through internal compunction or external intervention, there results in chimpanzee society the essence of Emma's decision: to be successfully dependent, one has to be dependable.

De Waal's point is that the components of morality evolve in the context of social necessity. He further insists that social necessity evolves in the context of environment. While food is plentiful in the forests chimpanzees inhabit, it is spottily distributed, and it is crucial that those who find it call the others to the feast. To find food and process it—and especially to provide meat—require skills that the young gain only through many years of learning from the group. If food were as evenly distributed as grass on the prairie, and education of the young were less critical to its provision, the evolution of morality in chimps would have advanced no further than that of cows.

As it is, chimp goodness doesn't reach very far. Fieldwork by Jane Goodall and other observers has revealed atrocious behavior among our closest relatives: opportunistic murder of unguarded strangers, planned raids against neighboring tribes, brutal rape of struggling females, infanticide, cannibalism. Far from being the vegetarians they once had been supposed, the chimpanzees Goodall observed capture and kill per year fully 10 percent of the red colobus monkey population, and they do not do so casually. In one of many observations, a party of eleven males, using drivers to herd the prey and blockers to prevent their escape, captured seven monkeys in a single hunt. As was noted previously, they tore apart the screaming prey as though the monkeys were merely animated food.

Yet these same individuals were the backbone of their community. De Waal emphasized in his work among captive colonies the political structure by which in-group aggression is defused and courage mounted for violence to others. We have to account for killing not as an exception to our good nature, but as integral to it: the combined work of Goodall and de Waal suggests that friendly cooperation evolved in the service of providing meat and disposing of enemies. The goodness found among apes concerns their behavior toward others of their group: beasts and strangers have never been the subject of their morality.

This is our animal past: the australopithecine within us. Our human present, however, differs in one critical respect. Our symbolic mind, by its ability to place a single object into multiple categories, can consider a stranger as threat or guest; a tree as utilitarian or sacred; a dog as meat, cur, worker, pet. Further, we can group ourselves within categories of others: identify with starving children of alien and distant tribes or with baby harp seals clubbed for their silvery-soft fur. And, we can assume that other life-forms and even inanimate objects are in identity with us: that a cat, like a loyal servant, can be the familiar of a witch; that a mountain, like an elder, can resent our disrespect. Culture has not created human morality, but each society can and does define for its members what is to be brought within its reach.

De Waal includes in his book an illustration of how the reach of our morality depends on the depth of our resources. The illustration is of a pyramid floating in water. At the top of the pyramid is individual self-interest. Just below selfishness lie the interests of family and kin, then increasingly broad concern for community, tribe, nation, and finally for the other life-forms to which altruism might extend. The water represents the buoyancy of material and social resources: the thinner the resources, the less of the pyramid will surface. Self-interest may be all that is revealed in the worst of times. As resources increase, the pyramid floats higher: people can afford to broaden the base of their generosity. At the highest level of prosperity and contentment, human nature naturally spreads its conscience over the entire environment that has raised it to that height.

Yet what has surfaced in these prosperous times is the "Me

Generation": abandoners of community, divorcers of family, shirk-
ers of public service. At the same time that our attentiveness toward
one another seems to have slipped badly, we have come to express
unprecedented concern for animal welfare: for protecting endangered species, improving the living conditions of domestic and captive animals, discouraging hunting, and even granting animals legal
rights in our courts of law.

Except for our buoyant ego, it would appear that the rest of de
Waal's pyramid is floating upside down.

In the opening scene of *A Death in the Family*, by James Agee, the
men in the neighborhood home from work in the early evening
stand hose in hand, watering their lawns. The image is of mutual
male display, but of morality as well as masculinity.

Opportunity to exhibit dependability is limited in modern
communities. Residents have not grown up together; they do not
share a common background; neighbors move in and move away
again; there is no daily meeting at the village store or post office;
people go to work, come home, and go indoors. Civic contribu-
tions—the committees people join, the charities they support, the
interests they espouse—are distributed over a broad landscape of
possible social connections. The work each person does tends to be
unrelated to the work that others do, and those who provide are
unknown to those who are provisioned. Even the children are prevented from casual congregation by the many and disparate after-
school activities in which they are engaged.

This is not the sort of society in which morality evolved nor
even the kind of community by which morality has been maintained in rural villages and close urban neighborhoods where interests literally collided in the streets. Morality and the precedents for
it in ape society are fundamentally in the service of maintaining stable relationships within the community: this has been achieved
through each individual remaining continuously aware of the status
of every other and each demonstrating reliability through publicly
revealed behavior.

Now, in our sacrosanct autonomy, we have little choice but to display status in the size and impressiveness of our homes and to proclaim our obedience to community interest in the nurturing of our lawns. In case we don't willingly comply, rules may be laid down: no bird feeders, no vegetable gardens, no laundry lines, no dogs. Conformity in outward appearance, to a large degree, has replaced conformity by conduct and reciprocity, and with the privatization of the nuclear family has come a sense of personal isolation from the group. Yet we are no less moral animals than we ever were, and I think we are uncomfortable to see our children maintaining their position among peers by the quality of their sneakers and the brand name on their jeans.

Several times I've run into an interesting statistic in the books I read: the people we count as friends—those with whom we comfortably share meals and other forms of visiting—number no more than 150 (and usually fewer). We are acquainted with many others by name and face, and by some rough idea of personality, but we seem to be biologically limited to a smallish circle of those whom we can know in a more familiar sense and who we feel know us. The number is about the upper limit of any group that can be sustained by a hunting/gathering economy and not much less than can be sustained by a subsistence farming community.

So it may be that, in addition to the fact that residents of a tract development or a block of apartment houses are not assembled in common purpose, the sheer scale of the community may stand in the way of our sense of belonging to it. We seem to realize the importance of social scale for children when we call for smaller classes and smaller schools within the neighborhood. The trend toward gated communities, neighborhood gardens, pocket parks, and local streets closed to traffic indicate our urge to safely congregate where we can consult the social mirror. But for many of us, and possibly for most, the urge is thwarted or was extinguished before it had much chance to grow.

Aware of that difficulty, many have proposed that we teach community and family values in school. The proposal is as hopeless as teaching children what an apple tree is without their experiencing the tree or instructing them on how to fish without going fishing. A sense of community is absorbed through experience of the actual community, just as family values are incorporated within the actual family. So we are left with our good nature flapping raggedly without the pole that once lifted it aloft, and we are lonely.

I think that is why the pyramid seems to be stacked topsy-turvy. We are adopting animals into the human family to vent a moral need. But having said that, I see another way of looking at the trend: we are turning from our human family in favor of those animals we idealize as more worthy of our grace than ourselves.

A woman confronted me about my attitude toward wildlife. I had made no effort to rescue an injured goose, and she couldn't see how I could be so callous. She believed that "if we happen upon an injured animal, we are meant to find and help it." She herself had brought a three-legged deer safely through the snowy winter by clearing a path to her feeder.

I wasn't troubled by the rebuke. I'd been advised by an ornithologist at my local Audubon chapter that there was nothing I could do for the hurt goose. It had been shunned by mate and tribe, and to save it would have been to offer it a lifelong agony of solitary confinement. But my correspondent was clearly reaching for an ethic.

Her concern was taken up recently at an international symposium assembled in quest of an ethic to guide our relations with wildlife. A friend who attended the symposium returned with an answer that satisfied her and that, at first, seemed unassailable to me. Animals, humans included, have a right to their habitat. Further, they have a right to protect that habitat against the depredations of other species. She illustrated with germs: germs have a right to live with us; we are their habitat. But if they cause disease, we have an equal right to defend ourselves against them.

When I tried to extend this ethic to deer, though, I ran into trouble. Deer habitat is light woods and open edges where bushes grow. Our habitat is scattered trees and open ground where we grow bushes. Deer can't see the difference. They eat it all and convert the extra calories to fawns, with the result that herds have increased beyond the capacity of their "rightful" habitat to support them.

I visited a woodland preserve where deer have been excluded for a decade. The entire understory was green with small trees, shrubs, and saplings in every stage of growth below the mature oak canopy. The ground was clothed with ferns and forest flowers. Beyond the chain-link fence, where deer roam freely, the woodland looked like someone had gone through it with a brush hog. The deer had consumed everything within their reach; the forest was beyond regeneration.

What good is it to defend deer rights to habitat that they themselves have made incapable of supporting them? In what sense is the residential landscape our habitat when it doesn't support us? If deer rely on my bushes for their food, isn't my yard more rightfully their habitat than it is mine? And yet I don't want them eating my salad garden.

"Shoot 'em!" Wayne would say, without a thought for ethics.

Wayne Paessler, Alma's stocky groundskeeper who speaks in bursts and growls almost as often as he smiles, keeps a crippled crow in his garage. Each spring he waits for his "baby" to arrive: one spring the baby was an orphaned squirrel that he carried in his jacket pocket and fed at three-hour intervals from a bottle. Another spring it was an injured fawn. One day Wayne pointed out two bucks in the meadow. "The boys of summer," he called them, explaining that male deer buddy up like that all season, best friends "until they try to kill each other in the fall." Wayne told me there's a famous painting with that title showing a bachelor party of antlered stags. He once saw the painting in reproduction and wanted to buy it. It cost $400. "Hell, I could get a new hunting rifle for that," Wayne said, "and hang the real thing on my wall."

Wayne's judgments are contingent and informed. He saves a fawn and kills a buck in the same breath, as it were, without a sense of contradiction: the fawn is in pain; there are too many deer.

Wayne is in perpetual swing between caring for and killing. "Shoot one and thirty come to the funeral," he growls when asked to cull the herd at home (he is showing us the forage crop he planted to help deer through the winter), and then—not as brute culler but as fair hunter—he does, in fact, shoot a home buck, dresses it himself, and deftly carves a venison roast for our Christmas dinner.

Wayne fed last spring's baby for two weeks, then put the young squirrel on a tree and said good-bye. I've heard him cussing the squirrels that dig out bulbs he's planted, and when one summer the population rose to the extent that hungry squirrels were eating his tomatoes, he did, in fact, shoot some. I prefer this circumstantial alternation of compassion with common sense to any moral certitude that plunges like a federal interstate toward a rigid goal. Rigidity undermines the purpose of morality, which is to negotiate among competing interests to preserve the common good.

But just as it is hard for children to participate in family interests when the basis for the home economy is opaque to them, and hard to participate in community when interdependence is not apparent, and hard to trust food without knowing who provides it, so is it hard to preserve the general good of the environment without having experienced the relationships within it. Those who defend deer from any attempt to control their number simply don't know that the woods they've ruined are bereft of even the young oaks that would replace their elders.

Our modulated response to dogs compared to our immoderate response to wolves says something about the difference between experience and ignorance. During just the last hundred years, American attitudes toward wolves has swung wildly between hatred so viciously expressed that one can hardly bear to read about it and love so blindly romantic that predation is ennobled.

Barry Lopez describes in *Of Wolves and Men* how by midway
into the twentieth century, wolves had been exterminated throughout the contiguous forty-eight states (except for a remnant population in northern Minnesota and an even smaller tribe on Isle
Royale in Michigan) through a pogrom conducted by gun, steel
trap, and finally through a federal program of massive poisoning
with strychnine (which also killed coyotes, mountain lions, eagles,
dogs, and children). Extermination was intentional. What had
started as wolf management to protect cattlemen from stock
losses—and at first was handled by hunters and trappers with intimate knowledge of their prey—was inflamed in the public mind by
such writers as William Hornaday, quoted by Lopez from *The
American Natural History*:

> Of all the wild creatures in North America, none are more
> despicable than wolves. There is no depth of meanness,
> treachery or cruelty to which they do not cheerfully de-
> scend. They are the only animals on earth which make a
> regular practice of killing and devouring their wounded
> companions, and eating their own dead.

This was in no way true, but neither are wolves wise cullers of
only the sick and weak. They are predators who, as the land where
"the deer and the antelope roam" was turned over to ranching, had
to switch their diet to the only remaining large prey. Finally, the
few wolves still living in the Southwest were those clever enough to
evade hunters' every ploy. They were called "outlaws." Ernest
Thompson Seton, naturalist, hunter, writer, and a hero of mine until I learned more about him, was called upon to kill an outlaw
couple, the Currumpaw Wolf and his mate, Blanca. Seton prepared
bait according to a complicated recipe of his own devising that included cheese, beef kidney fat, strychnine, and cyanide, only to
have the male wolf gather up four pieces of Seton's preparation into
a pile and defecate on them. Eventually, Seton caught Blanca in a

steel trap, which he and a friend approached on horseback. Then, "We each threw a lasso over the neck of the doomed wolf, and strained our horses in opposite directions until the blood burst from her mouth, her eyes glazed, her limbs stiffened and then fell limp."

Blanca's mate, the Currumpaw Wolf, followed the scent of her body to the ranch where her corpse had been taken, and there on the following day, he was trapped in a nest of steel jaws. Instead of killing him forthwith, Seton chained him for the night. The wolf was found dead the next morning and, in Lopez's words, "without a wound or any sign of struggle." Seton, he adds, "deeply moved by what had happened, placed his dead body in the shed next to Blanca's." There is no record of whether Seton accepted the thousand-dollar bounty that had been placed on the outlaw male. Did he bury the pair together? How can the same person kill with such unreasonable cruelty yet just as unreasonably suppose his prey to have died of a broken heart?

The year was 1894. It would be another three decades before field studies of wolves began to reveal what they are really like, some fifty years before Lopez differentiated for a popular audience the mythical wolf from the actual one, and close to a century before any effort was begun to achieve a balanced policy of wolf reintroduction and conservation.

Our broad concern with dogs, in contrast, encompasses leash laws, rabies shots, puppy toys, health foods, rain boots, adoption agencies, burial grounds, and such morally charged procedures as eugenics, sterilization, and euthanasia. Despite occasional idealizing, as in the *Lassie* television series, and flurries of demonizing, as when one pit bull's insane rampage leads us to indict the whole breed, on the whole, we remain flexible in our judgments about dogs, able to weigh, for example, an old dog's pain against our grief at killing it or a puppy's destructive chewing against our responsibility to train it.

Even so, I will get letters complaining that I "allow" Girl to kill mice and rabbits—and more letters still now that I'm admitting that she has also eaten fledging birds fallen from the nest. For all that Girl is adorable, she is a predator. Her evolution determined her recognition of grassy habitat, her alertness to rustling sounds, her chase and chomp response to small animals that move within her sight. We pick and choose among species, favoring bunnies over beetles and stags over snakes, not only because we are driven by innate recognitions of what is cute or awesome, creepy or sneaky; we lack the ecological experience to recognize the whole picture, in which authenticity must be granted to every creature's role in supporting the dynamics of its environment, including that of our own human species. Lacking that experience, our culture also has produced few narratives that express an ecological view.

We get stuck in the childish morals of the Bambi story, in which all deer are good and all humans bad (they kill; they set the forest on fire), without seeing that such black-and-white divisions are not different from racial prejudice. We identify with "our kind," the noble and gentle deer, and whoever harms them—us!—are the enemy. Speak of pitfalls of the symbolic mind!

And yet, Marjorie Kinnan Rawlings, living alone in the Florida scrub, supporting herself at first by raising oranges, gave us *The Yearling*. It is a rare tale that faces squarely the conflicts of interest inherent in community: the beloved deer; its threat to the corn crop critical to the family's survival through the winter; and, tragically but necessarily, its killing by the boy who loved it most.

Felix Salten's *Bambi* was read to me; I was given *The Yearling* to read by myself. I can't exactly figure the years between—maybe six to twelve, the central years of childhood. At first, children haven't much more to go on than ape morality—good and bad, them and us, the primitive basis for what culture is to elaborate, define, and make more sophisticated. At first, a child sees as "unfair" her exclusion *from* others who are enjoying a hayride; years later, her concept of fairness has grown to include herself *among* others. For that to happen, she has to have come to appreciate the larger picture— in fact, an ecological view of human relationships that is dynamic, involving a multiplicity of roles shifting over time and according to circumstance, and "fair" only in the sense of balancing one need against another. Like all other constructs—*round, salamander*—experience precedes comprehension. We can be fair to dogs because we have been among them.

To move from respect for a single species to Wayne's untutored moderation regarding many species or a naturalist's trained deliberation regarding whole ecosystems, we must gift children with the living environment that we presently withhold.

Ezra did not sleep through the night until he was nearly two, when he adopted as his sleeping companion a stuffed Mickey Mouse. Perhaps it is merely coincidence that Samantha, too, chose Mickey and that two generations earlier their grandfather Marty had been inseparable from his Mouse. But it is also remarkable that this particular Disney character has been used often by psychologists to illustrate our inborn bias for babyish shapes and faces.

The original Mickey was a skinny rodent whose behavior was ratty (or bratty) too. Over the years, animators shortened his limbs, plumped his body, enlarged his head, shortened his face, and gave him great big eyes. By the time of Marty's childhood, the Mouse had become childlike, and by now, he is positively infantile in features and proportion. Mickey no longer resembles a mouse; Ezra's version does not even have a tail.

Startlingly, a similar transformation occurs in animals as they are domesticated. Archaeologists can date domestication by an animal's bones: compared to the wild prototype, the limb bones of a domesticated sheep, ox, or pig are shorter and stouter, the skull broader and the forehead more rounded, the snout blunter and the eyes larger in proportion to the face. Recently, an accidental experiment showed how fast the process of juvenilization can occur. The animals were caged, untamed foxes raised for their fur. Hoping to make the foxes easier to handle prior to slaughtering, the fur farm decided to breed preferentially those individuals who were the most docile. Within thirty-five generations—only forty years' time—descendants of this selective breeding had changed in physical ways. They became shorter, fatter, and snub-nosed; their wild coloring was interrupted by white markings; their ears flopped; their tails curled. They became "cute."

It is well-known that young mammals are more docile than adults; it had not been guessed that juvenile temperament is in some way genetically linked with juvenile morphology. So, as our social needs changed us to plump-cheeked, playful humans, we, in turn, domesticated wild wolves to wag-tailed puppy dogs.

The original range of wolves was equaled only by the range of humans. Subpopulations—comparable to breeds but all the same species, *Canis lupus*—inhabited every environment, grassland or forest, mountain or plain, icy to tropical, jungle to desert, on every continent except Antarctica and Australia. Wolves vary in color from black through shades of gray to white, in size from modest to the great timber wolf, which can weigh over two hundred pounds, and in personality almost as much as chimpanzees or children.

Wolves' hunting way of life, and the social structure that enables it, so paralleled that of humans during the many thousands of years of our dispersal that it was inevitable that the two species should run together: run with the caribou, run with the sheep, run with the deer, the horse, the pig, and antelope, buffalo, bison, and gazelle before any prey at all had been domesticated. Except for the substitution of missiles for teeth, our hunting strategies were the same: tracking, herding, blocking, ambushing, culling, and group attack. As individuals, wolves and humans can bring down small game on the order of a rabbit or a grouse, but both species are specialists in bringing down large game by coordinated predation, and we must have friendship within our hunting tribe to do so.

There are other ways than ours and wolves' to achieve social cohesion. African hunting "dogs" (*Lycaon pictus*, not of the canid genus) maintain the peace by regurgitating to one another but coordinate their activities more by mutual appeasement and arousal than by political organization. Both wolves and humans maintain clear dominance hierachies, assign roles according to individual skills and circumstances, and communicate through facial expressions, postures, gestures, and sounds that are far more articulate than vomit. It is simply not in our vocabulary to throw up in love of one another, and so it is impossible for us to ally ourselves with *Lycaon*. But we bow submissively, stare down opponents, avert our gaze to avoid confrontation, kiss to greet, crouch in invitation to play, whine in supplication, growl in warning, and bark commands to one another. We also hunger for a hero who will lead us (both wolf and human relations barbarously deteriorate during periods of social disruption) and are fiercely tribal in our loyalties.

So it is hardly surprising that wolves were domesticated into what is now known as the separate species *Canis familiaris* earlier than any other animal—twelve thousand years ago, according to remains found in Idaho and Iraq; twenty thousand years ago, according to one find in the Yukon—and in many different places by dispersing tribes: wherever there are people, there are dogs.

The wild dingoes of Australia are descended from semidomesticated wolves brought to that continent ten millennia after the first dispersing *H. sapiens* arrived but before one could call them dogs. Dingoes, though given the name *C. familiaris*, have never been fully domesticated: they are not spotted, drop eared, or curly tailed. They are not used for hunting and are not purposefully fed or bred. They are taken in as captured pups and allowed to scavenge. Anthropologists studying Aboriginal cultures have come to the opinion that the dingoes' primary function in those societies is to huddle with people to keep them warm at night.

Like Mickey Mouse with Ezra.

Like me with Girl—who, I must say, has no more purpose in my life than to prolong my joy in motherhood and whose cute nose is definitely twisted out of joint when I cuddle a grandchild instead.

But poi dogs of the South Pacific were caged and fattened for the stew pot, and pariah dogs that hang about North African villages are treated as the outcasts that their name has come to mean.

In trying to figure out how it is that children who cuddle with teddy bears as though they were human babies can grow up demonizing or idealizing grizzlies—or simply indifferent to their fate— I considered the strange phenomenon of Tamagotchi, which in Japanese means "cute little egg":

These egg-shaped, palm-size toys required that the child nurture the image of an animal on a tiny computer screen. Beeps reminded the owner when the pet needed to be fed, exercised, cleaned, cuddled, or given medicine to nurse it through an illness. Neglect caused the pet to die. To keep the animal alive, children had to attend to its needs throughout the day, sometimes at five-minute intervals, and for weeks until, inevitably, it died anyway.

Within a month of their appearance in toy stores, Tamagotchi were being banned from classrooms. Children were so concerned with their cyberpet that they'd interrupt a test to care for it. Some were terrorized by guilt when they failed to meet their pet's demands, and many were inconsolable when it died. Virtual or not, Tamagotchi revealed the strength of children's urge to nurture and the depth of the emotional tie their nurturing creates.

Many parents and most preschools assume that it's important for children to take part in caring for a pet. The usual reason given is that children thereby learn "responsibility," as in cleaning the gerbil cage or feeding the parakeet. The word "responsibility," though, doesn't seem to adequately express the depth of feeling that young children may have for their pet. My first pet, a white mouse, loved me. It was therefore a tragic betrayal when I killed it by spinning it too fast in its exercise wheel.

An Indian woman, explaining to an outsider the ways of her tribe, referred to its origin in the time when "animals could speak to humans." We might refer to the era of childhood as the time when they and other animals speak the same language, for children talk to animals as though there were no barrier to their verbal communication, even supplying the animal's answer in the human tongue.

There is a biological parsimony at work here: the mind comes with clues to direct interest toward animals but is otherwise uncommitted, so the child must experience the elaboration of comprehension in whatever environment she finds herself. It does seem, though, that this circuitry is more complicated than that which alerts babies to the color red. It is selective, as is apparent from even very young children's reluctance to handle snakes and spiders compared to chicks and bunnies. More extraordinary is that children seem prepared in their earliest years to identify with animals, to assume kinship whether or not their culture grants other creatures equivalence with humans. Young children are certain that animals—real, stuffed, or virtual—not only understand their words and moods, but experience the full gamut of human emotion, awareness, intelligence, and pain. Children even seem to favor animals as enactors in their fantasy and play. We "know" this about children: the characters in much of childhood literature are animals. Interestingly, the characters in these storybooks often are of several species, as in the tale of Chicken Little, or *Charlotte's Web*, *The Wind in the Willows*, and *Bambi* itself. The settings, too, imply an ecological context—farm, river, forest—for characters that otherwise appear as humans in animal drag.

For a while, it became stylish to forbid anthropomorphizing in animal storybooks. Authors were to write in the detached manner of a field biologist who notes behavior but draws no conclusions as to the animal's thoughts or emotions. This not only made for boring books, but for ones that were unnatural and untrue. Emotions reside in an ancient portion of the brain, and we have no reason to suppose that the ferocious Nile crocodile, when she carries her hatchlings in her mouth to the nursery where they will be guarded in their helpless youth, feels any less tenderness than we do when we carry a baby in our arms.

I think, too, that the decision was immoral, or at least it rasped against the roots of children's humanity. What have they to work with?

An innate attentiveness to animals: a toddler is interested in a book, fascinated with an eggbeater, but excited almost to bursting by a dog.

An urge to nurture so intense that if nothing warm and cuddly is available, an animated image motivates their care.

An animistic assumption that all lives are enspirited in analogy with humans, and therefore a readiness to identify even with forms of life quite unlike our own.

A sense of relationships among species, toad with mole, rat with pig, fawn with skunk and rabbit, and all of these with humans whether they enter into or are merely audience to the tale.

Even if children's early assumptions are wrong—even if the worm really doesn't feel the fish hook, even if the mouse isn't capable of loving, even if the spider lacks the slightest perception of a pig, and the dog doesn't understand whispered confidences, and the teddy bear is as blind with eyes as without them—anthropomorphism is the only moral basis children have for relationships with other species.

And maybe, after all, they are right.

Aram worked afternoons in Samantha's nursery school. Mornings there were very structured, but afternoons were more lenient, a free-play sort of biding time until parents picked up their children at the end of the working day.

The latest movie in the *Star Wars* saga had just appeared. Unlike the previous films, which involved only adults, this one went back in time to explore the childhood of the arch villain, Darth Vader. Children brought to see the movie (and that apparently was almost all of them) were therefore presented with the etiology of evil, the possibility that good children may turn into not merely powerful adults, but monstrously bad ones. The children were frightened.

The boys in particular began to defend themselves by enacting the scary characters, and this led to aggressive encounters in which children were scratched, hit, hurt, crying.

One day, Aram, with gifted insight and without word or warning, turned into a gorilla. Fearfully and with cautious mutterings—"huh huh huh huh"—he approached a swing. He touched it; it moved: in alarm, he called, "hoo hoo hoo hoo hoo!" and jumped back. Then another approach: "huh huh huh." A harder push, a strong one: the swing could not hurt him after all. He stood tall and beat his chest: "UH UH UH UH OOH OOH OOH OOH!" in triumphant crescendo.

The children stopped midplay. There was silence. Then one small gorilla tentatively approached the swing. Aram laid an arm over his shoulder and began to groom his head, picking through his hair, grunting reassuringly. They pushed the swing together, then celebrated victory over the alien threat with mutual chest thumping. Power and aggression are to protect, Aram had said without a word.

Over the ensuing weeks, children came quietly to him to be groomed when they were upset, and groomed one another too. Though still on their minds, the bad guys—the monster men—dropped out of their enactments. They had gained an animal understanding.

I once with Girl was treated to that rarity of interspecies communication, a clear view of the workings of her canine mind. Girl likes to be covered with a blanket when she naps. Her signal for me to come and cover her is a high yip. One day at Alma's house, she called for a blanket for her morning nap, but the dog blankets were in the laundry, and I told her so, several times—and finally with irritation when she yipped in my face and nipped my thigh for emphasis. "*No blanket!*" I barked. I thought I'd snapped some sense into Girl, but no. In a moment, I heard her demand again coming from a hallway that led to guest quarters in a portion of the house that was seldom used and where she had never been. There, at the very end of the long corridor, I found her sitting on a wooden chest, on top of two folded blankets.

Wagging her tail. Grinning, I thought.

I am glad that my family encouraged my perception of canine communication and pleased, too, that Samantha's school allowed a teacher to speak the gorilla tongue. But I am still angry that Marty's parents and my own decided, when we were no more than ten, that we had grown too old for stuffed animals. We each were sent to summer camp, and while we were gone, Marty's Mickey and my Pluto were thrown into the garbage. This was wrong.

The teddy bear that Aram was so eager to show Samantha still lives in a cupboard in Aram's boyhood room. The bear wears the clothes I made him and sleeps in his own small bed. Turk and Isabella, the frogs that were Rafael's favorites, still hide in their secret room in the dollhouse we furnished together. These are treasures not to be disturbed, the very souls of the little boys who loved them. A child can grow out of blocks or trucks or Lego sets. They have no eyes. No fur. No soul. But not beloved animals: one can appreciate the difference by imagining sticking a needle into a teddy bear's eye.

A strong motivation for my learning to sew was that I couldn't stand to see my animals suffer from the sharp, stiff wires that had been inserted into their limbs to make them bendable. I would open the seams, remove the wires, and stitch the opening up. I knew this surgery hurt, but it was necessary. Eyes that were stuck in with wires were even worse. With apologies, but to relieve the constant pain, I would remove the wired eyes and substitute button ones. The animal was temporarily blind during the operation. I apologized for that too. When making the wooden animals now, I paint the eyes last. Eyes bring the animal to life.

Turk the frog, who is no bigger than a fist and made of green velveteen, suffered a difficult youth. Numerous times he had unfortunate run-ins with one or another of the dogs: his skin was ripped, and once he lost an eye. Due to eye surgery and the mismatched cloth with which I patched his wounds, Turk became a spotted frog with black button eyes. Isabella, presented as Turk's bride when he was about a year old, avoided dogs only to receive a worse fate. She became lost. This was a major tragedy from which Rafael seemed unable to recover. Then we went on a trip to Washington, D.C., and there, in a Howard Johnson hotel room, Isabella reappeared by Turk's side one night while Rafael was at supper. It was not until he was a man that Rafael thought to ask how Isabella had found her way back to him and Turk; even then, I was loathe to admit that she was, in fact, Isabella II. The magical reality of tooth fairies and Santa Claus is far less compelling than that of one's stuffed animals.

Sometimes they are kin:

Frogs became Rafael's totem animal and to some extent the family animal too. We celebrated Green Frog Day every year the first Saturday after the spring peepers started cheeping in the swamps. The boys played leapfrog, joined in a frog chorus, and tossed bread crumbs to one another to catch in their mouths like flies. Dessert was frog-shaped pastries. Lacking those, Joshua served green tapioca pudding (to resemble frogs' eggs) in his adult continuation of the holiday, and Aram managed to sneak a squishy toy frog deep into Joshua's bowl to surprise him on his spoon. Ezra's day-care center adopted the holiday, which, with the help of a visiting naturalist, now includes a frog field trip and the raising of tadpoles for release, upon their metamorphosis, back into their natal stream. What is there to outgrow in this relationship?

The boys give frogs in one form or another—T-shirts, candles, carvings—to each other and especially to Rafael. Samantha frog hunts with her mother; with a hand puppet, Aram enacts a dazzling Kermit frog for her. When I got to Maine after stopping over at Joshua's, I found a windup frog that swims (left behind by Ezra?). If we were a tribal family, we would surely think of frogs as ancestral beings with whose spirit we are embued: the Frog People, whose collective identity is still presided over by Turk and Isabella from their secret room.

A sense of kinship with animals isn't entirely lost in our modern maturity. A popular gift among adults is a Vermont Teddy Bear, custom dressed to represent the receiver's vocational or recreational interests. We name our athletic teams after animals: Tigers, Eagles, Wolverines, and Bears. Smokey Bear, dressed as a forest ranger, reminds us of our responsibility to protect the wilderness.

But this is still another example of the pitfalls of our symbolic mind, for childhood affinity with stuffed frogs does not determine whether, as adults, we will preserve the wetlands where the peepers sing, nor can the popularity of bear symbols protect the actual grizzly bear. Disney's sentimental rendition of Felix Salten's *Bambi* has contributed to the appalling overpopulation of deer, to the detriment of their own and our shared habitat.

Our nature takes note of salient features in our environment and builds in a special capacity for attention to and identification with animals, but it doesn't say what conclusions we are to draw. As always with the clues that biology provides, culture must provide interpretations that fit the urge to the reality.

In the kind of society in which morality evolved, the exigencies of our environment would mold innate alertness and interest in adaptive ways. The slight bias that makes a baby more cautious with a scaly animal than with a furry one, more awed by a large than by a small one, would grow into avoidance of dangerous snakes and fear of predatory leopards. In the case of prey species, the child's assumption of intimacy would develop into the detailed and close understanding of their nature that is necessary to hunt these creatures. And the identification that children feel with all animals would lead to their classification according to human traits—the proud eagle and the clever raven—and to observations of human nature embodied in animal myths.

Aesop wrote of the cautious carp and the persevering tortoise some twenty-five hundred years ago; some of his fables have been traced back to even earlier literature. For all that time, the tales have spoken to human nature through the animals they portray, and not exclusively to children, who are Aesop's audience now. The fables survived the ages because, in ages past, they mirrored adult perceptions of ways in which all animal species are like one another.

Children then did not have to outgrow childish notions as they are now expected to. The behaviors and biases with which they are endowed would have been modified and elaborated by actual experience. We're at most ten thousand years removed from the absolute necessity of intimacy with ferocious animals; only a generation or two removed from almost familial relations with the patient ox, the sly fox, and the dumb chicken. Our infants are born with the animal-attentive scaffolding that babies of our genus were born with ages ago, but the materials with which to complete the construction are not easily available. There is nothing wrong with Samantha choosing a mouse as her totem, if it were a mouse. But Mickey ("bigger than my mommy!") is not a mouse. What is to prevent the Samantha who is attracted to baby-faced creatures from being repelled by those that scurry in the night? Can *Stuart Little* save her from fear of rodents?

Maybe so and maybe not. To me as a girl, finding a mouse nest in a drawer in the barn; recognizing the fluffy material as the stuffing from our mattress; noting there, too, dried corn garnered from our crop (mixed with mouse droppings and white crusts of smelly urine); opening the nest hole to discover a heap of naked babies; quietly waiting; catching the mother in my hand as she returned (she bit me); moving kit and caboodle into a cage I'd made from brownie pans and hardware cloth—and learning, finally, that baby-faced, big-eyed, darling deer mice cannot be tamed as pets—was deeply grounding: real, stable, not like lions who, imagined only, can transform from benevolent protectors to roaring predators in the click of a psychological switch.

There is a reason why Girl no longer finds mice caught in the mop pail under the sink. I trap and kill them. She doesn't need to eat them, and I don't need their droppings in my kitchen drawers. Right outside, just where Ian was playing in the garden, are the grasses from which mice make their wild nests, the seeds they eat and, watchful in the trees beyond, the hawk by day and owl by night whose circuitry swoops them toward scurrying things that, if they were not eaten by their natural predators, certainly would overrun my house. Once you see the whole picture, there is no possible moral choice between the raptors that eat rodents and the rodents that raptors eat. The only transcendent expression of our ape-humanity is to maintain a community in which every creature can pursue "happiness," without guarantee that any individual will choose or will be chosen to succeed. That's life. The only sense that I can make of God's throwing up his hands, setting tribe against tribe, human against animal, is that in the resulting muddle and misfortune of experience, we would come to appreciate for ourselves the ecology of His creation.

Let us be practical.

Most children grow up now without the experience of either raising domestic animals or hunting wild ones that might guide them to more carefully considered relationships with these creatures. There are not, in most yards, very many creatures even to notice now that we keep the land so clean.

We could keep yard pets. I used to have a yard rabbit. He was so tame that caging wasn't necessary. He'd just appear from time to time to cadge a carrot. Girl, of course, eats rabbits, so I can't have one now. Samantha keeps chickens in her yard. They are doubly meaningful: she feeds them corn; they feed her eggs. I've considered guinea hens. Girl would eat them, too.

The closest barnyard to where I live in my euphemistically "rural" area is on a city lot. There, in a back yard the size of those in Lakeville, with neighbors' yards adjoining on all sides, a family keeps rabbits, chickens, two turkeys, several ducks, and an adorable dwarf goat. All but the goat are for eating. One turkey is killed for Thanksgiving, the other for Christmas. At an appropriate age, ducks are roasted, rabbits are stewed, and hens too old to lay are simmered to broth. The children, with their parents, take part in the whole process, from raising spring babies to butchering fall meat. One night I called the oldest boy, sixteen-year-old Brian, to ask if he could fix a glitch in my computer, only to discover that 10:00 P.M. was far too late for him. Brian goes to bed at 8:30 and gets up at 5:00 A.M. (Remember the television spot, "It's 10:00 P.M. Do you know where your children are?") Possibly one can't draw a connection between the diurnal rhythms of kept animals and of the boy who keeps them, but then how would one know the effect of a cock's crow on one's body chemistry if one hasn't ever even seen a chicken with its head on?

Again, we must sort of know something about the appeal of chicks and kids and bunny rabbits to young children, or we would not have invented such artificial meeting places as "petting zoos." I used to take our sons to the children's zoo in Central Park when they were little. They soon grew out of it. They wanted their own guinea pig, their own goat. Children want to live with, not visit, animals. Zoos make the point that animals live there and we live here. They may have vending machines that offer pellets to feed the guinea pigs and rabbits, and the pellets are probably made of good things like corn and alfalfa, but they leave mysterious what foods these animals might eat outside captivity—like salad from our garden or clover in our lawn. Outings to such places are brief episodes in a child's life and fail to say anything at all about how our and others' habitats are shared.

For evident reasons, what children find most in common with animals is that all of us must eat. And yet our yards are inedible. (In case you thought a dear dwarf goat might keep your lawn clipped for you, it will not: goats are browsers, not grazers. What mostly eats lawn are grubs and fungal diseases.) Fruiting bushes, graining grasses, seeding flowers, nutting trees—and the meaty insects that rich vegetation harbors—bring at least some wild animals to feed. They may not be thrilling ones to grownups who, safe behind their television screens, are gripped by dramas of great-cat predation, but chipmunks nibbling acorns or spiders snaring flies give children some sense that we all eat something, each in our own way. Add to those resources a birdhouse (don't we all need shelter?) and a birdbath (don't we all drink water?) and there will grow at least a modicum of understanding that we all need food, shelter, and water to be alive.

With patience, chickadees will take sunflower seeds from your open hand. Squirrels—but also chipmunks of a trusting temperament—will do the same for peanuts. My boys used to hand-feed a furry wolf spider with flies dangled at the end of a broom straw. The youngest of them perhaps thought the spider was his friend, as Charlotte dangling from her web is to Wilbur in his sty. The oldest of them must have known that, to the spider's mind, the human hand behind the broom straw did not exist. Yet he also learned by experience what time of day the spider was most likely to be lured to prey, and the spider learned to venture at that time of day from its basement crack to leap upon its daily fly. The form of intimacy with an animal changes over the years of childhood from assumption of its same nature to appreciation of its other nature. Is that not also the degree of moral sophistication that Emma, at ten, had achieved?

I cannot prove that relationships with animals make children better people, but there are clues. One is a farm-school for disturbed inner-city children that gives each child an animal to raise. These are children who can't get along with other humans: they fear or fight, talk back or won't talk at all, have histories of delinquency, truancy, violence, withdrawal. They are given infants— calf, piglet, duckling—that, like Tamagotchi, are dependent on their care. Something happens: the infant trusts their care, the children come to trust their care of it. Unlike Tamagotchi, whose programmed death defeats every effort at nurturance, the animal grows and thrives and becomes attached to its child. In time, the evidence that a relationship is possible, reliable, and rewarding seems to give the children a basis for trying again with those other animals, those humans. Children leave the school attached to friends and teachers, opened up, more certain, respectful: better people.

The logic of this therapy turns upside down an assumption adults have about children: that they become good people through our nurturance of them. That is true, of course, but these bad boys—they are mostly boys—become better by nurturing others. I think again of de Waal's pyramid, why it seems to have turned upside down. When Emma and Phoebe met infant Ezra, they couldn't keep their hands off him. They carried him about all day, making him laugh, letting him gum their fingers. We give children baby dolls and teddy bears to satisfy such urges, not thinking that the urge may have arisen in the long-ago necessity of older children caring for younger ones. Nurturing creates attachment in the young as well as in their elders. Our culture does not let children care for children; we don't ask their nurturance of us, not even to heat soup for a parent sick in bed or fetch the mail for an aging neighbor.

We should not wonder that, as cultural therapy for human detachment, we have flipped de Waal's pyramid over on its animal backside.

Emma's parents took her to the pound and let her choose her dog. I was afraid that her choice, a wild chow mix who leapt chairs and couches to get at the family cat, was a bit much. But Emma named her Natasha and persevered. She took her to puppy class, worked to control her on the leash, came to anticipate situations that overexcited her, introduced her carefully to other dogs until Natasha learned the rules of canine play, and groomed and fed her dog toward the bond that now ties them in mutual devotion.

And I, grappling with the larger implications of actual and symbolic relationships with animals, carved another animal for the ark:

At one of Ezra's early meetings with Girl, they shared a bagel. First, Ezra would take a bite, then hand the bagel to Girl to have a nibble, then take another bite, then share another nibble. Soon the bagel was reduced to a damp lump of dough, and the two of them were simultaneously chewing on it face-to-face. Ezra was neither put off nor amused by so close an eating encounter. He was straight-faced sober, as though this were the way one always eats with dogs.

He won't remember this.

I don't want him to grow out of animal understanding. I carved an image of Girl and placed it in the box that holds the Noah family. I was delighted to discover that the little whittled dog fit into Mrs. Noah's arms as comfortably as a baby, and that she could stand with her paws on the twins' shoulders to kiss their noses, and that Ham, who fathered a tribe that was doomed to disgrace and servitude, seemed very much to need that companion at his side.

Games They Play

 These are the games kittens play:

Hide and Pounce
Clutch and Bite
Belly Wrestle
Zigzag Tag

Each game is bound by rules. When hiding, the kitten crouches with heels and elbows high, belly to the ground. As the "prey" approaches—it may be your foot—the kitten lifts its rear and shifts its weight side to side. Then the sprint, the pounce: claws extended, it clutches its prey and bites. The rule says to bite the narrowest portion between two bulges. On a foot, that is the ankle (on a mouse, it is the neck). Perhaps the foot struggles, tries to shake the kitten off. The kitten clutches all the tighter and, maneuvering itself onto its back, rakes the belly of its prey fiercely with hind claws as though to disembowel it.

Zigzag Tag involves alternate swipes with the front paws while chasing something small. The play is to keep the ball (or mouse) from turning aside, and the object of the game is to hook it. The hooking motion changes with the position of the prey: if below (like a fish), the kitten scoops; if above (like a bird), it brings both feet together like clawed tongs.

Eventually, the kitten may string these games together into hunting sequences, but it does not know this and is unlikely to become an effective predator unless tutored by its mother. Pleasure in play motivates play, not the ultimate behavior that, in a social context, young mammal's games would lead to.

And yet I'm sorry for declawed cats who never learn how the skills they practice come together in the hunt.

After Sam moved away, a new family rented the house where he had lived. There were two boys this time, Alex, with whom I shelled peas, and his brother, Derek, then ten years old. They moved in with a very large television set and a collection of Nintendo games. I visited one Sunday afternoon to hear their opinions and to watch them play:

> Star Fox
> Smash
> Pokémon Snap

The speed was dizzying. The landscape hurtled at us and there was no way to slow it down. Things exploded (though silently because the audio wasn't working). Derek narrated for me. He said that it was all a matter of eye-hand coordination. His left thumb controlled the joystick that directed his movement through the landscape and his aim; his right fingers controlled a group of buttons, each of which empowered a tactic or a weapon.

Derek looks very like Harry Potter as depicted on the covers of the Harry Potter books: the same black, unruly hair, the narrow face and slender form, and the intensity, the glasses. I'd read all the Harry Potter books. So had Derek. There were similarities not only between the fictional hero and the living one who was demonstrating his prowess to me: the books and games follow a similar line. The hero is opposed to the forces of evil but, like Harry as the first novel opens and like a boy first opening a game, he has to learn se-

crets and earn powers to become effective. The dexterity by which
Derek careened and exploded his way through the landscape came
of hours and hours of play during which he had unraveled mysteries, figured out strategies, found new powers, and practiced to
use them. So it was not just a matter of eye-hand coordination: one
problem, Derek confided, had taken him a week to solve.

Each solution gives the player the opportunity to explore the
next level of difficulty, and each level reveals a new environment to
be mastered. This came clearest to me during a beginner game
shown to me by Alex. In one scene, he tried to scale a steep incline. But no matter which way he approached the obstacle and at
what moment he leapt or scrambled, he slipped or missed and skid-
ded to the bottom. He had not yet discovered the secret power—
gripper claws—that would let him climb slick heights. Alex retreated to an earlier, watery landscape in which he had gained the
power to swim, but only after having endured many times being
"killed" by a shark that truly frightened him.

I remarked that Alex seemed very skilled for a five-year-old.
Derek said that was because he had an older brother to help him
learn the way. I asked Alex whether he often played these games
with friends, and he said no—because, as Derek added, he was just
in kindergarten, not old enough for "play dates."

A wire came loose, and virtual reality was blackened for the day.
As I left, the brothers were mock wrestling over the sofa onto the
floor. Their father said, with apologetic pride, "That's boys."

I got this weird feeling reading the Harry Potter books. It was the
same shock of satisfaction I had known as a girl reading the Mary
Poppins books. This was the world where I belonged: magical,
powerful, mysterious, and real.

Ordinary grown-ups do not come off well in Poppins or Potter
books or in other classics of middle childhood: *Charlotte's Web*, *The
Secret Garden*, the Narnia novels. At best they are like Michael
and Jane's parents in the Mary Poppins series, the benevolent but

dithering Bankses, blind to the portents of shifting winds. At worst they are like Harry Potter's mean foster parents, the Dursleys, who loathe magic and won't allow it. Perhaps we have got things wrong. Maybe it is we mundane adults who are stuck in virtual reality while children discover the real world for which they were intended.

I used to spy on my parents and snoop through drawers and closets to find their secrets. One afternoon when the house was empty I found three narrow glass-lined cardboard canisters pushed far to the rear on a top shelf of the cupboard in my mother's bathroom. Each contained a single small white pill.

Poison.

This was as it should be. Adults are supposed to have dangerous secrets. A fundamental pursuit of childhood is to discover the secrets that give grown-ups power, and this may explain why Star Fox and Harry Potter are more gripping than the inauthentic world we modern moms and dads inhabit, cluttered with money talk and health concerns, lacking lore and wonder.

No doubt it has always been that children, like other mammal young, play mostly with each other. Only in modern times, though, has Hide-and-Seek become divorced from adult stealth and ambush, Shadow Tag from the grown-up hero's daring agility, or Concentration from the herbalist's spatial memory of where to find "facedown" plants when they are not in bloom or fruit. The transformations of string games are not enjoyed by grown-ups anymore; the power of spells and potions is realized in fiction only; jacks, once played with knucklebones, no longer spell the future.

We need to realize that the authenticity of childhood is not well supported in our modern culture. It must have been more comforting to children when everybody feared the dark and drew close around the fire, when everyone agreed that there was safety in the trees, when grownups knew how to propitiate the spirits of the dead and heeded the raven's warning that there were wolves abroad. I was a little better off than most perhaps, supposing that my con-

coctions of Prell shampoo stirred with toothpaste and iodine might
ultimately bring me into connection with doctor parents who had
the power to use poison and prescribe chloroform. On the whole,
though, adults have gotten pretty boring.

We have experienced an emphatic turning of children toward
their peers. We have seen the emergence of idols not yet beyond
their teens. We watch our children withdraw into other worlds
along the malls and behind computer screens where we don't—and
they don't let us—follow.

This is taking a great leap into the unprovable, but I would
guess that the interminable stage of life we call adolescence is, in
fact, a halting of development in cultures where childhood endeavor is not rewarded by adulthood as children imagined it would
be.

"That's boys," said Derek's dad of his sons' tussling with each other.
You would not be able to identify kittens' play by gender. Cats are
not cooperative animals; males and females hunt solo and in the
same way, so the games that kittens play do not differ by their sex.

Children's games also share underlying features whether they are
played by girls or boys. The play is spatially confined, whether formally, as in game boards, hopscotch patterns, and ball courts, or in-
formally, as in the precinct where it is legitimate to hide in a game
of Prisoner. Even outside of games, children behave as though the
ground were geometrically restricted. They step into spaces or follow the cracks, practice novel sequences of movement for getting
up stairs and down, swing on gates or vault them, jump to touch
the tops of door frames, balance on railings, leap puddles, run toys
along floorboards and fingers along fabric weaves and wood grains.
The intricacy of this play of movement through patterned and circumscribed space is hardly necessary in a landscape of lawn and
sidewalk, but the drive to maneuver through complicated terrain is
such that children seek the hardest way, not the easiest or most efficient, to get from one place to another.

All games, even the simplest ones like Mother, May I? and Follow the Leader, by definition are bound by rules. The rules are not instinctual as they are for kittens, but the universality of children's games that require prescribed movements, permission to move, and obedience to the leader suggests that there is some bias toward performing coordinated actions within a group. Children everywhere play versions of Hide-and-Seek that include the concept of "home," the place where you are safe, and forms of Tag with rules that say who is "it" or "out." Taking turns is equally practiced by children of either sex.

But forming teams is not. Teaming is a behavior that emerges spontaneously among boys but rarely among girls. I went to an all-girls school that was divided by color into two teams, Silver and Blue. We Blues were passionately devoted to our team, chose friends from among our teammates, and played fiercely against Silvers, whom we considered to be rather an alien tribe. So there is in girls the capacity to form strong alliances, but in after-school play, we did not choose games that required competing teams or opposing sides.

There is a contrast, too, in how girls and boys treat differences of opinion over rules. When boys have a falling out regarding fair play, they tend to negotiate their disagreement by reformulating the rules. When girls have a similar disagreement, they tend to dissolve that game and reform the group around some other activity. Social cohesion is preserved in both cases but not in the same way.

These differences and others I learned during several years of exploring the literature of gender identity at the height of nonsexist child rearing, when it was least popular to do so. Some of the authors I consulted were feminists: Margaret Mead, Letty Cottin Pogrebin, Carrie Carmichael. Others, like Richard Green and John Money, had studied the etiology of gender identity in gays and lesbians. A third category were data gatherers—I relied particularly on Eleanor Maccoby and Carol Jacklin—who searched statistically for subtle differences.

It was the subtleties that most interested me. The more a behavior slips by unnoticed, such as the way we present our nodding face to a newborn baby, the less likely it is to have been culturally determined. Yet slight cues can powerfully affect us, as in the discomfort aroused when a stranger tries to hold our gaze. Our dealings with children, after all, are not one-sided, the adult shaping and the child being shaped. From birth, children elicit certain behaviors in us, and our response in turn elicits their reply. Therefore, it seemed possible to me that regardless of the particulars of culture—whether women must be veiled to their eyeballs or cover only their genitals—contrasts between male and female might emerge based on slight cues that direct their social interactions.

We do not, for example, foist teddy bears on children because our culture insists we do; we respond to what we notice about their reactions to animals, their interest in faces, their pleasure in softness, and their need to cuddle. It is inconceivable that parents in any culture would put their child to bed with a scaly fake snake. In cultures where children share the bed with parents or one another, their need to cuddle is met without the stuffed proxy. The cultural difference is in *how* the young are soothed to sleep, not whether they are. By adulthood, the behavior of all animals that have been studied differs according to sex (female cats may mix and raise their litters together, whereas male cats kill the kittens). All human cultures express gender in contrasting ways. The question is what part children themselves play in their own identity as girls or boys.

I did not find that social inflictions upon neuter innocents constrained their development to cultural stereotypes. Quite the opposite, I found that children search their culture for clues to support a gender identity that accords with their sense of self and that the sense of self differs biologically between the sexes.

The strands veer apart early but in ways so subtle that they have been revealed only by elaborate investigations. Girl babies are easier to soothe both by voice and touch. They hold your gaze for longer and smile more often. They vocalize more too. As toddlers, girls leave their mother for shorter times and don't venture as far as boys do (this was plotted by stopwatch on a grid-marked playroom floor). When separated from their mother by a low gate, boys shake and rattle the barrier, trying muscularly to wrench it from its hinges, while girls stand crying, imploring their mother with their eyes. Unlike boys, who early on tend to mobilize their toys (Haul that wagon! Crash that truck!), girls draw their toys around them as they play. Although no remarkable contrast has been noted in either sex's potential for anger or nastiness, boys' activity level is higher and their play more energetic.

Statistics, of course, say nothing about any individual child. Statistically, people who smoke die younger than people who don't, but the last surviving Civil War veteran only gave up smoking at the age of 103. Among the infants and toddlers observed in these studies were surely girls who were hard to soothe and boys who continually babbled, as well as girls who wrenched the gate and boys who wept for rescue. The overlap is considerable. At the far ends of the spectrum are boys who are girlish and girls who are boyish. Statistics can say only that girls in general share certain forms of behavior that are less pronounced in boys and that boys in general behave in ways that are less usual for girls. There is, however, a striking consistency in how the earliest contrasts continue to develop.

By nursery school, differences have emerged in the ways children crayon pictures and build with blocks. Boys scrawl over the whole piece of paper, whereas girls contain their scribbling well within the edge. Boys' block constructions are mostly outdoor roads with tunnels, along which they careen small vehicles; in a few years, they will instead build tall and solid towers that end up crashing down. Girls, at first, hardly build with blocks at all; as they become more interested, they use blocks to form low enclosures with openings in the walls, and they arrange the inside with people, animals, and furniture. They rarely play with trucks or cars. Preschool boys begin to form groups for the purpose of completing a project—lining up chairs to make a bus, organizing a parade—whereas girls play in smaller clusters of two or three joined in a common occupation but without a specified goal.

By school age, boy groups are hierachical: the leader is supported by affiliates, each assigned status according to his role, which may be daring and aggressiveness but is just as likely to be to provide humor, good ideas, or mediating skills. When questioned about their status in the group, boys typically give themselves a higher rating than their peers accord them. Ask a group of girls to rank each other, and they don't know what to say.

Parents, too, have been scrutinized in this research into behavior and development. Responding to cues they are barely aware of, parents who, at first, invest equal energy in soothing a crying infant, as time goes by, give less attention to unyielding sons than to more easily calmed daughters, with the result that baby boys cry more than girls. Infants' differing threshold of stimulation—how loud the noise, how firm the touch that engages their attention or distracts them from distress—results in parents' more robust play with sons than daughters. Mothers and daughters weave a fabric of talk between them, whereas fathers more easily weld themselves to sons through shoulder hugs and tousled hair.

Parents reading these descriptions may be annoyed. I can't help it. Neither can culture. No one teaches boys to sprawl or girls to tuck their legs beneath them. It's no one's fault that boys delight in sound effects, and girls do not, or that by his second Christmas, Ezra had gone wild for trains yet Samantha never showed the slightest interest in them. Samantha's mother is a physicist; Ezra's father knits and cooks. Their children's stereotyped behavior is not their fault either.

At cultural fault is a denial of children's need to behave in sexist ways and a narrowing of their opportunity to do so. Derek has playmates by play date; Alex has friends among schoolmates during class hours. But gangs of boys in snowball fights or tearing about on bikes have become as rare as hopscotch. The only man around who could teach these boys what the crows are saying is Wayne who, in his disappointment with today's young couch potatoes, grumbles that "the only kids I like are roasted."

Of course, this isn't true: Wayne is very fond of the several boys in the neighborhood who join him and his cronies in the sugarhouse while the sap is boiling, attend to the smoking of the fish they catch, and heap the bonfires when Wayne burns the brush. Wayne arranged with Alex and Derek's father to make a bonfire to celebrate January 1, 2000, which was also the older son's eleventh birthday. But in the end, their father demurred, thinking his sons would be quickly bored by just a fire.

I had originally thought that our society's restrictions on children's freedom to congregate and the lack of occupations shared with adults should affect girls less than boys. Girls don't demand gang membership and risky ventures; their sense of inner space and their need for intimacy ought to be satisfied in more domesticated ways among just a few close girlfriends. Yet I had observed, too, that not many girls these days hold hands and link arms with one another as we used to do; they seem to have become more cool in both senses of the word. Reacquaintance with my nieces Laila and Nadia, whom I had met only twice and briefly during their childhood in Morocco, suggested a reason for our American daughters' seeming chilliness.

The sisters came for a long visit one summer when they were in their early teens. They were girlish, kissing and hugging, giggling and weeping, fond of cute things—stuffed animals and happy faces—affectionate with me and cuddly with their mother. Yet they were womanly, warm and sensual, concerned with others' feelings, modest, dignified.

So it seemed incongruous years later when the actually grown-up Laila, by then married and with a doctorate in engineering, mentioned that she was taking lessons in belly dancing.

Belly dancing!

Laila explained: she is home in Morocco for only a few weeks a year, so she gets out of practice. Belly dancing, which here is performed in front of men for their sexual enticement, is there enjoyed by girls and women with one another. They get together, eat, and gossip, and then aunt or mom or girlfriend will turn on some music, and they dance. Boys do not dance this way. Men are not invited.

Hearing this, I realized how deprived is the American female, subjected to bony and pseudosexy models, left as a girl before the mirror to somehow come to womanhood outside of womanly embrace.

We have been led to believe that sensuality is expressed through sex and intimacy through heterosexual relationship and marriage. When you think of the circumstances of our evolution, though, that version doesn't entirely make sense. Like other animals, we have to differentiate ourselves by gender in order to achieve the sexual orientation for reproduction. To some degree, that function is performed in utero, under the influence of hormones that shape, for instance, contrasts in male and female spatial perception and language fluency. But we are not toms and tabbies walking alone, dictated to by our relative proportions of androgens and estrogens. We are animals that require, for our adult social structure, love among men strong enough to uphold their mutual courage and intimacy among women close enough to nourish their mutual dependence. Children are inwardly pushed not only to differentiate by opposites—boys are rough and girls are soft—but by identity:

We girls and women.

We boys and men.

With this in mind, scenes from the past appear to me now in a context that I had not clearly seen at the time:

Three girls, ten-year-olds, borrow a neighbor's baby to dress, bathe, feed, and play with. They do this every day; it is more fun than Barbie dolls, one confides to me, as though letting me in on a secret.

Seven boys, ages five to eleven, play Hide-and-Seek in the gathering dusk of a summer evening. The youngest can't count to a hundred; the others show him how to count to ten ten times, using his fingers to keep track.

A Memorial Day parade: the volunteer firemen drive their polished trucks slowly up the street, with their sons beside them.

Marty and the four boys early in the morning pee in unison on the gravel driveway, aiming to dislodge the pebbles.

Laila, sweet sixteen, naps with her head in her mother's lap.

Among the various books and studies I consulted on gender identity was an unpublished doctoral thesis written in 1976 by Dorothy Z. Ullman. Unlike researchers who observe and record behavior as an ethologist must among animals, Ullman entered into conversation with her subjects. She wanted their point of view: how did they perceive, and explain, the differences between the sexes? "No," said a six-year-old when asked whether a woman should make as much money as a man, "because the man knows how to make more money because a man can do work better than a lady." Earning power, at six, is based on muscle power.

Here's more: women should take care of babies because "The mother's skin is softer than the daddy's skin. And daddies have hair all over their arms and stuff." Similarly, a woman can't have a job in an insurance agency because a man can get more money; he can do more things than a lady, and women can't learn the insurance business "because, as I was saying, a lady has delicate skin, a man has tougher skin."

Are you surprised? Did you realize that men can't be nurses because they have loud voices? And women can't be doctors because they're not strong? Men are smarter than women too—but not at all because of their innate intelligence. To a six-year-old (of either sex), men are big, strong, loud voiced, and tough skinned: therefore, they work; *therefore*, they are smart. Women are small, weak, soft voiced, and smooth skinned: therefore, they take care of babies and, since that is not "work" to a first-grader, women are not smart.

Many of the mothers of these children did work, in jobs or in professions. Ullman found that had no bearing on their offsprings' perceptions. But even if some parents did insist on traditional roles in the family economy, even if they themselves were sexist, it is absurd to imagine that they taught their children hairy-armed, soft-voiced sex stereotypes. The children were using salient physical features—ones that even babies are well equipped to perceive—to generate their own stereotypes of what male and female can and cannot do.

But why? At this early age, boys and girls are not at all sure their sex is permanent. They might turn into the other sex, as I, at six, still thought was possible. Whereas in a few years, they will be delighted to wear a Halloween mask, many now are frightened to "lose" their face behind it. It is as though Jane herself has vanished behind the witch and Johnny gone beneath the rubber monster. Their identity as "girl" or "boy" is similarly uncertain. To boost themselves into a sure and permanent sense of their gender, they seek obvious physical differences, and using these, they generate stereotypes such as that men are "smart" and women "nice." They scrutinize culture, too, for what it offers in the way of differentiation (after all, both boys and girls have smooth skin and high voices): this is the age of heartbreaking stereotypes, skinny boys in combat camouflage, gawky girls in tutus.

And then, lo and behold! They become nonsexist. By about eight years old, children have completed their effort to achieve permanent gender identity, and they relax. Now boys and girls can have long hair or short hair, fight or bake, throw footballs or dress dolls, wear the same sorts of clothes and, when they grow up, become whatever they wish (though boys are not quite as liberal as girls in these opinions).

Then again, they falter: by about fifth grade—ten or eleven years old—children cast about anew to reach an understanding of their sex's functionality. Now I am a boy, thinks the lad, What am I supposed to do about it? And the girl, How am I fit my sex to my society? Not incidentally, society, at this point, begins to require responsibility: for schoolwork, often for chores. The opposing views of children in first and fifth grades are almost a parody of the nature-versus-nurture controversy, for just as six-year-olds believe that biology is destiny, ten-year-olds believe that culture is destiny. They examine the social system, declare it immutable, and conform their behavior to what they believe will be their culture's rigid and inevitable expectations. Just as children learning to speak apply language rules consistently and so say "I goed" long before they learn "I went," these older children seek an underlying social grammar and ignore exceptions. Presidents are men; political office and the public sphere are for males. Women's purpose is to the private good through child care, teaching, nursing, and charity. Again, it's not important whether the actual parents fit the rule or that exceptions abound: the children are after a sexist division of labor in order to consolidate their own sense of responsibility within the larger society. Boys mow lawns and take out garbage; girls shop, baby-sit, and help with housework.

Once mastered, conventionality gives way to flexibility—a twelve-year-old may thoughtfully admit that right now, he thinks girls are smarter than boys, but that later, when boys go to college, they can learn to be as smart as girls. It's a sensible interval, but it doesn't last. By adolescence—somewhere between fourteen and eighteen—children generate a new theory of sexual difference, one that prepares them for heterosexuality. One could call it psychological determinism: girls, pronounces a teenager, "have a lot more emotions on things; I think they have more emotions than men do and they show it more than men do." Psychological differences now explain each sex's special abilities: "I think a woman's personality basically is more the type of personality to be staying home with children. Where men's personalities and lifestyle are different. They don't seem to me the type that could sit around; they would probably get bored doing it." On the other hand, because men are less sensitive than women and show their feelings less, they can "handle" situations that women can't. It is only by about college age, eighteen or so, when they have formulated for themselves their gender identity in biological, social, and psychological terms, that young men and women can blithely accept and enthusiastically join in celebrating the freedom of individuals to be and to do as they wish.

And, comically, after all the effort put into generating rigid versions of masculinity and femininity, this is when youth disparages stereotyped sex differences as behaviors learned in childhood from old-fashioned parents or an unjust society.

My mother had a Victorian plate that showed a little girl in ringlets wearing her father's boots. The caption read, "Don't I look like Papa?" If you try the joke the other way around—a little boy trying on his mother's shoes and saying, "Don't I look like Mama?"—you will see how aware you are of an essential difference between the sexes. Masculine identity must be built by boys, and is easily threatened, whereas feminine identity is just there, in no danger from Papa's boots.

The reason for the difference is not cultural homophobia, but a psychological reality. An infant's first identity is with the mother; or, more accurately, it is fusion with the mother. A girl can formulate her separate self without giving up that first sense of sameness, for she *is* the same as her mother: the same sex. A boy, in separating himself from his mother, must disidentify with her sex. The job is harder, the structure shakier, and the more we try to make boys be like girls, the greater the assault on the boundaries they are trying to construct. In the years since feminism began to intrude adult ideals of sexual equality into the realm of child rearing, G.I. Joe has grown from a slender youth to a muscle-bound brute, and John Wayne has given way to Darth Vader. These super-male images are no more foisted on boys than are teddy bears on infants. They are a commercial response to boys' fervent, and often undersupported, wish for masculine identity. Yet the idea persists that letting boys be boys sharpens their aggressiveness, dulls their sensitivity, and perpetuates patriarchal attitudes toward women.

It is true that violence is in our nature and that it is more pronounced in males than in females. It is also true that we come by our violence naturally through our descent from apes. Yet reassuring shoulder hugs among males are just as ancient. As Aram so aptly conveyed in Gorilla, male power is as much for protection as it is for predation.

You can see a primitive balance between the two in boy gangs. Once accepted into membership, a child becomes the responsibility of the leader and considers the other boys his family. However, loyalty to the gang, obedience to the leader, and care of one another often serve predation on outsiders. Boy gangs have traditionally congealed at the borders of ethnic neighborhoods, where adults themselves may condone a degree of brawling. The gangs whose violence we have come to fear most, though, arise in communities where fathers are often absent or irresponsible and adult males in general are not politically unified in leading their community. In those circumstances, boys look to their peers for protection and guidance. What they receive is a raw version of humanity.

The taming of the brute is less accomplished by the gentling influence of mothers and women teachers than by helping boys ally among themselves and with grown men who can better define for them what their affiliation is to uphold or oppose. Marty had earned the rank of Eagle Scout, the highest level a Boy Scout can attain, and also been elected to the Order of the Arrow. He was to uphold fortitude. He was to oppose helplessness. The boys wanted badly to follow in those steps, to be brave like Peter Pan paddling the Serpentine, but also to chivalrously aid young Maimie, lost in the park after lock-up time, and old ladies crossing streets. More than anything, they wanted, as in Marty's final test, to build, with fellows, a bridge across a swamp using only logs they had cut themselves by hatchet and that they bound together using only rope. Boy Scouts by that time and in our community had deteriorated to basketball games punctuated by parent-attended ceremonies conducted by a stranger-man wearing an elaborate feather headdress. The boys quit the Boy Scouts.

Had they been available at the time, I think our sons might have turned to Pokémon adventures, as Derek has. A particular charm of these virtual scouting expeditions is that the "enemies" are not killed, but are captivated into goodness by their capture: they join the gang.

Pokémons are the latest and adamantly conformist craze among middle-childhood boys. The theme of the video games that started the craze is, as usual, the triumph of good over evil. The hero is a child, twelve-year-old Ash. His goal is to capture all 150-plus non-human creatures called Pokémons, train them to be good, and use them to capture the remaining wicked Pokémons that so far have escaped. In the games, Ash is not your ally: he is you.

Each of the Pokémons has its own sort of power which, after conversion, accrues to Ash's (your) favor. Battles won thus inflate the hero's strength—badge by badge, one might say, thinking Boy Scout. Each character also has a piece of information that is necessary to capture other characters. The more elusive the Pokémon, the more information required from previous captures; the 154th character can be caught only by using knowledge from every one of the others.

The particular game Derek played for my education was a shoot-'em-up by camera. He not only had to learn how to track his prey through shifting sands and yawning chasms, but to penetrate each Pokémon's defenses and counteract its elusions so as to get a full-front close-up in realistic pose. The game presented a considerable intellectual challenge and one strikingly similar to how a boy, gradually gaining knowledge of the ways and weaknesses of prey, would once have accrued power and stature within his community. Uncannily to me, though, the computer acts as the adult who knows what the boy must learn. "You play with the computer," Derek told me at one point and, again, "You play against the computer."

Pokémon cards based on the video game are sold for between $7 and $9 a pack. The relative rarity of a character in the set, and therefore its trading value, is rigged by the manufacturer: previous characters are taken out of publication; new ones are added. The same is true of the figurines based on the games and the cartoons and movies that Nintendo also produces. *Pokémon: The First Movie* premiered on a school day, a Wednesday. It made over $10 million the first day, another $9 million on Thursday, and had grossed over $50 million by the end of the weekend. So many parents let their children stay home from school on a weekday that the absence excuse came to be called Pokéflu. Nintendo's worldwide earnings from all Pokémon-related products reached $6 billion in 1999.

An axiom of ecological as well as of evolutionary theory is that where a niche opens, someone will move in. We are well aware that prosperity offers green pastures to those who would exploit the young. We are far less clear about why boys should be so eager to comply. It is as though the niche itself demands to be filled, that boys experience an inner vacuum, an emotional hunger to sate their boyishness. They might well prefer to be fed by men the venturesome inclusion that they crave, but their hero, Ash, is likely to remain perennially twelve as long as the best that grown men offer to boys in promise of eventual manhood is paid tutors to coach Little Leaguers in the art of the pitch.

I think Nintendo is about to make a grave mistake. Pokémon characters were sexless in the original versions. With the newest videos, children will learn whether the one they have set out to capture is a girl or a boy. The move is politically correct but risky: boys may well resist fighting against or allying with female Pokémons.

It's been remarked to me many times that it must have been some job to raise four sons. It was not. The house was noisy, yes, and boisterous too when they all were home together, but mostly they were gone and so were the friends they played with. The group at its height, during its most exciting ventures, numbered seven boys from six to twelve, and they were as disparate in personality as they were in age. One, who had a limping gait but racing mind, had the idea of building a full-size chariot. Another cadged an empty cable reel off linemen doing repairs along the road. A third had the mechanical know-how to convert the wooden reel to a pair of wheels on an axle and to direct the building of the carriage and the poles to pull it. The youngest were the horses (I keep a snapshot of small Joshua and smaller Aram abreast in their traces).

There is among free-formed groups of boys an element of continual induction. The older boys, through tests and trials, gradually let the younger ones in on the secrets of their superior knowledge: the password to gain entry to the hideout; how to make a fire and piss it out. But the youthful cohort (our sons' gang was born during the decade of the 1960s) grows up, and the information the older boys have unwound for the younger ones knots with pubertal sexuality and falters. The younger boys are not ready yet to go with girls, and the older ones are as unwilling as they are unable to take them there. The division between boyhood and manhood happens like the end of a string that was supposed to be picked up and spliced into the next length but isn't. Boys entering their teenage years are left dangling, without apprenticeship for or initiation into the brotherhood of men.

There has been an equivalent abandonment of girls. The anthropologist Sarah Blaffer Hrdy, in her book *Mother Nature: A History of Mothers, Infants, and Natural Selection*, examines feminine ambition and finds that there is nothing new in women's pursuit of success and effort to achieve status within the community. Women's status—and this is true of female chimpanzees as well—helps to determine the status of their offspring: the children of the most respected mothers gain the most attention from their peers and the greater tolerance from adults for their prankishness.

Respect always has been due to women in the economic sector. As gatherers, they supplied the nuts, roots, and grains that are the nutritional basis of human diet in almost every culture. What's more, women could hoard, store, and barter their gathered produce for other goods. The behavior of female chimpanzees suggests that domestic technology may also have been in women's hands from ancient times: it is the females, not the males, who teach the young how to strip grass stems or twig probes for extracting termites; how to choose and use sticks for cracking nuts and bone picks for prying out the flesh; how to prepare leaf sponges for soaking up rainwater to quench their thirst or clean themselves; how to construct sleeping nests for naps and overnight; and (probably, but this is not yet certain) how to identify medicinal as well as food plants.

At least one primatologist has been led by such observations to theorize that human toolmaking arose in the context of food processing, not prey killing; that tools for digging and pulverizing preceded tools for butchering; and that we may thank females for the repercussions that ensued. (Given women's softness toward baby animals, I wouldn't be surprised to learn that they played the main role in domestication too; certainly in later times they kept the chickens and ran the dairy.)

Paleolithic "Venus" figures, dating from twenty-seven thousand years ago and among the first-known sculptures, had been presumed on the basis of their exaggerated breasts and hips to be "fertility" figures. They have recently been reinterpreted as possible advertisements for women in the weaving business: the Venuses wear string hair nets, brassieres, and skirts. A fascinating book, *The Mummies of Urumchi* by textile expert Elizabeth Wayland Barber, illustrates exquisite wool tartans woven by prehistoric women four thousand years ago. Quillwork boots and beaded belts, fringed cloaks and feathered headdresses have been the peacock dress of tribal men, but they were made by women. I have two tiny, intricate, and perfect baskets that are examples of pieces made by Papago Indian women two centuries ago for no other reason than to compete among themselves for the most skilled work.

In terms of services, women have been better positioned than men to dispense primary education, herbal medicine, midwifery, nursing care, charity, and marital advice—all services that, in the past at least, accorded women additional status within their social group.

The critical difference between the then and the now is that the ambition of women to earn and to excel in the field of their expertise did not require them to leave their children in others' care. Women's businesses were home based; markets were nearby. Daughters' ambitions and skills grew at the knee of their mothers' success.

And not just one mother, groups of mothers, a womanly surround:

I was a consultant during the 1970s to a cooperative women's venture called the Freedom Quilting Bee, in Gee's Bend, Alabama, where women of all ages, many with daughters or granddaughters in tow (the boys were in the fields with their daddies), came together to stitch the product, cook the midday meal, supervise the children, and run the business all at once.

And weren't they wicked! Didn't those women just skewer the do-good, up-north minister who didn't know what to do with the contents of his chamber pot! And the Vista worker! How could she be so brazen as to use *mouthwash*, when anyone could see from ads that it was intended as an aphrodisiac! (And wouldn't I be mimicked too for my finicky insistence on quality and disapproved for suggesting that elderly women who could no longer see well enough to sew be dropped from the cooperative group.)

This used to be another aspect of women's clustering that was of social consequence: the role of busybody, the glue of gossip. Because women did not *go* to work, they could keep a close eye on their neighbors. The subject of interest was the real and living soap opera of others' goings-on. The exercise of ridicule and outrage—but also the charity of economic inclusion—was very much the prerogative of the ladies of the club (and must have been a lot more fun than *Oprah*).

The women of Gee's Bend called themselves Ladies. The Freedom Quilting Bee's board of directors followed *Robert's Rules of Order* for its quarterly meetings. The members were bastions of the

church, teachers in the school—and had lost their jobs as domestics
in Selma by refusing to pee in the back yards of homes where they
were not allowed to use the bathroom. The per capita income in
Gee's Bend in 1970 was $500; most of that was due to the enter-
prise of its women. I keep a photograph of Louise Wilcox, daughter of the leading matron of the community, riding a mule with
Lincoln who, at ten years old, was smitten by her bearing, surety,
and warmth: "role model," as in Hillary Clinton, hardly begins to
suggest how female dignity is achieved.

The New York Times has taken to assigning themes to its Sunday
Magazine. One that appalled me almost as much as toy catalogs do
was devoted to "What clothes reveal, and mask, about identity."
     Adult identity. Erotic identity. Homoerotic identity. But mostly
no gender identity at all. Instead, there was a confusion of unisex
sports, leisure, and business clothes, including an "austere" Prada
"primacy-of-work" design featuring the (female) model's belly button. In fact, belly buttons were *in*, big time: I could count them on
all ten fingers and again on my ten toes without reaching the number that ad and feature photographs revealed.
     This jolted my mind: belly buttons are the only physically inti-
mate topographical feature that both sexes have in common. They
are beloved by toddlers just because they are not determinate of
sex. A belly button does not preclude the later growth of breasts or,
by analogy, a penis. Both seem potent organs to young children. "If
you eat your cereal," my three-year-old reassured me one breakfast
long ago, "your penis will grow." At the same age, he tried to nurse
his infant brother at his navel.
     Unisex styles, with their emphasis on gender neutrality, preserve
that fantasy; in fact, they are meant to liberate both sexes from the
masculine and feminine stereotypes that once constrained them. Yet
relinquishment of the hope to be everything is among children's
struggles to grow up, and the ambiguities we model for them sabo-
tage their effort.
     I've been able to summon old snapshots to this chapter, like the

one of Lincoln and Louise on the mule, because the house was just painted, so I've had to clear closets of boxes containing forty years' of memorable litter, including this pic: Rafael in curls below his shoulders, dressed in a tie-dyed dashiki and velvet-patched jeans, attached to his same-dressed first girlfriend by an umbilical cord of tinkly bells (I also found the bells). I wasn't shocked in those long-haired days that our pretty sons with their luxurious hair were often mistaken for girls, though I got a strong clue about the necessity of differentiation when Joshua, maybe four years old, cut a hole in the red silk kimono an aunt had given him for Christmas so that his penis could stick through. I found that snapshot too.

And there was Aram, perhaps six years old, with an oarlock clamped below each knee like some spiked armor a knight might have worn to battle, and there was another photo of him, in a bandanna like a pirate, belted heavy with weaponry. I came upon Aram's sword in the attic closet, and Rafael's air rifle too. But also, wrapped in tissue paper in a cracked cardboard box, my uncle Saul's ringlets, now more than a hundred years old and, in a metal strongbox among other vintage photographs, one of my aunt Naomi as a little girl, with her hair tied up in the enormous bow that was stylish at the time, cockily aiming a toy gun. The photo was labeled (in her own but grown-up hand) "Be prepared!"

How snapshots present children depends on when the shutter opens on their inner life, as well as where they fall on psychologists' masculinity/femininity scales. In my overalls, a jackknife in my pocket and a bow across my shoulder, I certainly fell on the tomboy side. Yet for all my railings against the color pink, my block buildings were, sure enough, hollow rooms, not solid towers. And when in the hollow of my womb a child grew, I became a woman in ways culture cannot dictate and men cannot know.

There is nothing in male experience so profoundly passive as pregnancy. Men make new sperm by the hundreds of thousands all through their lives; the eggs a girl carries are numerous at birth, but only a few hundred survive to her adulthood. The egg, not the woman, prepares its bed and accepts the sperm. The embryo, on its sixth day of life, burrows into the womb lining by digesting its cells. The placenta, an organ entirely encoded by the father's, not the mother's, genes, takes from the mother's blood the calcium her fetus needs, even if in doing so it depletes her teeth and bones. The woman's body would reject this foreign tissue were it not that it chemically disguises its presence. It is the baby, not its mother, who initiates the contractions that will expel it from the womb. I very much enjoyed pregnancy (including the exhibitionistic protrusion of my belly), yet I remember toward the end this scary image: I was on a train hurtling down the tracks toward a dark tunnel, unable to see what lay beyond and with no brakes. Birth was going to happen; I could not stop it.

Pregnancy is a bodily invasion, and femininity has far more to do with acceptance of that invasion—with fusion and confusion of self and other—than it has to do with pink and frills. Mothering is a relinquishing of boundaries, a regression to infancy in the service of union, a regrowing through childhood as the years go by. The girlishness of girls—their whispers and giggles, their grooming and dressing, the apparent pointlessness of their intimate coteries—prepares them to remain permeable to their infants' needs.

At each step during children's construction of their sexual identity, the biological, social, or psychological theory they formulate precedes their conformity to it. Ullman concluded her study with college students; had she gone on to question men and women in their thirties, she might have found that the interplay between nature and culture doesn't terminate at reproductive maturity. In our society's latest enactment of sexual destiny, we are able to go on to stay-at-home fatherhood, to off-to-work motherhood—though not in painless defiance of our natures, since these choices are hardly without conflict even during middle age.

But then we are old and the struggle that seemed so critical to our younger selves loses its grip. Having gone through all that reproductive business—and emerged out the other side of the tun-

nel—my view is retrospective. The boys are up and gone. My work
is more important to me now; I travel. Marty's work gives way to
home: he doesn't want to leave it anymore. We have become more
like each other; distinctions that once were focal have blurred.

Our evolutionary destiny is done.

Another difference between boys and girls: girls stand closer together and touch each other more than boys do.

Another difference between fathers and mothers: fathers jazz up
their infants and engage them more vigorously in novel things and
games, while mothers soothe them.

"Outside! Outside!" cried Ian, and it will be his fathering role
to reveal the outside world to his children.

"Mommy, Daddy, Baby," Samantha insisted, and it will be her
mothering role to hold the family together.

Or so says Mother Nature in her biological shorthand. She had
to write her memo toward the goal of reproduction: had she not,
we would not be here to interpret it. Had she not also graced us
with a symbolic mind, we also would not have been here: we could
not have raised children without the community support that
promises made possible. Yet it is exactly our biologically symbolic
nature that gives us that astonishing capacity called insight: we can
read our own minds; we can catch our thoughts and change them.

Ian and Samantha will, as they grow up, acquire free will. They
may not do as Mother Nature says to do or become what we dictate either.

Becoming

I am trying to align disjunct images:

There is the snapshot of Emma, haloed in pale curls, cradling her broccoli bouquet. And here is a newspaper photograph of Jennifer Love Hewitt, starlet and youth idol, baring her flesh.

The latter is from a *New York Times* article titled "Daughters of American Evolution" that decries the blatant sexual come-on style of dress that is popular now among what the author calls the "tweens," children between the ages of nine and twelve. Whatever happened to Scout's bangs and overalls as depicted in *To Kill a Mockingbird*? wonders the writer.

Yesterday I cleaned the surface of my desk, a more or less monthly operation that reveals what I have gathered from here and there over the preceding weeks. Here is another clipping: an article that worries about tween boys who build muscles in order to feel acceptable among their peers. Could that be in store for Ezra, naked and rinsing tomatoes at the kitchen sink?

Recollections surface as I clear papers down to bare wood: a letter from my friend in the mountains of Virginia; the rolled-up poster-ad for a talk I gave in Pennsylvania.

In Pennsylvania I was invited for dinner with a family that was not, as far as I could tell, a family. That is, there were two tween children, a boy and a girl, to whom I was introduced through the doorways of their respective bedrooms. It was a glancing introduction: they glanced at me. Neither rose to greet me. Neither came to dinner either. Later in the evening, the boy rummaged for something in the refrigerator; the girl warmed herself something in the microwave.

In Virginia I was brought to meet the Feetes who, with their teen son and daughter, run a dairy farm. The boy came out to greet us, smiled broadly, shook our hands, led us to the house, opened the door, and took us through the mudroom into the kitchen where the girl was baking the daily bread. Mrs. Feete was away taking a course on cheese making. Her daughter had taken on the hosting role: she sat us at the table and poured our coffee.

It was March, calving season. Mr. Feete came in from the barn to call his son for help delivering a calf, and we went with them to watch. The day was cold with drenching rain. I stood shivering under the drumming roof of the calving shed as the cow heaved and circled and grunted her wet-sacced infant, front feet first, slowly from her womb. The boy dried the calf with towels.

And here against the finally clear grain of the wood lies Marty's old bar mitzvah Bible, still opened to Genesis, atop *From Lucy to Language*, a lavishly illustrated, oversized tome also opened, in its way, to Genesis: the first of a series of photographs of *Homo sapiens* fossils.

I stare and stare at them, these ancestors. One was barely grown up when he died. I wonder if even then, some children did, and some did not, grow up to be what they had seemed to promise in their broccoli-flowered youth.

"To become": to grow, to come to be; to be appropriate or suitable; to show to advantage; to be the fate or subsequent condition of.

What a difficult word! All of childhood is a becoming in the sense of the dictionary's final definition: the fate or subsequent condition of a child is to become adult. Yet becoming also means growth in the sense of development—the process that children undergo to arrive at adulthood. The verb carries as well a social sense, as when a person's behavior is appropriate; and an esthetic one, as when a hat shows the face to advantage.

I remember with what sinking heart I sent my first son off to school. He would be judged; I would be judged. There is in all of us the concern not only that our children will turn out okay in their own behalf, but in ours: we want them aesthetically, behaviorally, intellectually, and morally to do us proud, to be becoming *to us*.

Since children start out with that same desire, one has to wonder why adults and adolescents often seem like different species, neither one very likable to the other. It is almost custom for youth to disparage adult culture and for us to disparage theirs. That there should be a youth culture at all surely can't be right: youth customs, yes, like childhood games and toddler ways, but how can children become grown-ups when they are aloof from the grown-up culture? I suspect they can't, and many aren't, and that they are sullen with disappointment that we have not enabled their becoming.

I read Hrdy's *Mother Nature* late in the writing of this book, when I felt the need for more perspective. Going back through human evolutionary past, Hrdy explores what it really was to mother an infant in those times when separation of infant from mother meant its almost certain death from starvation or predation, and when the drain of carrying and nursing a baby placed a woman perilously close to the limits of her resources. Hrdy's purpose was to uncover the ambivalence of motherhood: women have always had to balance their desire for children with the resources available for their rearing. Those resources have been limited by the energy the mother could expend in their care, the reliability of food within the home environment, the help she could rely on from friends and kin, and the contribution of her mate.

In those foraging societies still available for study during the twentieth century, breast-feeding on demand for four or five years prolonged the mother's period of infertility, and marital relations were also suspended for some years. A woman gave birth to about five children in her lifetime, of whom an average of 2.6 survived to reproductive age. That was our prehistory.

With the greater resources that agriculture provided, children were weaned to other foods much earlier. Women might give birth to ten children in twelve years, twenty in a lifetime, but even with the reliable help of kin, it was rarely possible to raise them all to maturity. Mothers made choices: a shockingly common choice was to abandon or kill a newborn who could not be supported without detriment to existing older children or who by its low birth weight or other signs of physical disadvantage could not be expected to thrive.

Hrdy marshalls gruesome statistics as evidence that motherhood is not an instinctual drive to nurture whatever conceptus is produced, but is a commitment taken on according to a calculation of benefit versus risk. The benefit is the rearing of high-quality young that will carry parents' lineage into the future; the risk is that the progenitor herself (fathers are less vulnerable) will be so depleted in the process that she, along with her immature offspring, will perish without issue. Inherent in this calculation is an expectation of return from the investment.

The terms now have changed. Mothers in our society generally give birth only to the number of children they wish to raise. Neither parent expects offspring to return the investment in money or labor. Yet the calculation persists: we expect the product of our effort to reward us psychologically, to become our success.

But we do not live in Egypt past, when a child's process of becoming adult clearly led to being adult, and adulthood was what it had been for ages and could be expected to remain. Participation began early in childhood and grew as children grew. Religion was a shared worldview, inseparable from both group and individual identity. Customs were restrictive; artifacts were stylized: neither were to be created anew by an upcoming generation. Children had only to do what children naturally suppose they are to do: learn the skills, obey the rules. At the proper time, adults ritually conducted them into their midst. Youth went then from being offspring to bearing offspring. The round trip was completed. That was "success."

I'd call such a culture a moral landscape: a proscribed, consistent, and undeviating way of life.

Whether "moral" meant then what it means now, though, is another question. Behaving well through fear of punishment from angry gods or jealous neighbors' magic seems primitive to us, how children think, not grown-ups. We cope with concepts barely formed in early cultures: individuality, autonomy, opposing value systems, equal opportunity, even choice of the group to which we belong. Such ideas would have been bewildering to Egyptian villagers and certainly to those fossil ancestors, frozen in antiquity.

Yet so are relativistic ideas of morality bewildering to children, whose minds are equally ancient. The landscape they are to maneuver is bewildering too.

To a middle-class child, baffled by the abstract nature of adult endeavor, it is clear only that adults "make" money. Few customs extend beyond the immediate family: they are personalized, not explanatory of a cultural worldview. What parents and children "belong" to—a place, a church, a social class—is not ordained: it can be chosen, or it can change. We can't show children their future because it is unrelated to our past (only one of our sons entered a field that existed in his childhood, much less in his father's time). As to artifact, we have little to teach: no traditional iconography, such as the decorative themes once incised in clay; no traditional dress, such as the tartans of Scottish clans. Participation that used to be central to a child's cultural identity—songs, dances, dramas, games, and crafts—are now "extracurricular." By the tween years, participation in arts and sports is reserved for those with special talent. The rest are audience.

We do not even have much in the way of ceremony—I think,

for example, of those children in Pennsylvania who barely lifted
their heads in introduction and whose parents also ignored formalities of greeting, escorting, seating, and serving guests. Unmodern-
ized languages encode in their grammar proper ways to address
others according to age, kinship, and social status. Our society has
even dropped *sir* and *ma'am*; my friend's sons in Virginia call her by
her first name, Carol. "It's like, it's like," teenagers say, like all is
simile, like what is real.

That quirk of speech is quite recent. So is virtual reality. So is
meaningless ritual: at a bar mitzvah I attended recently, the boy
who through the traditional drama was supposed to have become
an adult was given a party separate from the grownups, who ate
other food, danced to other music, and sat apart. At my oldest
niece's wedding, no children were allowed. Nevertheless, the bride
wore white as symbol of her (long-vanished) virginity, and the
couple took their vows, exchanged rings, shared wine, opened the
dance, cut the cake, and were separated within the year. Compared
to traditional cultures, ours is slithery, hard to get a grasp on, hard
to find a place in, hard to belong to, and hard even to believe in.

Beginning at puberty or soon after, children start to form ideals
such as human equality, true love, and the sanctity of life. Earlier,
they would not have been so moved by *Romeo and Juliet* or *The Red
Badge of Courage*; they would not have been elated by the nobility
of tragedy. Ideals become literally "to die for." This is, on the face
of it, a surprising culmination to moral development: idealism is as
nonnegotiable as much earlier and rigid rules of conduct—don't
snitch, take dares, fight back, get even. Emma's more thoughtful
weighing of what is fair under the circumstances seems more mature. Ideals are independent of circumstance, do not convey rules,
and appear transcendent, not authored by the humans who hold to
them. "Thou shalt not kill" is an uncompromising prohibition. Justice, blindfolded and holding her scales in perfect balance, is the
ideal. Mature morality is the *practice* of justice. We shoulder the responsibility for it: we define who may be killed, which killings are

murder, and how the fate of killers is to be suited to their state of mind, circumstance, motive, remorse, and potential for reform.

Ideals are unrealistic and unattainable, yet the timing of their emergence at the gateway to adulthood and their often spiritual or heroic coloring suggest some critical significance. Idealism connotes sacrifice, a giving up of self in transcendence, a bliss of belief. I have thought that this feeling is similar, perhaps, to what infants first experience in their mothers' physical commitment, before they have a separate sense of self. The adolescent yearns to belong and, by belonging, never to be forsaken.

Our culture—as I need not tell you—doesn't score particularly well on transcendence, belonging, or any assurance that lip-pierced, green-haired, tattooed teenagers will not be forsaken by any but the youth tribe that they, in disillusion, have joined.

I am exaggerating. So are they. Exaggeration, by increasing contrast, focuses more sharply on what is to be understood. These alienated adolescents are making a statement: the variety of our customs, the cauldron of our ethnicities, religions, and secular beliefs, the choices that each of us can make, the play of individuality that we prize, and the extent of autonomy we require have failed to define what adolescents should be at their confusing age: if we won't clarify their definition, they will define themselves. Our culture is blurry, a maze rife with possibility. That's good; that's an improvement over what those old fossil bones could tell me about how to become human—their way only; one path; follow the straight and narrow.

But realizing that morality arose in the social necessities of community, its mature development must have to depend on a strong sense of belonging. That, at least, is a starting point in making our way through our foggy landscape.

I found out some awfully good news: Guess what, I'm not responsible for my children's personality! Or hardly at all: very prolonged studies of identical and fraternal twins (the Minnesota Twin Study and others) show that most of personality is genetically guided, influenced somewhat by the intrauterine environment, somewhat more by peers, with only a minor contribution from parents. Same with intelligence or height: given enough to be smart about and enough food to grow on too, children become as bright and big as they genetically can be. This revelation doesn't quite get parents off the hook, but it was a relief to me.

The catch about personality is that it is genetically *guided*, not determined. The genetic components of personality are emergent, tendential, awaiting the particular milieu that gives form to their expression. In this sense, childhood is a process of authentication: the person is there; the culture is to aid in his or her articulation. This is a pretty important concept for parents to understand in helping children feel that they belong. It means that you can't *make* them belong, can't shape them to be outgoing, competitive, intellectual, athletic—whatever it is you (or they) think it takes to "get in," to be a success. You have to notice what *they're* like, like my niece Alix.

Already at three, Alix was flamboyant, big voiced, dramatic, and not a little exhibitionistic. Susie, my not-dead sister, provided this burgeoning show-off with heaps and heaps of odd thrift-shop dress-up clothing, the more eccentric the better. Alix, by age five or six, was changing costumes as many times a day or more. By middle childhood, she was belting out songs of Ethel Merman proportion. Now she's a wonderfully loud-mouthed, extravagantly enthusiastic, and irreverently charming radio disc jockey. That's Alix, always has been.

It's not that children should just suit themselves—that's what the Pennsylvania children did, and their behavior was unbecoming (I'll get to that later). Sam and Sam, Alix and Alex, need to suit their interests, pursuits, talents, intelligence, and social style to the kind of person they sense themselves to be: to be their own shape and, as they fully come to realize who they are, to discover how their unique shape fits into the larger puzzle.

Obviously, our support of our sons and daughters as they try to fit comfortably into their own skins includes provision of goods and services, as in my father's encouragement of my interest in bugs. Just as importantly, it includes validation: what if he had scorned my interest, called it a foolish waste of time to run around swishing through the grass with my silly net?

That was me, always has been and still is.

While trying to articulate for myself what a moral landscape is, I happened to see *The Wizard of Oz* for the umpteenth time—this time with young Ezra and this time more vividly colored by my ponderings than by the Technicolor that appeared on movie screens for the first time with Dorothy's red shoes.

The characters—the creaky Tinman, the flammable Scarecrow, the Cowardly Lion—suffer from outward limitations but exhibit inner strengths that they do not realize they have. When Oz is revealed as a fraud unable to give Dorothy's friends the heart, the brain, and the courage he had promised for defeating the Wicked Witch of the West, Dorothy accuses him of being a very bad man. "I am a very good man," Oz contradicts her. "I'm just not a very good wizard."

None of us is, yet children seem unable to know their parents as simply people, with human faults and foibles. In the movie, it is only Toto the dog who sniffs the human behind the curtain and pulls it aside. I suppose that if, in the course of evolution, we had become wise to ourselves—learned that there is no good outside our own construction of it—morality would not have worked. It is also true that, during childhood, moral injunctions do, in fact, emanate from outside us through the voice of elders thundering from their literal height above us. And we play along: if children hear injunctions like "That isn't yours; you may not take it," amplified, as though from a wizard, so do parents meet that expectation by pronouncing rules in absolute terms, even though they are aware that they may not always have followed the rule themselves nor will their child. Without quite knowing it, we are giving children the wherewithal to internalize our voice: the voice of conscience.

There are voices and voices, though. Here is Marty's mother
when he, at seven or eight, told her that he hated a certain boy, let's
call him Johnny: "Don't say that! Don't even think it. You can't
hate Johnny." But he did.

And here is my mother when I, verging on puberty, said the
same thing to her about a girl who had borrowed my sweater and
refused to return it. She explained that the friend had taken a piece
of me, and that I was understandably angry, but that I should recognize the jealousy of those who steal what is not freely given.

I certainly thought my mother was a wizard (she was a psychoanalyst). But she did as Oz did when he pinned a heart to Tinman,
hung a medal for courage around Cowardly Lion's neck, and presented to Scarecrow the diploma that proved he had a brain. She
authenticated what I really was inside (and made me see into another too). She didn't validate the act of theft; it is wrong to steal.
She validated how it feels to wish to steal and how it feels to be
stolen from. She conveyed to me a maturity of conscience that better suits our modern world than unexamined prohibitions: people
may *like* to do what they may not do.

One day when Emma came to her father complaining that she
had told Phoebe to stop teasing her and Phoebe wouldn't, Rafael
asked, What should he do? Beat her up and lock her out of the
house?

"Yes," said Emma, in her honest and serious way.

We are not very good wizards. However, if we can testify to our
children's uniqueness, acknowledge the validity of their feelings,
and bestow recognition of their character, we will be very good
people indeed.

Let us now stand on ceremony: back from Oz, blown clear to
Pennsylvania.

Those children I visited were plain rude; so were their parents.
The entire evening was spent in the kitchen, adjoining the living
room into which I was not invited. Not for cocktails and appetizers

learned earlier. I had to take care of my mother-in-law during a terminal illness. We'd never liked each other much; our personalities did not fit well together. Still—feeding her, cleaning her, serving her, spending long hours in what, at first, was forced conversation—formality gave way to spontaneity: I came to know her and to love her, and she me. The lesson, although it had to do with validation, was an outside-in version of what I had learned from my mother: we launched from the superficial and arrived at the deep.

It now seems to me that codes of conduct bridge for children the seeming gap between relative morality and absolute ideals. Only by learning to behave well with others can people come to see that ideals cannot be approached but through negotiation: this is what children learn by dining with us in mutual civility.

Tigers (a tale):

Peter Matthiessen explains, in *Tigers in the Snow*, why these great Asian cats are nearing extinction. On the surface, their extirpation is the oft-told tale of increasing human population, decreasing prey population, poverty, warfare, exploitation, and wanton habitat destruction. Underneath, though, runs a kind of morality play that caught my attention because of its similarity to Samantha's lion drama.

Historically, among forest tribes in tiger habitat, the beast was known by such names as "Grandfather" or "The Gentleman." He was considered the protector of the forest and depicted as the sweet-faced guardian of its people. The people believed that a tiger's ferocity was aroused only toward those who transgressed the rules of the culture he protected or despoiled their and the tigers' shared forest realm. A person who showed disrespect by felling trees or taking more game than was needed would surely be killed by a furious cat.

As modern misfortunes befell both the forest and its people, just the opposite happened: the people turned against The Gentleman who had let these bad things happen. In disillusionment and anger, they began to kill the tigers—for the beauty of their skins, the power in their powdered bones, the aphrodisiac of dried tiger penises simmered into soup.

I see in this sad tale children whose piety and restraint was intended to prevent their being forsaken, and who were disappointed in that expectation, and who took, in consolation and retribution, whatever symbolically they could.

Young children harbor just such tigers of the mind. I can imagine that Samantha thought her own badness had caused her parents' anger and turned her great cats against her. She was only three. For many years of childhood, boys and girls can't acknowledge that their lions—or policemen, ghosts, gods, God—are actually their parents because they do not want to know that "sweet-faced" mothers and fathers could turn bad, abandon them, or kill them (witches and ogres do that). If bad things happen, it must be their own fault.

They get wiser as they get older, though. Disappoint the older child too much, and she will turn against the tigers who failed to keep her safe. Or she will simply turn away.

Hrdy makes clear that, historically, abandonment by parents was paramount to death, that fear of abandonment (we give it the overly mild term "separation anxiety") still haunts the modern child, and that childhood traits we find "charming" evolved in the interests of eliciting adult care. She means those traits that children cannot help, such as chubby cheeks and silky skin, innocent prattling, imploring eyes, and sobbing tears (we are the only species that weeps).

No parent can raise children, though, without noticing that they also manipulate our care. I once caught Rafael fake-crying in front of a mirror, practicing how to make us sorry for the poor small boy. I remember as a little girl pretending to be asleep, hoping my parents would tenderly say how sweet I looked. The urge to *appear* good is at least as strong as the desire to *be* good.

It's not hard to detect falsity in little boys and girls. Marty's mother used to say she could see a lie written on his forehead, and he believed her. As children become more independent—as they construct an inner and private self—they also become able to convincingly present themselves as they think others wish them to appear. That's a human talent: everyone puts on one face for a cocktail party, another for a job interview, while within the family and among friends, we can "be ourselves." We don these masquerades in circumstances where expectations are narrow and poorly matched with who we know ourselves to be, but we are seldom really comfortable in such ill-fitting skins and may resent that we are made to wear them.

A child psychiatrist told me that, in recent years, the most frequent complaint he hears from his teenage patients is that they feel fraudulent. These "frauds" are "successes"; they perform well in school and are popular too. Yet, though they have fit themselves to peer and parental expectations, they experience themselves as superficial and inauthentic. Among the articles piled on my desk were several that reported a similar "dis-ease." In the plaintive words of a boy in the article about building muscles, "No one knows who I am, so I have to look the way they like."

Another article related the latest in girls' styles. Tween girls, claimed the reporter, tyrannize one another over clothes: a tube top has to be of a certain color; jeans must be rolled to just the proper length; the right handbag a month ago is wrong today. Such exactitude of dress is necessitated by what the style slaves themselves call "sizing." They size each other up with a double meaning to the term: a wrong size is a bad fit, and a girl who deviates from the continually mutating dress code is scorned aloud ("So what's with the layered look?") or shunned with silence for her failure to fit within the group. The opening photograph showed four girls, all with long hair parted in the middle, all wearing the same jeans rolled (I'd judge, but I could be wrong) exactly five inches above the ankle, and all in tube tops revealing a uniformly placed belly button. One girl remarked that it's, like, she has this other life inside; the clothes are what matter outside.

I don't know these girls as individuals, or whether their parents, by emphasizing their looks, had indicated disinterest in who they were inside. I do know two boys, grandchildren of a friend, who suffer similarly from monetary narcissism. Since they were in elementary school, they have needed to display wealth: a Rolex watch at nine, then their own credit card, cell phone, top-line laptop, and—at sixteen—a costly brand-new car. Ask their parents how the boys are, and they answer in grades. But how *are* they? All A's. The bargain struck is pay for points, and I have seldom seen such disengaged, disappointed, and incomplete boys.

If children aren't acknowledged in plain dress as the person that they sense themselves to be, then they will attempt to become whatever it takes to belong, and by whatever masquerade.

In fact, the older boy did not graduate from high school. He was expelled for cheating.

One of the nicest things about the human race is our abiding juvenility. This was an evolutionary accident, a result of our big heads. Human infants can't complete their gestation to the same stage as an ape at birth because the human skull would grow too large to squeeze through the pelvic canal, and if the mother were to have a pelvis broad enough to accommodate the infant's skull, she would wobble as she walked. Compared to chimp infants, who from birth can cling to and climb upon their mother, we are born not only premature but developmentally retarded. Chimps are fully mobile by six months, forage for food at three to four years, and are fully grown and sexually mature at seven years. Whatever genetically enabled our early birth apparently slowed the rate of our subsequent development as well, both prolonging childhood and curtailing maturation well short of perfect sobriety. We're fun; we're funny. There is probably no species, not even chimps or wolves, in which there is as much behavioral congruence between adults and children.

Yet how unfun we've gotten! Biking has gone pro; it is to be performed seriously (exhaustingly!) and properly attired. Even

taking a walk has been transformed into *walking*—stylishly, with
striped sweats and weighted mannerisms, to the purpose of fit-
ness—and without an eye for what might be of interest along the
way. In an article I read about dismantling playgrounds and aban-
doning school recess, a principal was quoted on the subject of improving academic performance. "You can't do that," he said, "by
having kids hanging on monkey bars." A student, a little girl, was
quoted too: "I'd like to sit on the grass and look for ladybugs," she
confided, gazing out the window at the sunny day.

Parents still support their children's interests but hardly with the
lightness of a butterfly net. A boy likes music, so he is sent to music
camp. Or tussling is translated into karate; or dressing up into child
beauty contests; or impromptu games of ball into Little League,
now coached by paid professionals.

I fondly remember the dramas our sons devised throughout
their boyhood. One memorable piece of theater—after I had gotten furious at them for something and banished them from
my sight—involved an elaborate stage set with ropes and pulleys
arranged in such a way that when I consented to enter their quarters to hear their practiced apology, a blanket descended from the
ceiling with a note: "We're sorry, Mom." For Green Frog Day, they
invented a chorus in which each was a different species, croaking,
peeping, grunting, and trilling in splendid syncopation.

No lessons were offered in frog song—nor would I have paid
for them—nor did either of us ever nag our sons over the years to
practice lute, banjo, sitar, mandolin, violin, guitar, cello, trumpet,
flute, recorder, or drums (no piano!) as each in his turn explored his
instrumental voice. As an adult, one son sang tenor in the Boston
Christmas Revels, and in an a cappella group, and now in a group
specializing in madrigals. All unpaid, all amateur, just for fun. Two
of them go circle dancing and Joshua with his friends and drums
has formed a homemade rock group. Marty and I are musical mis-
fits: let the boys enjoy.

Snapshots of them as children are hilarious: one shows Aram, in

slack-jawed, cross-eyed, knock-kneed pretense, holding a sign that
reads "Won't you help this child?" It was taken on our village Main
Street. There is a certain stepping back that allows humor to happen. Close-up, Aram's plight as the youngest of four was not funny;
comic relief, like all family jokes, acknowledged the burden while
lightening it. We have laughing gas, we humans, to buoy each other
up.

I've seen snapshots of those two sad grandchildren too. Like
Emma at four with her broccoli bouquet, their faces at that age are
alight, their smiles spontaneous and bright. In later snapshots, their
smiles seem forced, stiff—a smile for the camera. Finally, they
smirk.

That fading of joy seems echoed in the fading of our own joy
when we take their performance so seriously. At first, we play with
children and enjoy it, as Aram did enacting gorillas with his young
charges, as we all did that day playing Hide-and-Seek with the two
Sams, and as Joshua did the following Christmas laying tracks with
Ezra, who by then had fallen madly for Thomas the Tank Engine.
In those early years, we are curious about our children, continually
surprised by what they do or say, and delighted with their novelty.
When parents of preschool or kindergarten children are asked how
their son or daughter is, they relate an anecdote that aptly depicts
some new twist of personality they have discovered—he insists on
wearing his new boots to bed; she won't eat broken cookies.

We give children all sorts of things to experience—paint, dress-
up clothing, drums; fish to feed and beans to sprout; a sandy beach;
a puppet show. It is as though we ourselves have a new toy, and it is
our pleasure to discover how to play with it, what it can do, and
what makes it work. Our play with young children is as much our
exploration of them as it is their exploration of the environment we
offer. By the time they are six, we and they, in delicious conspiracy,
have well begun the narrative of who they are.

Then two things happen, one by nature and one by culture:
children turn to their peers for further definition, and we turn

them over to school to define them for us. Again, I'm exaggerating to make a point: neither the turn to nor the turn over is so sharp. Yet, if you examine your memory-pictures from six to twelve, you'll find your parents in the background, your mind-camera focused vividly on friends. The heart sinking I experienced sending a son to school is, I believe, mirrored in your own anxiety concerning report cards and parent/teacher conferences.

Both turnings are culturally natural: wherever formal schooling exists at all, it begins at six. My first "best friend," Lucy, also dates to then. Children's peers are those whom they traditionally would work with as adults, and it is primarily among them that they find their social fit. (One small but telling indication that peers, more than grown-ups, define social fit is the nicknames children give to one another—Doozy, Biscuit, Sneak, Gweek, Flea. These nicknames—from the Maine island where tradition still holds—have significance to the namers and the named but remain opaque to elders.)

In our suburban culture, though, the turn toward peers is frustrated and the turnover to schools constricting. Children have lived fewer than half the years of childhood when they leave kindergarten. They have been immersed in process. Samantha, now just shy of five, sings "Itsy Bitsy Spider" with her friends, unaware that there could be such a thing as a musical misfit. Neither does she know yet that she might be "good" or "bad" at art or that her pleasure in painting could be usurped by paintings for exhibit. She does not experience as performance her intense Mommy, Daddy, Baby game or the nursery scenes she enacted using the ark animals.

This fall, Samantha will be sent to kindergarten at a Chinese school known for its academic standards. The school day is eight to six. She will spend Saturday mornings in an "after-school" activity: learning to speak Mandarin. I am so sorry for her.

I had an interesting conversation with one of the Huisman children, another Ian as it happens, but spelled Jan and pronounced Yan in the Dutch manner. He's the middle child, age ten. I, along with his parents and sisters, had just been to hear him perform in a school concert. All of us were in the living room, comfortably seated around the fire having cookies, cider, coffee, drinks. I asked Jan if he or other members of the assembled choir, band, or orchestra ever made music together just for the pleasure of it. Jan explained, as though to a foreigner (which I guess I am to him), that American schools close their doors at three o'clock to all children not scheduled for practice, leaving the rest no headquarters in which to congregate for after-school interests. They made music only as rehearsal for display—and "they" were only those who had passed the audition.

Jan's main complaint about school was that it makes friendship so difficult. Each of his classes is a different group of children, so a friend he makes in one course may follow a different schedule entirely during the rest of the day. Then the buses come, the doors close, and the children go their separate ways—often to after-school activities that, like school classes, reassort them asocially by subject.

Jan, alone among his peers, rides his bike to school. He hides it in the bushes two blocks away; his older sister Claartje's bicycle was kicked in and spat on. She "belongs" to her high-school sailing team, in fact was awarded its prize for "most enthusiastic and dedicated sailing." At term's end, she invited her twenty-four teammates and their coach to a cookout. They all accepted. Three showed up, the coach not among them.

I can see them now, this unbelonging, unbecoming tween/teen crowd: they come upon Tinman on their way to class, look him over appraisingly, and say, "So what's with the metal look?"

So what is with the metal look? Piercings, for example.

I came upon a gripping piece of chimp information: even though they're sexually mature, postpubertal youngsters don't immediately have babies. Between her first estrous period and her first pregnancy, a female chimpanzee typically copulates 3,600 times! She's sexy but not yet fertile. Males, too, don't immediately father offspring. Older males don't let them. For both sexes, there is a period of about five years during which they first tentatively approach the adult troupe, gradually feel out their place within it, and only finally, after each has consolidated his or her status among same-sex adults, does either produce offspring.

The human period of postpubertal infertility is briefer (only a couple of years for either sex) and less reliable, yet culture typically has provided youth just about five years of preparation for parenthood. In old-fashioned America, girls were allowed to baby-sit beginning at thirteen and often were engaged to be married (or did marry) at eighteen. Boys, who mature later than girls, were expected to begin earning wages at sixteen and postpone marriage until they could support a wife somewhere in their twenties.

In the interim, adults took responsibility for introducing boys and girls to one another through established customs: dances, socials, and by-invitation-only family occasions. Courtship procedures were taught—opening doors for young women, escorting them, giving them corsages—and courtship was supervised. In the meantime, too, young men joined older ones in social rituals: the bowling team, fall hunting trip, stopping by for a beer at the neighborhood bar. And young women the same—perhaps joining the church choir, Junior League, or hospital candy stripers, which was still popular among adolescent girls in my generation. Supposing that parents themselves had not arranged the marriage, a boy, nevertheless, had to ask for a girl's hand, and the consenting father gave his daughter to him.

In Western cultures, this introductory period hasn't ever been so constrained as in those where, for example, young women are strictly segregated from men until they marry. Nor have our coming-of-age rituals ever been so savage as they have been in more primitive societies, as when a Masai boy was required to kill a lion to prove his manliness or a girl to endure facial scarring to display her womanhood. Now, though, we hardly make a gesture at all: don't conduct adolescents to their social coming out, don't induct them into their country's service, and don't mark either sex's arrival at physical maturity in any way, not by face paint, costume, hairstyle, or ornament.

All these things youths must manage by themselves. They do so savagely.

Yet bravely, I think, for all their sadness and anger:

Youth culture, with its body piercings and sexy dress, its leap to copulation without benefit of courtship, and its dangerous speeding-car, drugged-out displays of daring, is adolescents' painfully invented way to induct each other into, and conduct each other through, those years when we offer no adult hand to guide them.

"We're the Generation of Individual Choice," remarked a young man about his coming-of-age. "Which? Which? Which? In the end, the bottom can fall out from some of those choices. And, in the end, we're orphans. We're supposed to take care of ourselves. That's our only choice."

The last article:

Realizing that their children had too little time to just fool around together and were stressed by the level of performance demanded in after-school activities, a group of Midwestern parents got together to ease things up. They asked athletic coaches to stop dropping a child from the team for missing practice; they asked all teachers to release children from after-school activities by six o'clock, in time for dinner. That done, they arranged a workshop for themselves in how to conduct a family meal.

I was about to be appalled. I caught myself up fast, though.

If tweens and teens and almost-adults can mark their own coming-of-age and invent their own social customs, and do so in fellowship and according to the urgings of their human nature, why can't we mature adults similarly get together and come to some agreement about how we are to proceed? The young feel abandoned by us; we feel abandoned by tradition. They take what is salient to them, dress or drink or boom boxes, to create youthful standards in which they enlist the conformity of their group. We can do that, we grown-ups. Deciding that dinner shall be at six o'clock is a good beginning. Who knows but what the Midwestern parents might decide to host get-togethers for their adolescents too?

We have a pretty good inkling of our own human nature—or we do once we dare to pull aside the curtain and take a good look. We have an advantage over green-haired youth of at least some modicum of gray-haired wisdom. They don't know where to go; we've all been there. Our own nostalgia-scented album gives us some guidance: whatever landscape we individually and communally create, both materially in the form of old wooden tables and ritually in the order of the meal, it is our job to keep it faithfully for our children to return to in Thanksgivings yet to come.

Noah walked into my mind as I was thinking through these things. He arrived accompanied by that throng of children: there are more individuals of this one species than of any others I have carved, even the flock of sheep. They came to me outsize—Noah is taller than the mammoth, bigger than the whale—and with more personality than even the sweetly smiling mother polar bear. Although I created them, they arouse my curiosity:

Whose baby is held in lady Noah's arms? Where does that chubby and wildly running girl fit in? Is she running to catch up or running in the lead? Is that pride or arrogance that I see in Seth's face? What will become of that odd dark-skinned, blond-haired child whom Japheth, resting his hand on her shoulder, seems to have taken a shine to? I know from the story that Ham, Noah's middle son, is destined to behold his father naked in a drunken stupor, and I'm bewildered as to why covering his father with his cloak will be punished by servitude to his brothers. Ham looks innocent to me.

Each of them will have a story. I, their whittler, have already contributed to it. I've seen the mischief in the faces of the red-haired twins and Japheth's budding tenderness. So, too, will my grandchildren who play with them place each piece in the context of some narrative only that child could invent and that is fitting only to the particular figure.

Like the Noah family, children arrive; they arouse our curiosity. We provide them certainly with standards—the staff we arm them with, but also the hound that dogs their heels—yet not knowing ahead of time who they will be, it is at least as important that we enjoy the suspense, let them unwrap themselves to our astonishment. We are not the authors of our children; biology did that. We're not their editors either; that's their job. I'd say parents are more like stage managers who, taking cues from the players, place the scrims and supply the props their children need for their own enacting.

Yes. That behind-the-curtain role is right for us. It is becoming.

The Rainbow Sign

It became time to build the ark. I started to draw up the design on a snowy Sunday more than a year after I had whittled the first sheep. It was enormously difficult.

I worked first on the floor plan. Each partitioned area had to measure at least two inches wide to accommodate the animals—three-quarters of an inch thick, two to a stall, plus a little breathing space. Even the hooved animals vary in length, though, from the tiny burro to the hefty musk ox. I erased partitions in the four corners to create more commodious box stalls. No way could the long-tailed triceratops cram aboard (it would have to remain extinct). And where, in this mammoth-proportioned boat, might mice feel comfortable?

Marty, who that weekend was designing a new dormitory complex for a state university, could treat the living quarters uniformly, for the occupants are all one species that differ in size by a foot or so at most and have the same needs. He was at one end of the table, I at the other. He had sketched out housing units for 550 students by the time I added a loft space for the middle range of creatures—ferrets, possums, armadillos, anteaters, muskrats, beavers, raccoons.

These were among the earlier whittlings. Toward the end, I had carved a bunch of beetles; then, enjoying the contrast, finished with Leviathan. He could remain outside the ark, and must. But an

ocean floor of flopped fishes (for they are not, like the whale, supported by broad bellies) seemed a poor thing to offer the playing
child. Even a toy ark requires varieties of habitat.

Once a floor plan is sketched out, one draws the sections. I
learned this watching Marty. A section is a slice through the building that shows floors, ceilings, roof, and openings—doors and
windows. I'd worked out the placement of the windows. Now I realized that the animals should be able to look out the windows, but
I hadn't thought of that when whittling. How tall should the windows be, and at what height from the floor? That depends on
whether the viewer is an ostrich or a penguin. I compromised: the
big workhorse can poke his head out; his wild stablemate cannot.

Ceiling height had also to be considered. I went back to the lay-
out and drew a semicircular cutout in the first-floor ceiling to give
the giraffes some head room.

The "basement" in an ark is the space below the deck: the hold,
which had not been apparent to me when laying out the floor plan.
But there it appeared in the section as I drew it, nearly a two-inch
depth of additional space that might be reached through hatches. I
added to the floor plan a hatch cover that, lifted, reveals an on-
board, below-deck aquarium for the fish.

Then I drew the elevations. And disliked them: the fenestration,
which had worked so well with one window per small stall and two
for the big ones on both upper and lower stories of the ark, made
the boat look from the outside like a floating Hilton. I erased the
end windows; that was better.

The shapes of prow and stern were easy enough to design in
profile—what child cannot draw a boat?—but when I tried the
front and rear views, I discovered that geometry poses certain co-
nundrums that I could not picture in three-dimensional space. I
won't (I can't) go into the details, but the obstinate fact is that a
prow formed of plane surfaces ends in a triangle if you cut with
perfect accuracy, a trapezoid if you do not.

Because Marty had a deadline on his project, and it was a Sunday when art stores are closed, and we had only three sheets of large graph paper to share between us, and Marty absolutely needed two of them, and I was drawing this big boat at full-scale, I had to overlap the sections, elevations, and floor plans on one sheet. I asked, Would he be confused by this overlapping when he cut the pieces for me? And he said, How could he cut the pieces for me since he had no saw that could possibly do the job at that small scale? What is small to him is big to me (another difference).

So come Monday, I ordered an electric scroll saw for myself.

By the time it arrived, the ark had multiplied: there was not one boat, but four. Yes, I had decided chapters ago that Noah's Flotilla was as absurd as saving fish from floods, and the animals had for some time been happily stashed in boxes, but in the event I couldn't stop the playing of my mind.

Once I saw that I could hinge a roof to open over a loft, I wanted nest boxes for the ducks and geese, a breezy space for penguins, and somewhere to keep safe the mottled, speckled, blotched, and luminous eggs I still have not carved, but will, I promise. I drew a floating coop.

Then, with hinges and hatches enlivening my invention, I designed a boat-barn with a pigsty on the poop deck and a bilge bin for the rodents.

None of these quarters quite suited that flock of sheep with which I had first launched the whole endeavor. I drew a fold.

In the end I added still another craft: a skiff. One doesn't know how a child may wish to play. He may need to transport animals from one boat to another or isolate an animal that may be dangerous from those that are not. And Ezra may have a sister with whom this expansive toy must be shared, and either child may bear another generation that may have its own issues to play out.

You have to make room for everyone.

I shy from bigness. I pull back from Education, Politics, Culture like a snail from salt. How could I make schools stay open until

evening when they barely can afford to get through the day? How
can I convince municipalities that the dangers of playground swings
and monkey bars are more than offset by children's need for risk
and motion? How can I convey to a whole culture the shame of
professionalizing activities that used to be just fun? My land is a
small place; my community is a few people. The substrate that I inhabit is not the Environment: it is more to the scale of the tide pool
that a single starfish could affect. There, within my own reach, on
my own ground, and among my own people, I am free to act.

At the deepest reach of our humanity is our conviction of free
will. Within each of us is that "I" that thinks its thoughts and
makes its choices. No one else ever or anywhere would have made
the ark and its inhabitants exactly as I did.

And yet biology determined, through the generality of my sex
and the individuality of my inheritance, that particular nimbleness
of fingers that I enjoy. Evolution anciently bequeathed the symbolic
turn of mind by which I could conceive the project, and the narrative that gripped me almost certainly predates written history. The
urge to pass cultural values to descendants arises outside my voli-
tion, as does the urge to produce, amass, possess, and give. If something like 60 percent of intelligence and personality is biologically
determined and the remainder shaped by physical environment,
upbringing, education, and peer culture, there would not seem to
be much room for the exercise of free will. Only about 1 percent of
our brain work is available to our awareness anyway. Most brain activity occurs without our knowledge of it: this sentence was formulated in my mind microseconds before it was revealed to the "I"
who wrote it.

Then is our conviction of free will a trick of our nature similar
to that which makes us assume the inherence of moral dictates and
human rights? Perhaps knowledge of how far behavior is determined by the accidents of our nature or our nurture would paralyze
us in fatalism, place the blame for who we are on our genes or on
our stars. (Or on our parents.)

But I do not think we deceive ourselves in our conviction of free will. I think we misunderstand what it is. Where freedom lies is in our capacity to realize our biological self and to willfully extract from our environment what best suits us. As modern research suggests, intelligence may be less a "thing" than it is an appetite for learning certain kinds of things—including manipulating the physical environment to our material and social advantage. So yes, it is our human nature to mow the lawn to maintain the value of our real estate and social standing. It is natural, too, to indulge children with gifts that show them to advantage among their peers. It's unlikely that we adults really want to crack nuts the hard way when we can buy them already shelled. But, having realized these things about our nature, we can look again: reexamine ourselves, our ways, and our surroundings. This is what I wish in behalf of children: that by recognizing the significance of their urges and expectations, we will come to *re*spect them.

Joshua, at three, explained to me the elements of matter. They included "juice" (meaning wetness—sap and blood), dirt, and string. I didn't correct him: string (thong, rush, rope, flaxen fiber!) is elemental to children, whose primitive compulsion is to attach one thing to another. Lincoln, who never did learn to draw, became fascinated at about twelve by the intricacies of knots and three-dimensional constructions held in improbable suspension by the tension of fishing line. What these endeavors had to do with his later work in bioinformatics is beyond one's wildest guess. But I wouldn't, for that reason, have denied him string.

Lincoln and others of his unexpected ilk invented computer software to keep track of and distribute medical and biological data two decades after he tied for me the Turk's-head knot that I still pull to turn the light on in the storage closet in Maine. Among his first "toys" was the discarded turntable from an old phonograph, which he spun to hurl marbles across the floor. He was fascinated by magnets, prisms, lenses, and anything that burned. It was he who, with clothesline and pulleys strung between two bunk beds, created the mechanism by which the boys' apology note descended to me as I opened their bedroom door. In retrospect, one can say Lincoln was headed toward becoming a scientist, but his idea was more like that of a mad scientist—producing phenomena, flash of light and puff of purple smoke.

Childhood is to the purpose of growing up, but it unfolds in childish, not adult terms. That the transition seems to be so fraught with difficulties—with reluctance on our part to admit children into our company and on theirs to join us—indicates some mismatch between the biology of development and the environment that enables it. Are we failing to give string? Because we see no purpose in it? Because knotting is not a saleable skill? Because our eyes are on our children's future and not on them?

If I had to come up with a single metaphorical device to express what is missing in childhood now it would be something on the order of string: the tie that binds, the thread of connection, the weave of narrative, the web of life.

The bell rope:

One of Marty's recent projects was the design of an elementary school on a constricted and odd-shaped city lot. He created on paper an angel sort of building: two wings flung back to enfold a playing field open to every classroom and, where the school faced the street corner, a bell tower that marked the entrance. The bell was real; there was a rope to pull it. At eight o'clock, when the school opened for the day, a child who had earned the privilege would be allowed to ring the bronze bell to signal the start of classes. There was no one on the selection committee who failed to see the intimacy, the meaning, the thrill of the plan, and so it was chosen.

But the bell cost $8,000. Was it really necessary? The client insisted that the bell could be formed just as well of fiberglass as cast in bronze.

What is the sound of fiberglass? Marty asked. Thunk?

No problem, he was told: a bell would be recorded; a switch would run the tape.

Does that make you cringe?

It should. It is style at the sacrifice of life.

Children seek authenticity and genuine connection. Dough, not Doh—and not "dough" as in money, either. The total construction budget for the school was $6 million. All that, and nothing spent on the ring of truth.

Usually the connections children seek are not for sale anyway. One day, when clearing our land with the boys, we came upon an arrowhead. It was chipped of white quartz by the hand of an Indian who must have hunted here, right here, in what is now the garden where Ian hunted bees. The hunter lost his arrowhead (his tribe lost the land); we found it buried in a farmer's stone dump. I could have bought an arrowhead; I could have bought a plastic reproduction. I could not have made the heart of a boy beat with the substitution.

I could have paid to have the stone dump hauled away. So, on my childhood farm, may the present owner choose to clear away that one remnant unremarked-on pile of stones where possibly some blacksnake still survives to sun on summer mornings. We chose to use the stones in building the retaining wall that edges the terrace garden, and to build it ourselves, and without cement (using string to mark the top course and keep it level). And along came Ian's crying toad to live there, and a blacksnake too, and one August when the garden was open to the public, the snake came forth and swallowed a frog right there in front of a dozen visitors, there where the Indian lost his arrowhead, there where we were serving lemonade made from real lemons (not ReaLemon), there where we, in our freedom to choose, had chosen to make a garden.

I watched a historical mystery on PBS one night. The mystery had to do with the origin of a strangely elongated, very stylized, highly polished, and exquisitely carved wooden figurine that the narrator had bought at an auction. He eventually found two others like it among stored artifacts at a museum in Russia and, tracing further through an expedition diary kept by one of Captain Cook's crew during his South Sea explorations, discovered that the figurine had been carved on Easter Island centuries ago.

Woven through the narrative was the history of the island and its inhabitants. They were Polynesians, expert sailors who, to reach this speck of land over a thousand years ago, had crossed two thousand miles of open ocean in large dugout canoes rigged with sails and navigated by sun and stars as their ancestors might have forty thousand years before. Easter Island was then forested with palms and a species of hardwood tree, the toromiro, that grew nowhere else. Toromiro was a dense, fine-grained wood, the material from which the figurines had been carved. Two of the three existing carvings were human—a man and a woman; the third had the head of a frigate bird, a giant species with wings nearly eight feet from tip to tip that soars above the sea and lands only to sleep and nest. This bird the people aptly chose to be their god.

Each year, the Easter Islanders named a new chief and crowned him with a frigate-bird headdress. The chief spent the year in a certain cave, hair and fingernails uncut (as were those of the figurines), and fed by others. He emerged after this feat of endurance a "wise man," and while the next chief took his place in the cave, a huge stone statue of the previous chief was cut and hauled to take its place high on a headland among rows of statues representing all his bird-chief predecessors. Archaeologists duplicating this Stone Age feat found that it took fifty to one hundred men to erect such giant stelae.

Easter Islanders farmed a little but lived mainly by fishing. As their numbers increased, they had to depend more on agriculture. They cleared the trees for fields. Eventually, they came to the last tree and cut that too (the toromiro is extinct). The last of their dugouts rotted. There was no wood to make more boats. Fish close to shore were insufficient to feed the growing population. The tribe split; each group fought against the other over the barren and eroding land until only stragglers were left, barely subsisting, devoid of any memory of how to carve.

This would be just another tiger tale but for one quirk: about the last shred of tradition these weary and malnourished islanders abandoned was erecting giant statues to their failed frigate-god.

I was dumbfounded.

There were no "outsiders" to blame, no modern temptation to kill the trees for money as forest tribes have killed Asian tigers. Easter Island is small, a volcanic remnant so isolated that few species had ever reached it. Its ecology can't have been entirely beyond the ken of its inhabitants. Seafaring had been their livelihood not just for centuries, but for millennia, perhaps since that first overwater dispersal of *Homo sapiens*. Like frigate birds, they sailed the sea in search of fish. How could they have willfully destroyed their means to do so? And those statues! Is the human mind so insistent on symbols that it loses common sense?

Yet common sense is symbolic thought. We have no other way to think, at least no way that consciousness can be aware of. As much as I would like to confine my good sense to some small scale that lets me feel effectual, that trick of nesting one category within another in the myriad overlappings of human intelligence forces even the smallest things to expand like the dimpling of raindrops on a pond.

Take the ladybug the little girl wished to hunt for in the grass. Overlap the beetle with the concept of ownership. Ask the question: Who do ladybugs belong to?

Common sense tells me that a ladybug belongs to no one. Unlike a pet, it comes without a bill of sale. Unlike migratory waterfowl, it is not under government protection or regulation. You're allowed to deprive the ladybug of its livelihood by removing the plants that feed the aphids that are its primary source of food. You may also, if you wish, kill it outright with pesticide.

But then, think again: the beetle's limbo outside the law gives you virtual ownership of it. Your land belongs to you with all that's on it. You are allowed to keep out your neighbor's dog; your neighbors are not allowed to pick your flowers. The ladybug is on your property: if you don't want it there, so much the worse for it.

And then again, the ladybug doesn't recognize your boundaries.

A dog may well have knowledge of its and your mutual territory and may tacitly agree to stay within it, but that idea of property isn't shared by any of the other creatures that live on your land, or live from it, or cross over it.

I've bought many of the plants that grow on my property: they are things, and I possess them. But I don't possess the systems that maintain them—their pollination, their seed dispersal, the recycling of soil nutrients that feed their roots. Since pollinating insects, seed-dispersing birds, root-nourishing fungi, and the many kinds of predators that control herbivorous pests don't recognize boundaries and may perform their services on others' land as well as on my own, any claim to virtual ownership of even a ladybug would be at least unneighborly, if not downright dumb.

In an even broader sense, the ladybug is enmeshed in a web of relationships flung over the land at every scale from microscopic soil bacteria to massive oaks, and from the mud on my shoe all the way to the little girl, wherever she is, gazing out the window at the sunny day. In this ecological view, and despite the fact that I have license to harm what really isn't mine, what I do on my private property affects what happens to yours.

Private actions also affect what happens to a little girl looking for ladybugs in the grass where, in these days of sprayed yards, she is not very likely to find one. Consider her: she is human. Like all of us, she was born with a bias to attend to red objects and to notice especially those things that are animate. And she, like all of us as well, has a soft spot for plump, cute, babyish animals. Moreover, in those hours when the girl isn't wasting her time hanging on monkey bars, she is probably being introduced by her teacher to ladybugs in books and by her schoolfriends to the "Ladybug, ladybug" rhyme. When an interest is preset by biology and also so emphasized and symbolized in culture, one has to suppose that the interest isn't altogether idle and that a nice fit between biology and culture may make sense in some way whether we fathom it or not.

I myself can't fathom an ultimate reason why ladybugs should delight us, but even so I wouldn't want to be responsible for that child growing up ignorant of their charms, unable to relate to her own children how, once upon a time, she used to sit on the grass and hunt for ladybugs on sunny days. Finally, in that sense, the ladybug does very much belong to the little girl. She should not be deprived of it.

And you! You mean principal! You son of an ape!

And us, all of us, all descended likewise: all of us are responsible for pursuing common sense beyond the tiny island that we call our own.

So here I am at the old table writing about string and symbols, and there on the floor is the finished flotilla in total disarray. Ezra was here yesterday.

If ever I wore for even a moment the cloak of wizardry, I am disrobed. Stalls! Why, he piled every animal into the ark in heaps, without regard to partitions, much less to what kinds of animals he loaded by the fistful aboard the boat. He noticed the windows: windows are to stick whales through (he called Leviathan "seal"). I do take credit for striping the zebras clearly enough that even a two-year-old could to name it, but the little wooden Girl went unobserved—possibly because we had just brought home from a pound in Puerto Rico his own real dog, named Tiko, Pico, or Poco; take your choice. Or Puppy, as Ezra so far calls him.

The mechanics of the boats were what really interested the boy: the hatch lids and hinged roofs, the ramp and removable loft. I had dyed cotton masons' line with tea so it would look like rope, fitted the hatch covers with simple loops to lift them, and the ramp with a fancy-knotted loop that holds it to a peg when it is closed. Funny what a child will notice: Ezra liked that he could pull the skiff by its string.

Still, he found my hand-carved, homemade metaphor less compelling than Thomas the Tank Engine. Children now inhabit an environment where powerful creatures have wheels or treads, not hooves. Their roar is engines. They are controlled mechanically with sticks and electronically with buttons; they are ridden on a seat. On our Caribbean vacation, Ezra rode from one island to another on a small plane—small enough that he did not, like Joshua at that age, ask where the airplane was. He knew he was flying in the sky. He rode motored boats over the water. He stood in awe of the back-hoe working the next-door yard, gulping and spitting soil from its toothy maw. The noise! The strength! But the beasts are made of steel.

Ezra was born human—which is to say, obsolete: few of his childish practicings will contribute to his adult survival. Even his fears are wasted in an age when tigers do not hide in the shadows and vacuum cleaners really can't eat little boys. Nothing will convince him, though, that his perceptions are anachronisms. He insists on traditional food, mac-n-cheese. He recognizes Jeep as a species. He struggles to build with Legos the walls and tunnels that at his age and in previous times a child would have built with sticks and stones and dirt. So far he appears undeterred by the discrepancies between what his nature leads him to expect and the analogies we offer, but then Ezra is only two. No one has removed his monkey bars, not yet.

My generation is handing on to his an environment that needs repair—home repair, I mean, fixes to our human habitat. Handyman work, like digging a garden or building a coop. And headwork, as in considering in a Neolithic sort of way whether, in inventing the letter *s*, we must lose the hissing snake: Do we discard wind song for white noise? Roses for aromatherapy? Gossip for chat groups? Gathering for shopping? There is only so far that we can stretch analogy with the conditions in which we evolved before too many threads are left dangling, and we come unraveled. Has anyone considered that we buy so much because we have so little?

When measured by actual number of years, childhood accounts for only about a sixth of a lifetime (maybe a little less these days when so many live beyond their eighties, probably a lot more when people were old by their forties). But when measured by retrospection, childhood occupies a much larger chunk. This is partly because our sense of time's passage speeds up as we get older, so the summer you were ten passed more slowly in your perception than the summer you were thirty. But more also happened during the summer you were ten—or six, or twelve.

Childhood is momentous. (The word came to me, then sent me to the dictionary: it is from the Latin *momentum*, which now means the impetus of a moving object but is built on earlier meanings— "movement, change"—with the added sense of "brief space.") Childhood is brief happenings of what the dictionary calls "great weight" and "consequence," what I would call *loaded moments*. One that I remember is when my father let go his hold on the two-wheeler I was learning to ride, and I pedaled free, down the road's slight incline toward the stream where the wild watercress grew— and crashed into the wooden bridge, too rattled to apply the brakes. That's *momentous*, not brought to you by Nintendo.

My parents, in their Neolithic and not so Neolithic ways, took their time with me. They didn't rush me off to elsewhere or turn me from the present toward pursuit of distant goals. Except for that damnable insistence that my future depended in some obscure way on finishing my spinach (and the unforgivably premature disposal of my stuffed animals, which was momentous in its way), they let me live as a child wild with wonder and primitivity. I think they enjoyed my childhood too, as I would later enjoy its repetition in the long, slow summers of my children's youth, and as Joshua now enjoys with Ezra the child's naked pleasure in rinsing tomatoes— unhurriedly, perhaps pointlessly, neither of them knowing which moments may become momentous to the someday grown-up man.

We no longer need children in an economic sense any more than we need Tiko-Pico-Poco-Puppy to herd sheep or retrieve dead ducks. We want children as heirs to the past and ushers of the future for no better reason than that we are procreators of our species: hard-wired baby lovers, biologically ambitious child rearers.

Just let's not ascend to symbol heaven while the earth is still beneath
our feet.

I've earned a whole new category of catalogs: woodworker's supplies. I guess I first got on that list when I bought the Japanese
carving knives; then I ordered brass clamps and hinges, which led
to a slew of catalogs for hobbyists: knobs and handles, dowels and
turnings, wooden toy kits, dollhouse furniture appurtenances,
miniature tools, gadgets. Some bodies must be out there busy with
their hands.

The boats gave me four busy weekends. I loved the wood. It
was sheets of three-eighth-inch plywood, one veneered with rock
maple, the other with black cherry, both species that I know in
many ways: as my childhood maple bed and the antique cherry
four-poster I've slept in almost ever since; as the source of maple
syrup and the active ingredient in cherry cough drops; as the mature maple forest on the once-was farm and the pioneer cherry of
fields growing through a weedy phase on their way back to woods;
as the maple pollen that now makes me wheeze in springtime, the
maple wings we used to stick on our noses long ago, the cherry log
my father made into a horse for me, the cherries that more than
any tree hereabouts feed the birds in early summer. And both trees
as firewood.

I had to go out of my way to find such plywood: ordinary lum-
beryards don't carry it. I found it at a specialty yard that supplies
sculptors and cabinetmakers. I found there, too, a small chunk of
walnut: Joshua has asked me to carve him a scarab to wear around
his neck.

My Dremel scroll saw arrived; also my Dremel drill. I'd redrawn
the plans. They were now on a much larger sheet of graph paper
cut from a roll and showing ark, barn, coop, fold, and skiff in plan,
section, and elevation. A piece of work!

Rather, ninety-one pieces of work: lines on paper somehow
had failed to convey the number of partitions, roofs, floors, side-

walls, end walls, prows, ramp, and covers that actually had to be cut. And openings! Thirty-two windows, eight doors, three hatches (the barn hatch is for rodents). To cut windows, you first have to drill a hole in each; then you remove the saw blade from the saw, stick it through the hole, reattach the blade, and then saw out the opening. I'd made it to the ninth window when the saw broke— faulty wiring; it wouldn't turn on. So in the end, it really was Marty who did most of the cutting: large pieces with his table saw, detail work by hand. I got to file the roughly hand-cut edges straight; and I sanded, and I glued.

Slowly, deck by deck and stall by stall, the boats came together. It was not like building a house, where the walls and roofs go up first so you get to see the finished shape of your home before it's divided into rooms. This was insides first, outsides last: it took two days to see the first boat.

This inside-out approach may explain why, when at last the ark itself was done, there turned out to be no place for Noah to steer his ship across the rising sea. He could stand facing the prow in the family's living quarters under the high-peaked roof; it's just that he couldn't *see* the sea: there was no window there.

Alma dropped by the day the ark was done. It was her very strong, indeed unshakable, opinion that not only must the man have a window from which to captain his ship, but also the baby lifted in his wife's arms must be able to see out of it and, she added, What good was the dove if it had no sill to sit on? If anyone in the future wonders why Noah's afterthought window is tall and arched and has a sill, unlike any other in any of the boats, that's why. Alma got her way.

And then she started to play. So did I (but not Marty who, as usual, was *seriously* at work). The toy might as well have been a baby for all we could resist its invitation. Out with the boxes and off with their lids! Sheep to the fold and fish down the hatch! Pigs in the sty and raven on the roof! The boats became animate: elephants trumpeted from windows, penguins strutted the deck. Two by two and hoof to paw the creatures filled the stalls and crowded fore and aft until—can you believe this?—I found that there was not room, not even in a whole flotilla, to house all the animals I had whittled (unless one were to load them, as Ezra did, by the fist-ful).

There were children to be named. We tried biblical names—Hanna, Jemima—then played with names that we imagined might be in the vocal range of australopithecines: Og, Ooma. There were jobs to do: Ham to herd and Seth to guard; the twins to feed the bunnies. The baby often had to be saved from falling down an open hatch or crawling among hooves. I firmly installed all the bears with both the pandas, only to find the baby panda visiting a walrus. ("He wants to explore," Alma explained.) We two played this way through suppertime and past the evening news, then went to bed.

And in the morning, the figures had moved! Seth had left his station at the ramp to pole the skiff. The raven had flown from the roof to perch upon the sill. The piglets had ventured from their sty. The rhinoceroses had heaved themselves onto their hind legs to better see the view from their box-stall window. Had I been a child, I might have accepted the magic of their moves, but I know better now:

Marty, the old chimpanzee, had been playing in the night.

Acknowledgments

Writers are thieves: they take from others' looks, dress, speech, actions, and stories what they wish to rework into their own narrative without the subjects realizing at the time that anything is being taken, or that anything will be made of what seems to be an ordinary encounter. I don't like this stealth, but how am I to know during the encounter what, if anything, will come in handy as I pursue my later thoughts? If I were to announce my intentions to gather material every time I visit people or they visit me, their awareness of scrutiny would result in dishonesty too. And to announce intentions would also be dishonest, for I don't intend what telling details happen to fall my way. I see no way around this innocent lurking. I nevertheless feel like a thief.

When the observations I use of people I meet are sure to please them, I may identify them by name. I acknowledge by name the Feete family, the Huismans, the Wordens, Wayne Paessler, and my sons and grandchildren. Sometimes I use only first names—Sam, Max, Ian—just because the surname seems superfluous when describing a child so young. On other occasions, though, what I notice implies criticism, and I wish to give no clues at all to identity, although the context may be recognizable to the subjects themselves or a few of their intimates. Since my purpose in writing is to reveal difficulties and suggest ways to extricate ourselves from them, I owe as much to those I criticize as to those I praise. Many families have helped me find the thread of the story I want to tell, and I thank them all equally for that help.

I am also painfully aware that no one I have ever met wished ill for their child, yet they were seduced or pressured or simply drifted into behaviors that did their child ill. I thank all parents I have talked with and all teachers I have known for keeping in focus the most basic of human aspirations, to raise children well. Most especially, I thank the children I meet, for they have told me more about where to begin my inquiry into what is human than any other source can tell.

I wish also to thank my editor, Becky Saletan, for seeing where I was going through thickets that sometimes obscured my own sight; Shelley Roseman, the researcher who dug out obscure facts I needed to articulate my thoughts; Frieda Duggan and Karla Eoff for their sharp eyes on the text; my husband, Marty, for his forbearance (I think he really doesn't like scrambled eggs for dinner); and Alma Tuchman for her often contentious but ultimately clarifying challenges to my work.

Index

302